Last Steps to Freedom
The Evolution of Canadian Racism

Last Steps to Freedom
The Evolution of Canadian Racism

John Boyko

Cover design by Terry Gallagher/Doowah Design Inc.
Author photo by Alasdair Wallace

Published with the assistance of the Manitoba Arts Council
and The Canada Council for the Arts

Printed and bound in Canada

Canadian Cataloguing in Publication Data

Boyko, John, 1957–
        Last steps to freedom: the evolution of Canadian racism

2nd ed., rev.
Includes bibliographical references and index.
ISBN 1-896239-40-4
        1. Racism—Canada—History. 2. Canada—Race relations—
History. I. Title.
FC104.B69 1998   305.8′00971   C98-900885-1
F1035.A1B595 1998

This book is dedicated to Roman and Victoria Czkowski and Daniel and Elana Boyko. They are my great grandparents. They came from the Ukraine to Canada near the turn of the century to pursue a dream. This book is also dedicated to Jennifer Boyko. She is my daughter. May she continue in the pursuit of that dream.

Table of Contents

Introduction

Facing a Racist Past

When a stranger resides with you in your land, you shall not wrong him. The stranger who resides with you shall be to you as one of your citizens; you shall love him as yourself, for you were strangers in the land of Egypt.
—Leviticus 19:33

A public meeting created an angry mob. It rampaged through Vancouver's Chinese and Japanese neighbourhoods throwing rocks and swinging clubs. Homes and businesses were attacked and burned. Those who emerged to run or defend themselves were beaten, and others were driven to the harbour, pelted with rocks and set adrift on makeshift rafts.

One warm summer evening an overflow crowd assembled at Toronto's Willowdale Park to see a Jewish ball club play. Nazi flags were unfurled and insults filled the air. A fight broke out in the stands and soon spilled onto the field, then into the streets. For six hours a riot swept the neighbourhood.

An east-end Montreal neighbourhood had grown brittle with tension after a Black family moved into a local apartment. A group of young people planned an assault. Three days later they were bolstered with reinforcements and armed with rocks, bottles and baseball bats. The confrontation began with shouting, but soon the family's car was aflame and their apartment smashed. They were beaten and chased from their home with cries of "White Power! White Power!" When Black youths arrived the melee escalated into a riot involving four hundred people that lasted over five hours.

The stories are all disturbing. All tell of Canadians violently attacking other Canadians due to their belonging to an ethnic minority. What is most jarring is that the first happened in 1907, the second in 1933 and the third in 1991. In nearly a century little had changed. Newspapers, police and politicians reacted to all three incidents with appropriate pleas for calm and understanding. All were dismissed as aberrations in a normally peaceful, accommodating, egalitarian country. They were not aberrations. They were merely bubbles in the cauldron of racist hatred that has brewed in this country throughout its history.

Racism is based upon two main ideas. Ethnic allegiance implies that those who belong to a particular ethnic group share common histories, traits and aspirations, and that all those of other ethnic groups are outsiders to be seen as different and possibly dangerous. Social Darwinism, which has little to do with theories postulated by Charles Darwin, implies that those enjoying status and influence owe their position partly to their biological superiority and that it is necessary to protect and enhance their power for the overall good of society. Although the terms were not coined until much later, the two closely related ideas played important roles in the development of New France, British North America and their child Canada. Leaders in each of the states appealed to racism's primal sense of belonging.

With the two ideas at the core of Canada's evolving political culture, the Canadian state became an ethnic as well as a political or civic construct. As the function of a state is to serve and protect the nation, those ascribing to the concepts of ethnic allegiance and social Darwinism, and their attendant narrow definition of nationality, supported the notion that the state must enact and enforce laws and regulations to protect and enhance the power of the dominant ethnic group. Actions taken against ethnic minorities become necessary and justifiable, for ethnic minorities should have no rights, and certainly no power, within such a state.

A state so defined becomes intolerant as it strives to protect or create a homogeneous nation. History is dotted with cases of ethnic states striving to fulfil their mandates through violent purges of ethnic minorities. In the 1990s, the new ethnic states of the disintegrating Yugoslavia coined the phrase "ethnic cleansing" to explain both their actions and their goal. States with long democratic traditions have shared similar goals but have applied more humanitarian, or at least subtle, means to attain them. One such state has been Canada.

At Confederation, Canada was an ethnic state, sixty percent of which was comprised of people of British descent, thirty percent French and only ten percent Native or others. The nation changed quickly. Immigration was encouraged by Canada's first governments as the only way to build the young country and stand against the pressure of American expansion. Canada was built on the backs of the millions of immigrants, without whom it would have failed. As immigration disrupted the nation's ethnic balance, pressure was brought to bear on the state by those of the ethnic majority, who by virtue of controlling all social, political and economic institutions held all the cards. New laws and regulations were demanded to preserve the power, rights and opportunities of that majority. Meanwhile, demands were made that the nation's ethnic purity be regained and then guarded through restrictive immigration laws and wholesale deportations of ethnic minorities. The state declared war on the nation.

The war was fought on many fronts, with many leaders, with small victories on both sides. From before Confederation until after the Second World War, racist forces were powerful and nearly always victorious. Liberal, egalitarian ideas were slow to take root. The war continued even as Canada entered the 1990s. Throughout Canada's history, excuses were made and myths created, but the truth is clear. To understand Canada one must understand racism, for Canada was born and grew as a racist state.

The manner in which racism evolved in Canada can be best understood by seeing racism as a ladder. Actions of societal leaders moved the state up or down the ladder. It was often on one rung with respect to one group and on a different rung with another. The racist ladder is unique in that many rungs may be occupied simultaneously.

The racist ladder's first rung is stereotypes, which are characteristics attributed to a particular group. They are often created and perpetuated by popular culture: newspapers, magazines, cartoons, and later movies, television and other media exploit them as cultural shorthand. Racist jokes also play an important role. They would fall flat if the stereotypes were not known.

The racist ladder's next step is prejudice, which is the belief that stereotypes are true and that, consequently, all members of a group possess the stereotypical characteristics attributed to it. Prejudiced beliefs are betrayed by phrases such as "They are all...," "Those people...," and so on. Prejudice allows no room for individuality.

11

The ladder's next rung is discrimination, which is an action taken based on prejudice. A prejudiced employer, for example, may refuse to hire a person who belongs to a particular group because of the stereotypes attached to that group. Since all members of the group are the same, the logic goes, all are suspect and deserve the same discriminatory treatment.

Officially sanctioned discrimination is the next rung. Discrimination becomes entrenched in laws, practices, regulations and rules. It is natural that people who grow up in a racist society learn to harbour racist views and, consequently, when they attain positions of power, act according to those views. A racist society thereby becomes more racist and self-perpetuating as racism becomes engrained into all facets of social activity and all social institutions. A systemically racist society can overlook or condone racist individuals, groups, or incidents in the house because the house itself is racist.

Systemic racism is seen first in laws promoting racial segregation. Services such as restaurants, hotels, public transit, recreation clubs and parks either keep races separate or ban certain races altogether. Housing and education may be separated. Employment and promotion opportunities may be limited according to race by employers or unions. Many of the rights and responsibilities of democratic citizenship such as voting, jury service, military service or holding elected office may be sanctioned according to race. In all cases where racial segregation has occurred the dominant race has ensured through either direct action or benign neglect that the services, lifestyles and opportunities available to certain races are of an inferior and often dangerous nature. Separate is never equal.

A widespread and popular system of racial segregation often leads to the next step up the ladder, to attempts to "purify" the nation through the exclusion and expulsion of minority groups. Exclusion is accomplished through the creation of immigration laws and practices that erect walls to keep some races out while welcoming others. Expulsion laws allow a dominant race to gather and deport those of unwanted races. Prejudice allows for the exclusion and expulsion of racial groups while refusing to recognize individuals within those groups. Infant children can become dangerous enemies of the state. In a systemically racist society, the collective conscience of those within the racist walls remains clear even if they become accessories to murder.

The top rung on the racist ladder is genocide, which is the deliberate extermination of a race. The twentieth century is riddled with cases such as Turks killing Armenians, Americans slaughtering Indians, Stalin starving Ukrainians, Hitler gassing Jews, and Uganda, Bosnia, Rwanda and more. Genocide need not, however, involve the physical murder of a group of people. A more insidious approach, recognized by United Nations Resolution 96, involves stealing a people's soul. Cultural genocide witnesses the theft of a race's religion, customs and language. It takes longer than mass murder but its effects are much the same: the ethnic or racial group ceases to exist.

Canada has occupied every rung on the racist ladder. The ladder is white, Christian, and French in Quebec and British in the rest of the country. It is propped against a wall of suspicion, fear, pride and hatred. Without those emotions, and the ignorance from which they grow, the ladder would fall. The stirring and exploitation of those emotions give it strength.

The purpose of this book is to explain the evolution of systemic racism in Canada through the stories of some of its victims. Through anecdotal evidence, the book will describe actions taken by business and labour groups, school boards, professional organizations, the media and all three levels of government that often created and nearly always reflected and exploited emotions to move Canada up the racist ladder. Only through the enthusiastic support of those societal leaders, secure in their belief in ethnic allegiance and social Darwinism or willing to exploit the fears and ignorance of others, was systemic racism constructed and maintained. They created and enforced the laws, regulations and practices that wove racism into the fabric of Canadian society.

The book is organized chronologically, by region, and by ethnic group. This structure is meant to suggest that systemic racism has always been a part of Canada's political culture, that no region is clean, and that its victims were not restricted to one race, ethnic group, or religion.

The groups and stories were chosen to illustrate the many masks behind which racism often hides. The experiences of Chinese, Black and Native Canadians illustrate the degree to which many Canadian leaders supported the inherently racist, pseudo-scientific theories of genetic purity. Their experiences also show how actions ostensibly taken to protect jobs were often merely excuses to move against undesirable races. Nativism is the impulse to protect one's country when threatened from without, and it was used to justify actions taken against Ukrainians in the First World War and Japanese in the Second. Often ignored by those hiding behind the nativist mask is the plethora of racist restrictions and attempts at exclusion and expulsion aimed at Japanese and Ukrainian Canadians and others long before either war. Economic nationalism and nativism were claimed to have motivated actions taken against Jews, while a closer look reveals that systemic anti-Semitism, which began in the 1700s, was the true motivation even as Jews were being murdered in Europe. A desire to save misguided people by showing them the supposed error of their ways and the route to salvation has been used by many Christian and liberal activists to justify blatantly racist actions taken against Native people. The book will peel away the masks.

A few points should be clarified at the outset. Many more groups could have been discussed. The experience of Italian Canadians who were interned in the Second World War, for example, could have been used to illustrate Canada's presence on the exclusion and expulsion rung of the racist ladder and to expose nativism as an excuse rather than the reason for all that happened. One must stop somewhere, however, and the main points are made in the six stories related.

The first five chapters briefly explain why the people under examination came to Canada, and all six note some of the major contributions they made to the country's development. No attempt has been made to tell the full stories of each of the six groups. Many fine books have been written, especially since the 1970s, that do that job. They are valuable. There is value too, however, in pausing a moment to look beyond the trees to the forest. Rather than undertaking extensive new research in these areas, the book attempts to draw together many fine secondary sources to invite a new look at our history.

Each chapter ends abruptly. The rather arbitrary endings are not meant to suggest that problems were suddenly solved or that groups somehow vanished, but that, it is hoped, the relevant points have been adequately made.

In examining Canada's racist past it is not my intention to relate sensationalist tales of misguided individuals. Neither will the actions of racist groups such as the Ku Klux Klan, the Heritage Front or others be told. Explorations of the loony extremes will be left to others. The focus will remain on systemic racism. Racist groups or individuals are discussed only if they were either supported by or a part of the leadership of the day and thereby contributed to, or reflected, the systemic racism in their community.

It is discomforting to shed unflattering light on well-respected historical figures. Canada has few heroes. A candid examination of racism in Canada must, nonetheless, view some that we have with a dispassionate eye. Sir John A. Macdonald, Sir Wilfrid Laurier, Goldwin Smith, Abbé Groulx, Jean Chrétien and others are indicted as supporting racist policies. Surely we are sufficiently mature to assess our leaders honestly rather than cloaking them in half-truths. It must be stressed that stating that someone supported a racist policy should not be construed as branding that person a racist. It is more often the case that normally well-intentioned and fair-minded people supported racist policies because of political or economic expedience, cultural myopia or intellectual stubbornness rather than a hatred of the group victimized by the policies. The book seeks only to have us accept the bad with the good, not to deny the good that many of the people and groups examined may have contributed to Canada's development.

Moral relativism is an important factor in any consideration of the past. One must be careful in judging people and actions of the past with today's sensibilities. Some sins, however, transcend cultural and generational change. It is the contention of this book that acting against individuals because of their race is wrong now and, despite the fact that it used to be more widely popular and openly practised, it was wrong then.

Finally, in recent years, Canadians have been educated, amused and outraged by the zealous hunt for politically incorrect thought by self-appointed soldiers of the new left. The often well-intentioned lot may be chagrined to find that the lines between good and evil in Canada's past are quite fluid. This book is not a hunt for bad guys or innocent victims. All those of the ethnic majority were not bad. While the book's focus is not upon those who fought racism, many white, British and French people who led those fights will be noted. All members of racial minorities were not good. When Japanese Canadians were being persecuted in the Second World War, for example, many Chinese Canadian people and groups spent more energy publicly proclaiming that they were not Japanese than in trying to help their fellow citizens.

The book is meant to challenge the lies we tell ourselves. Canadians are often guilty of ignoring or warping our past while sanctimoniously feeling somewhat removed from, and superior to, countries struggling with racial problems and harbouring histories marked by slavery or racial violence. Political activist Rosemary Brown has stated that if she were to write a book about Canada she would call it *Let's Pretend Let's Deny*. The lies often begin in school. Nearly all secondary-school history textbooks used prior to the 1980s portrayed Canada's development as essentially the history of Ontario and Quebec and the French and British people. Other regions and ethnic groups entered the story only as they affected the main characters. Native people, for example, were portrayed stereotypically as noble savages blindly clinging to anachronistic ways while serving European masters. After the Riel Rebellions, which were themselves reduced to French-British struggles, they simply disappeared. There were no Blacks among the United Empire Loyalists, no Chinese navvies on the railway; racial segregation did not exist; Canada's doors were always wide open to all; and influential people such as Mary Ann Shadd, Big Bear and Ivan Pylypiw never lived.

Let us end the lies. Let us look truthfully at our past, admit our mistakes, atone for our crimes and celebrate our progress. Canada's progress with respect to race and racism has, in fact, been remarkable and serves as a model for the world. But there remains work to be done. An honest acceptance of our racist past may lead to our deciding that the pursuit of a non-racist future is not only morally responsible but in the naked self-interest of us all. It is hoped that this book will contribute to that process of reflection, debate and renewal.

1

Chinese Canadians 1858–1924
From Gold to Steel Rail to Bolted Door

It is not advantageous to the country that the Chinese
should come and settle in Canada, producing a mongrel
race.
   —Sir John A. Macdonald

From its snow-peaked mountains to its primeval forests and thun-
dering shores, British Columbia is home to humbling natural
beauty. It is sad and somewhat ironic that in the bosom of such
natural splendour should grow the cancer of blind, violent racism.
Racism was born and grew with the province. It shaped its history.
It shaped its people. It defiled its beauty.

Like much of Canada, British Columbia is the child of the
Hudson's Bay Company. By the early 1800s, the HBC was competing with Russia, the United States and Britain to win control of the
resource-rich coast of what would become British Columbia. The
company built Fort Victoria on Vancouver Island. It was a clever
ploy, for the relationship between possession and the law was well
known. Finally, the Russians were ignored and the British, the
Americans and the HBC agreed to the extension of the 49th-parallel
border and to a curve southward at the end to allow the company
to retain the island and its fort.

Nowhere in the negotiations or the final agreement was mention made of the more than three thousand people of the proud and
culturally rich Haida, Kwakiutl, Cowichan and Nootka nations.
Like other Native people that the company and governments had
encountered, they were used when beneficial and thrown aside
when they were not.

The threat of American encroachment remained quite real. To counter it and legitimize British and company claims to the area, the HBC undertook an organized settlement of the island. Immigration was restricted to white, British subjects. A few wealthy British landowners and people to whom the company or government owed favours were given land. Soon a number of large, tidy, model farms were established. The town of Victoria that grew around the fort was moulded by transplanted British aristocrats intent upon cementing well-engrained British values into their new society. As noted by social historian Douglas Hill, "Victoria was born with the snobbery that has since become (for outsiders) basic in her traditions."[1]

By 1857, there were one thousand white inhabitants on the island. Roads had been built, a sawmill was operating, the fur trade and farms prospered. The company's representative, the handsome, regal-looking James Douglas, was the dominant force on the seven-member governing council. Douglas reported to company officials that all seemed to be progressing well. His only complaints were of isolation and loneliness. Douglas and his cronies had no way of knowing that everything was about to change. Gold was discovered in the Thompson River.

Gold is magic. Gold is a drug that suspends reason. Within a year of its discovery, a thousand prospectors swarmed to the Fraser Valley. Nearly all at the crest of the madness were American. Most were experienced prospectors, having played out their hand in the California gold rush with enough spunk left to try again. They were the mirror opposite of those who had created Victoria. Historian James Morton called them "the white dregs of the earth."[2] On the heels of the prospectors came the echo invasion of saloonkeepers, gamblers, prostitutes, criminals, ne'er-do-wells and lawyers all thirsting to turn human frailties to profit. Two or three ships arrived every day for months. Most of the scruffy lot quickly disappeared into the Interior. By the end of the summer of 1858, nearly thirty thousand people had swept into or through Victoria.

Douglas acted quickly, albeit with dubious legality, and claimed control of the entire Fraser Valley. He sent officials to address land and licensing squabbles and to quell the violence that had become commonplace. Douglas' initiative was praised by both company officials and the British government. The mainland was declared a crown colony under the rule of the British Colonial Office. James

Douglas was appointed governor of both it and the island. Queen Victoria suggested the name British Columbia for her new colony.

With the white rabble came the first Chinese immigrants. Like their white counterparts they came from the United States. They too had grown tired of trying to scratch a living from the over-staked and largely worn-out California mines. Further, they sought to escape American racial violence. In June 1858, approximately two thousand Chinese prospectors left Portland and arrived in New Westminster. Many more left San Francisco and sailed for Victoria.

They were soon joined by great numbers of Chinese immigrants who came directly from their homeland. China was at that time in the throes of the long and bloody Taiping Rebellion. By the late 1850s, ruthless landlords had taken control of the land. In the southern provinces, land rents had ballooned to between fifty and fifty-seven percent of harvests. The old Confucian values of respect and obedience, which had for centuries been the glue of China's culture, were thrown into question. Private armies looted and pillaged at will. Over twenty million were murdered.

Among the hardest-hit areas were the southern provinces of the Canton delta called Guangdong and Fujian. The people spoke Cantonese. They had been exposed to Britain's language and customs in the early 1850s when British soldiers and traders infiltrated the cities in the First Opium War. The British came to respect the people of the Canton delta. Fine traditions in poetry, philosophy, cuisine and the arts spoke well of the pride of a strong people. For thousands of war-ravaged, impoverished, but determined people, Britain's North American colonies were like a dream. These people comprised the bulk of Chinese immigrants to Canada.

The immigrants were of two types. Chain migrants travelled at their own expense. Their intention was to secure work, save money and return home. It was generally believed that three hundred dollars in Canadian funds would be sufficient for a family to live in relative luxury back home in China. The second type of Chinese immigrant was the indentured labourer. These people were gathered together in Canton or Hong Kong by an agency with ties in Canada. The first and largest of these companies was the Kwang Tung company of San Francisco. In 1858, it established offices in Victoria and Hong Kong to move indentured labourers to British Columbia. The labourers' passage and expenses were paid by the agency, and an agreement was signed whereby a portion of salary was paid to the agency until all expenses, plus a fee, were cleared. The immigrant was then free to continue to save to return home or remain in Canada. As most chain migrants and indentured servants planned to return home, few made substantial efforts to learn English or adapt to Canadian ways.

The first ships from Hong Kong arrived in Victoria in June 1859. When taken together with those continuing to arrive from the United States, the number of Chinese people in the colony soared. By 1860, an estimated four thousand Chinese immigrants had arrived, and by the end of 1861 it was between six and seven thousand. Nearly all were men.

The majority of Chinese arrivals joined their white counterparts in the Fraser Valley. Finding the best spots already staked, many resorted to working abandoned mines along river banks. As with the whites, only a small minority were successful. A diligent few turned a tidy profit digging jade. White miners initially recognized no value in the green rocks and left chunks scattered about abandoned mine sites. Once jade's worth was established, many white prospectors reclaimed the areas that rendered the newly prized mineral, and fortunes were made.

The success of some Chinese prospectors became widely known and was generally credited to their willingness to work exceedingly hard and long while living frugally. The majority of Chinese people in the field were also reported to refrain from the destructive personal habits typical of their white counterparts. Methodist missionary Rev. Edward White wrote in 1860,

> while others are grumbling and hesitating, or in too many instances drinking and gambling, the Chinese go at once to the mines, work hard, and spend as little as possible. I have not seen one of them either drinking or gambling since I came to this coast.[3]

By 1860, the Fraser gold rush was subsiding. The short Caribou gold rush had offered more excitement than profit. It had been discovered that panning worked only in the lower Fraser and that success nearly everywhere else depended upon large-scale excavation. This type of mining begged the formation of mining companies and rendered the lone prospector an anachronism. Many Chinese prospectors joined their white counterparts in seeking employment with the new companies. Others left the fields to find jobs in new towns and villages.

In 1863, in response to demands from the growing mining companies, Governor Douglas commissioned the first roads to the Interior. Douglas ordered that only white labourers should be hired to complete the project. Walter Moberly was placed in charge of the Caribou Wagon Road construction between Lytton and Spencer's Bridge. Moberly found that there were simply not enough white labourers willing to work on the road. He was left no alternative but to hire Chinese workers.

Moberly found that the Chinese labourers were far more honest, hard-working and trustworthy than the white men in his employ. In a report to Douglas, he explained that the problems with white workers had

> compelled me to employ, much against my wishes, a large force of Chinese labourers. It will thus be seen that the bad faith and unscrupulous conduct of the white labourers was the cause of the employment of Chinese labour in constructing the Caribou Wagon Road. All the other contractors on this road experienced the same treatment from their white labourers that befell me. I found all the Chinese employed worked most industriously and faithfully and gave us no trouble.[4]

Douglas was forced to re-evaluate his decision, and, somewhat after the fact, he officially allowed Moberly and all other road contractors to hire Chinese labourers. Soon there were approximately one thousand Chinese men at work building British Columbia's first major roads.

The well-publicized lessons of the roads projects were not lost on white business people. Many shared Moberly's disdain for white and admiration of Chinese workers. Beyond their dependability and productivity, it was widely believed that since Chinese men had grown used to slave wages at home they were willing to work for significantly less than white men. This belief led to a situation where Chinese labourers earned an average of 75¢ to $1.25 a day while white labourers earned an average of $1.50 to $2.50.

This assumed willingness to settle for less helped many businesses. For example, coal mines were the basis of Nanaimo's economy. A worldwide depression hit the coal industry in 1866 and coal prices plummeted. Mine owners negotiated with white miners to accept lower wages but they refused to budge from their $2.50 a day. While no white workers were fired, and white wages were not changed, most mine owners began hiring Chinese miners when jobs became available and paid them only $1.00 a day. Many of the mines that may have closed during the depression remained open due in large part to the influx of the lower-salaried but harder-working Chinese miners. The 1885 Royal Commission investigating Oriental problems in British Columbia stated that not only the coal-mining industry but also the canning and gold industries would not have succeeded without Chinese labour.[5]

Not all Chinese workers toiled for others. By the 1870s, there were thirty Chinese-owned mining companies. The largest were owned and operated by Quong Lee, Dang Sing Dang, Sing Dang and Loo Gee Wing. The four produced an average of $3 million worth of gold a year throughout the decade. In 1878, a Chinese businessman purchased British Columbia's largest mine, the Dancing Bird Mine, and produced $9 million worth of gold in that year.

White businessman Robert Collier praised Chinese businessmen at the time as hard-working and able to be trusted to fulfil their contracts.[6] In Victoria, most Chinese-owned businesses were located along Johnson, Cormorant and Fisgard Streets. The area became Canada's first Chinatown. A particularly successful Chinese business was Kuong Lee, established in June 1858. It was an agency of a San Francisco company that specialized in imported Chinese teas, sugar, rice and other goods. Kuong Lee, which loosely translates to "expansive profit," had by 1885 become second only to the Hudson's Bay Company in terms of sales and number of employees. Its owner, Lee Chong, was the first Chinese immigrant to bring his wife and family to Canada.

By 1862, eleven companies owned by Chinese business people were paying taxes in Victoria. Subsidiaries of Chinese-owned companies were seen in towns throughout the colony. A Chinese doctor named Ah Chi established a successful practice. A Chinese-owned inn called the Sacramento House was built. Restaurants, laundries, an apothecary and many more thriving businesses were owned and operated by Chinese business people. Initially, most customers of Chinese-owned businesses were Chinese. Soon, however, a great number of white customers appeared. White women were reported to be especially willing to venture into Chinatown to take advantage of what became generally accepted as superior selection, cleanliness and service.

When not providing goods and services to white customers, Chinese men and a few women were working as servants in their homes. The first Chinese servants were hired by American families in Victoria in 1864. They were reported to be responsible and hardworking. A prominent Victoria man told the 1879 Select Committee on Chinese Labour and Immigration that "Without the Chinese in British Columbia there would have been no domestic service at all."[7]

The Chinese immigrants had arrived as part of the gold-rush flood of new residents and had played their part in the growth of the young colony. A grand jury in Lillooet made this point in 1860 when it wrote that the Chinese people were "a steady source of profit to the trader and materially increase the revenue of the colony and in addition greatly benefit the country by the extreme development of its mineral resources; they are also a well-behaved, easily governed class of the population."[8] An editorial in the May 10, 1858 *British Colonist* stated that the building of the new colony "now assumes a more tangible form by the initiative taken by native Chinese merchants themselves in consigning vessels laden with labourers and Chinese produce to our port."[9] They had become responsible and valuable members of the community.

•

Anti-Chinese ideas and actions had been rampant during the California gold rush. In 1852, the governor of California had run for re-election on the promise to rid the state of Chinese people. A number of towns and mines had banned Chinese inhabitants and workers, and newspapers had cried out against further Chinese immigration.

The imported anti-Chinese attitudes were present with the arrival of Chinese immigrants to B.C. In August 1858, for example, a number of Chinese prospectors arrived in Hope, in the Fraser Valley. Their boat was met by angry white prospectors, many of whom had come from California only weeks before. They hurled insults and rocks, and would not allow the boat to dock. The mob was turned back by a Hudson's Bay Company official named

Donald McLean who, with his young son's assistance, drew a revolver and forced the increasingly violent mob to retire. The boat moored and the passengers were escorted ashore. Violence perpetrated against Chinese prospectors quickly became routine. That same month, the *Victoria Gazette*, founded by two Americans, reported, "A Chinaman was found shot dead with five bullets in his body. He was on his way to a spring to fetch a bucket of water and had to pass a camp of miners. Further comment unnecessary."[10]

Newspapers actively supported British Columbia's climb up the racist ladder through publicizing and legitimizing anti-Chinese stereotypes. For example, the *Victoria Gazette* editorial of June 1858 warned,

> We have not yet seen a Chinaman in Victoria, though a small number of citizens of the Flowery Kingdom are known to have left California in the Fraser River exodus. From a sign which appears in our streets, however, it may be presumed that John is among us and bears the euphonious and suggestive legend, Chang Tsoo. Doubtless ere long the familiar interrogation of 'Want washes?' will be added to our everyday library.[11]

Chinese people were popularly referred to as "John." One reason for the pejorative monicker was that many Anglo-Saxon people could not be bothered to learn difficult Chinese names. Another explanation is that John is a bastardization of the French word for yellow. It joined other words variously used by newspapers in referring to Chinese people, such as "moon-eyes," "slants," and "Mongolians." The epithets became increasingly less polite.

The newspaper that seemed most intent upon stirring racial fear and hatred was the *British Colonist*, created by Amor De Cosmos. De Cosmos was a Nova Scotia-born reformer who, as editor and politician, played a significant part in shaping public opinion and in British Columbia's development. The charismatic man's real name was Bill Smith, but while working as a photographer in the California gold rush he had it legally changed to what translated as "lover of the universe." De Cosmos often reprinted articles verbatim from San Francisco newspapers. In June 1859, as the first immigrants were arriving from China, the *British Colonist* reprinted a *San Francisco Bulletin* article that appealed to ideas of ethnic allegiance while mixing notions of social Darwinism and fears of genetic impurity with class and economic paranoia. It read,

> when a white man is placed alongside a company of these creatures, imported from abroad, and fed on rice and dog-fish, and made to measure the price of his day's work by the price of theirs, there will be complaining and dissatisfaction. And for our part, we sympathise with and take the part of the white miner when he is drawn to meet such unnatural competition. We say it is the prosperity of the white man in this state that makes up her prosperity; that the aggrandisement of the Chinese does not make us a particle richer—adds nothing to our fixed capital, builds no cities or towns, erects no churches or school houses, or, in short, does anything to advance us in wealth, power or greatness.[12]

Perhaps community leaders and the shapers of public opinion could have acted to kill the racist stereotypes and prejudice before they took root. Unfortunately, the very people who could have tried to eradicate the ideas instead fed and nurtured them until a monster grew. Racism became institutionalized and cemented into the foundation of British Columbia's political culture.

Perhaps business leaders could have stopped racism's insidious growth. Most business people, however, found themselves in a quandary. Their business instincts told them that Chinese labour was necessary, cheaper and, in many cases, preferable. On the other hand, their competitive instincts told them that Chinese business people were more than worthy competitors and that they would naturally benefit from the elimination of that competition. With one eye on the cash register, most white business people scampered quickly up the racist ladder.

Joined by municipal government leaders, the business people of Victoria formed the Working Man's Protective Association in September 1878. It was led by Noah Shakespeare. The group's aim was "the mutual protection of the working class in British Columbia against the great influx of Chinese...." Its members pledged to "neither aid nor abet or patronise Chinamen in any way whatever or patronise those employing them [and] use all legitimate means for their expulsion from the country."[13] Chapters of the organization were formed first in New Westminster, then in a number of other communities. Surveys led to the publication and distribution of lists of businesses that were to be boycotted for employing Chinese labour or having intercourse with Chinese businesses.

Perhaps the church could have thrown itself before the growth of racism. Christian churches, however, found themselves in a quandary as disturbing as that of the businessmen. How could they address the paradox of recognizing Chinese people as children of God in need of support and protection while the Chinese culture, according to popular belief, posed a threat to Christian beliefs and hegemony?

The Protestant and Catholic churches' tacit support of anti-Oriental racism was heard from pulpits. Their official support of racist paternalism was made clear in a great many church documents. A Methodist report stated, "Let our attitude be one of sympathy, of welcome, of invitation to assimilation and it will yield a result diametrically different from that of coldness or persecution or ostracism...."[14] The churches chose to save the Chinese people from themselves by turning them into white clones. The Acts of the Proceedings of the Presbyterian Church said that all Orientals must be saved from "the centuries of darling superstitions, demonolatry, ancestral worship, and faith in false gods which meet in him."[15] Stating that the Chinese people should be accepted if they could be assimilated suggested that they were to be rejected if they could not.

Some brave church officials objected to the racism they saw festering around them and demanded that a stand be taken against it, but anti-racist ideas were seldom made public. Methodist Rev. Edward White was a rare exception. He wrote,

> Although the popular cry of California and with many here is 'Stop them!', 'drive them back;' I say, let them come! While we are trying to get their country open to commerce and our Christianity, it is right that we should treat them kindly who come to our shores.[16]

Perhaps elected political leaders could have tried to stop the racism. From the arrival of the first Chinese immigrants, however, politicians reflected, inflamed and entrenched the racism of their constituents. Instead of enacting legislation to protect all citizens, a plethora of racist, exclusionary laws was passed restricting suffrage, limiting employment and housing opportunities, and attempting to end immigration while promoting deportation.

The first of the racist laws came in 1859 with Vancouver's Franchise Act. It stated that only British subjects could vote. Since regulations made it very difficult for Chinese people to become naturalized citizens, the law effectively barred Chinese people from an essential democratic right. That the Vancouver city council acted with the support of a majority of its constituents was made clear in the return of the entire council in a subsequent election. The views of Vancouver's white community were reflected again in an article written by a leading citizen of the town. He wrote in opposition to a proposed tax on Chinese people, but his prejudice was glaringly evident. He wrote,

> They may be inferior to Europeans and Americans in energy and ability; hostile to us in race, language and habits, and may remain among us as a Pariah race; still they are patient, easily governed, and invariably industrious.... Hereafter, when the time arrives that we can dispose of them, we will heartily second a check to their immigration.[17]

British Columbia joined Canada in 1871. Its infant provincial legislature wasted no time in enacting a great deal of racist legislation. In its first session, the Qualification of Voters Act was passed. Where Vancouver's Franchise Act implicitly and imperfectly robbed Chinese people of the right to vote, the new provincial law robbed them explicitly and completely.

Newly appointed lieutenant-governor Joseph Truth could have refused to grant royal assent and stopped the racist bill but he did not. The British North America Act, the Canadian constitution at that time, afforded the federal government the power to disallow provincial laws that it deemed *ultra vires* or not in the interest of the country as a whole. Prime Minister Sir John A. Macdonald was a strong federalist who had proven himself quite willing to use this power. He and his cabinet apparently saw nothing wrong with the Qualification of Voters Act, for it was allowed to stand.

The Vancouver and provincial laws restricting suffrage according to race led a number of municipalities to enact similar legislation. In Nanaimo, for instance, Chinese people were not allowed to vote in the January 1873 municipal election. Some Chinese men who appeared at the polls were beaten up. The *British Colonist* applauded the decision of the Nanaimo town council and the roughneck tactics used to enforce it. It reported,

> so sensible were the Freemen of Nanaimo of the impropri-
> ety, the degradation of allowing these heathen slaves...to
> stand side by side with themselves at the ballot box and
> have an equal voice in the management of affairs....[18]

Governments did not stop at restricting the franchise. They sought also to work in harmony with business leaders and white workers to restrict employment opportunities for Chinese people. In 1875, it was proposed that no Chinese person be employed in Victoria's public works. The bill passed unanimously.

Taxation laws were also racist. In 1879, a motion supporting the imposition of a head tax on all Chinese people in Victoria was passed unanimously by city council. The new tax was levied on every Chinese person over twelve years of age. It forced them to purchase a ten-dollar licence every three months. White employers had to submit lists of Chinese people in their employ and ensure that their licences were up to date. They were fined one hundred dollars for having unlicensed Chinese employees and were often counselled by city hall officials as to the wisdom of employing them at all.

While Chinese people had not liked the other racist laws, licensing inspired an organized reaction. Petitions were signed and sent to Ottawa and London. Chinese merchants refused to pay the fees. On September 16, the Victoria police broke down the doors of protesting Chinese businesses, seized their goods and auctioned them for a fraction of their value. The next day the Chinese commu-nity undertook a general strike. All Chinese businesses closed. No Chinese workers reported to their jobs, including two hundred domestic servants. For five days the city teetered on the brink of racial violence. Tensions eased when a court injunction forced an end to the auctions and ordered the police to return all unsold goods to their rightful owners. Finally, on October 28, the federal govern-ment disallowed the law.

The support given to the racist laws, and to the politicians who espoused them, plainly shows the popularity of anti-Chinese be-liefs. Arthur Bunster, for instance, was a fiery man who represented Nanaimo in the colonial assembly in Victoria before Confederation. One day he had stood in the legislature to propose a fifty percent poll tax on all Chinese people working in the colony. His red jowls shook as he pounded the table and screamed in the legislature, "It's going to be a test question in the next election—see if it ain't... I want to see the Chinamen kept to himself [sic] and foul diseases kept away from white people."[19]

The proposed tax did not come to a vote but his remarks showed prescience. By the early 1870s one had to publicly subscribe to anti-Chinese beliefs to enjoy any hope of electoral success. This remained the case for decades as municipal, provincial and federal political leaders appeared and left the scene either sincerely espousing racist beliefs or lacking the personal or political courage to gainsay. The people of Nanaimo expressed their opinion of Bunster's racist beliefs by electing him to serve as Nanaimo's first federal member of Parliament.

Newspapers continued to both reflect and inflame the racism of the community. For example, the *Victoria Gazette* editorial of March 31, 1859 stated that Chinese people were, "a species of slavery...and they are, with few exceptions, not desirable as permanent settlers in a country peopled by the Caucasian race and governed by civilised enactments."[20] A decade and a half later, the July 24, 1875 *Caribou Senital* editorial stated that it would be a

> delightful relief to both sight and senses not only of residents of Victoria but of visitors, if that pleasant little city could be freed from the forbidding presence and vile habitations of the majority of the Chinese residents, and the comfortable cottages of white labourers, with happy wives and troops of smiling children substituted in their place.[21]

By the 1870s the Chinese people were without friends. In the struggle against compassion, racism won the day by default. The Chinese people had been abandoned by fellow workers, the church, the business community, the law, the press and all levels of government.

A British essayist named R. Byron Johnson travelled much of British Columbia in the 1860s and was appalled by what he saw. He wrote,

> It is the fashion on the Pacific Coast, to abuse and ill treat the Chinaman in every possible way.... He is treated like a dog, bullied, scoffed at, kicked, and cuffed-about on all

occasions...and yet, withal, be betrays no sign of meditated revenge, and pursues his labours calmly, and is civil and polite to all....[22]

In only a few years, the racist ladder had been built and ascended to its fourth rung. The Chinese people were friendless at a time when they needed all the friends they could get, for everything was about to change. The railway was coming.

•

Sir John A. Macdonald enjoyed the odd taste of gin when political or personal tensions were intense. Everyone in Ottawa knew what was meant by the whispered suggestion "Sir John's off again." Despite his occasionally insalubrious personal habits, he possessed a keen wit and an agile mind. He also possessed the most important attribute of leadership; he had vision.

Macdonald knew that in 1867 Canada was a country in name only. He knew that if it did not quickly claim the great prairies and beyond, the Americans would pursue their insatiable desire for land by filling the North-West with settlers. Thus surrounded, the rump of the four original provinces would not remain independent for long. Macdonald promised British Columbia's colonial government that he would have a rail line to them in ten years if they would forget ideas about American annexation and join the young dominion. Half believing the promise could not be kept, but anxious to maintain British ties, the colonial leaders struck the deal.

Liberal leader Alexander Mackenzie called the railway "an act of insane recklessness."[23] In many ways it was just that. It was to be one thousand miles longer than any line in the United States and the longest line in the world. As work progressed, the unforgiving ruthlessness of the Canadian landscape was brought to bear. Near Savanna, Ontario, for instance, an entire train and one hundred feet of track were simply swallowed by the muskeg. Life was cheap. In one fifty-mile stretch of track thirty men were killed in blasting accidents. As hard and dangerous as the work was, there was a general consensus that the Ontario and prairie sections of the line were relatively easy. The mountains loomed.

Andrew Onderdonk was a reticent, fastidious man from a rich New York family. He was awarded the contract to build the line through the mountains. Before the job was done he would build hundreds of trestles and bridges and hundreds of miles of roads, create a lumber industry and an explosives factory, develop a banking system, and invent new types of land and water transportation vehicles. The first thing he needed, however, was workers. There were only thirty-five hundred able bodied workers in British Columbia when Onderdonk arrived in Victoria in 1880. He estimated a need for ten thousand.

Tenders for the railway contracts had been announced in October 1877. The announcement revived interest in the Victoria Anti-Chinese Association. The group had been formed in May 1873. It was comprised of prominent business people and civic leaders intent upon pressuring the provincial and federal governments to restrict immigration of Chinese people to British Columbia. Members of the Anti-Chinese Association told Onderdonk that every effort had to be made to hire white British Columbians and then to import white workers from other parts of Canada and the United States. They even gulped hard and suggested that as a last resort he should consider hiring French and Native workers. He must, they insisted, at all costs avoid hiring Chinese people to work on the railway.

Onderdonk had expected such a reception, for he had been well briefed about the racism that pumped British Columbia's heart. The Working Man's Protective Association (WPA) had already sent petitions to Ottawa demanding that no Chinese workers be hired. With the fear of hordes of Chinese railway workers pouring into the province the WPA, and other like-minded racist organizations, had grown in membership and power. By 1881 the WPA boasted over one thousand members and had chapters in a number of towns. It had organized harassment campaigns in which Chinese homes and businesses in Victoria, Vancouver and New Westminster were ransacked. Windows were broken, houses burned and residents beaten. Some Chinese shops were boycotted while others were looted or burned. A number of Chinese men who dared to walk alone, even in broad daylight, were jumped and their ceremonial queue, or ponytail, cut off or their heads roughly shaved. Victoria's Mayor Shakespeare had a queue thus obtained mounted as a trophy in his home.

Prime Minister Macdonald had lost his Kingston seat in the 1878 election. Although he had never visited the city, a seat was made available in Victoria and in a hastily arranged by-election Sir John became that city's member of Parliament. He needed to be aware of the concerns of his new constituents, including anti-Oriental racism, and to placate the growing anger over delays to the promised railway. The prime minister needed an education.

Amor De Cosmos had left the editorship of the *British Colonist* but before doing so had become one of the main proponents of Chinese expulsion. In 1862 he had written in his newspaper,

> Chinamen are not the most desirable population. The social evils connected with a Mongolian population [include] their inferior civilisation, their language, their religion, their habits of living—all so hostile to the customs and prejudices of the higher and dominant race.[24]

By 1878, he had become a federal member of Parliament and simultaneously, in an odd but legal political two-step, the first premier of British Columbia. Premier De Cosmos had already sent Macdonald long letters and a 1,497-signature petition indicating Victoria's violent opposition to Chinese people in general and Chinese workers in particular. He volunteered to tutor the prime minister.

Macdonald created a committee to study the B.C. Chinese situation and appointed De Cosmos as its chair. Only white people were allowed to appear at the public hearings. Testimony was seldom accurate. Arthur Bunster, for example, appeared with the old ruse that Chinese workers were depressing wages. Another witness accused Chinese men of introducing a virulent strain of syphilis. The committee's report was tabled in May 1879, and, predictably, it recommended that Chinese immigration be restricted and that no Chinese workers be employed to construct the railway. Sir John responded as he no doubt knew he would from the beginning. He ignored it. As he stated three years later in the House of Commons, "It is simply a question of alternatives; either you must have this labour or you can't have a railway."[25]

This was the same conclusion to which Onderdonk had already come. He listened politely to the representations of various groups and individuals, then set about to complete his work. Like a good politician he took one step at a time and began by hiring only white labour.

The centre of railway activity began at a small community

called Yale. Yale quickly became a town reminiscent of old-time Hollywood westerns. The saloons were full, there were fights on muddy streets, and busy prostitutes waved from second-storey windows. Many of the white railway workers who swelled the town had been hired from within British Columbia. Others were experienced railway workers from the Northern Pacific Railroad in Oregon and the Southern Pacific Railroad in California. All were paid between $1.50 and $1.75 a day. Skilled tradespeople, such as carpenters and the like, could make up to $2.00 a day. Room, board and other expenses were, of course, deducted.

Work began slowly. Onderdonk blasted through the mountains, creating dangerous and innovative tunnels, for nearly a year before laying a single mile of track. He watched the granite, the weather and his men make a mockery of his schedule. He saw many white workers doing their best but most simply wasting his time and money. Onderdonk wrote that his workers were for the most part "the most useless lot of broken down gamblers, barkeepers, etc. ever collected in one place."[26]

Within a month of starting work, Onderdonk announced his intention to hire Chinese workers. Many were hired from railroad companies in the United States. They were not enough. Ignoring a torrent of criticism, Onderdonk arranged with the Six Companies of Kwang Tung, the most important of which was the Lian Chang Company, to bring workers from China. In May 1882, two ships called the *Escambia* and the *Suez* brought the first lot of two thousand directly from Hong Kong to Victoria. By the end of June over sixty-five hundred had arrived. By the time construction ended in 1885, approximately 170,000 Chinese workers had been brought to Canada to build its railway.

The first ships were met on the Victoria docks by angry, stone-throwing mobs. An average of ten percent of those arriving had contracted scurvy on the voyage. The newspapers, perhaps expectedly but certainly inaccurately, reported it as venereal disease and smallpox. Those arriving in New Westminster were deloused, then penned like cattle on the docks. They were transferred to steamships for the treacherous trip up the Fraser to Emory. They were then loaded on flatcars for the trip to Yale. Most were swinging a pick one day after their arrival in Canada.

Their fellow workers did not greet them warmly. They were pejoratively dubbed "coolies." Typical of the relationship was a confrontation near Lytton in May 1883. After a white foreman refused to pay his Chinese workers, he and a Chinese navvy wrestled each other to the ground. The proper payments were made. When darkness fell, a group of white workers armed with shovels and picks descended on the segregated, sleeping Chinese camp. The Chinese workers were mercilessly beaten, the camp burned and personal property smashed. The victims were moved to another work camp. Although the rioters' identities were known they were neither arrested nor reprimanded. Compensation was not offered to the victims.

Chinese navvies were paid less than the whites. They worked most often for $1.00 a day less expenses. Onderdonk was pleased to hear reports indicating that they apparently required less in terms of supplies to live. They did not sleep late, fight or carouse. They worked hard all day and were willing to march long distances to perform roadbuilding and other collateral tasks without complaint. Onderdonk wrote to Macdonald that he was very pleased with the production and conduct of the Chinese workers. He wrote that they showed an "obligation to family and friends [that] made them thoroughly reliable, unlike the white workers, who tended to desert the construction site as soon as they received their pay."[27]

Onderdonk's initial reaction was born out over the long haul. In the 1885 Royal Commission report on Chinese immigration, commissioner J.A. Chapleau wrote, "as a railway navvy, the Chinaman has no superior."[28]

Chinese workers shared the misery of difficult, dangerous work and brutal living conditions with white workers. Food was often scarce and nearly always of wretched quality. Tents and wooden shanties welcomed the wind, rain and snow. Winter's cold was numbing. Clothing was often torn, boots old, and gloves threadbare.

While the situation was hard for all, the Chinese workers were subjected to especially poor treatment. B.C. Chief Justice Matthew Baillie Begbie wrote that "the terrible outrages against Chinamen...in its wholesale unconcealed atrocity equalled anything which I have read of agrarian outrage in Ireland."[29] Often the outrages to which he referred were the result of careless or vindictive decisions made by white foremen who led segregated thirty-member Chinese work gangs. Precautions that were standard practice with white workers were often forgotten when Chinese workers were involved. This tendency resulted in deaths among Chinese workers being much higher in proportion to their numbers than deaths among whites.

The British Columbia press often failed to mention these disturbing facts. For example, the diary of Henry Cambie, Onderdonk's chief engineer, notes the following for one month in 1880:

August 13: A Chinese drilling on the ledge of a bluff of Alexander Bar is killed when a stone falls from above and knocks him off.
August 19: A log rolls over an embankment and crushes a Chinese to death at the foot of the slope.
September 4: A Chinese killed by a rock slide.
September 7: A boat upsets in the Fraser and a Chinese is drowned.[30]

On September 9, 1880 the *Yale Sentinal* ran an article about the progress of the railway. The article stated, "There have been no deaths since the 15th of June."[31] Apparently Chinese workers did not count.

Besides work-related accidents, many Chinese workers suffered from diseases for which life in China had provided no natural immunities. While scurvy was a problem, the largest killer was smallpox contracted after their arrival. While medical treatment was provided for white workers, there were few and, in many cases, no doctors sent to Chinese camps.

The work went on. Railway workers died by the score. Careers and fortunes were made and dashed but the work went on. Finally, on a dull November morning in 1885, the last spike was driven at Cragellachie. Sir John's dream had been fulfilled and his promise kept.

Under Onderdonk's direction, white workers had laid twenty-seven miles of track from Yale to North Bend. White and Chinese workers had completed a twenty-six-mile section from North Bend to Lytton. Exclusively Chinese work gangs had laid seventy miles from Lytton to Savanna's Ferry and another ninety miles from Port Moody to Yale. Over two hundred Chinese workers died from smallpox and hundreds more from normally preventable or curable ailments. Approximately four thousand Chinese workers gave their lives laying the majority of the track of the most difficult portion of the Canadian railway.

It has been convincingly argued that the railway could simply not have been built without the Chinese workers. Pierre Berton has concluded that "Cheap Oriental labour undoubtedly saved Onderdonk from bankruptcy. Without the Chinese it is probable that he could not have completed his contract."[32] Berton estimates that the Canadian government saved approximately $3 million to $5 million by employing cheap Chinese labour and that these savings may not have only rescued the railway but also the debt-burdened country itself from financial ruin.[33] Canada's national dream was built on the backs and with the blood of Chinese labour.

•

It may seem reasonable to believe that the white majority of British Columbia would have acknowledged the invaluable contribution of the Chinese railway worker by turning their backs on racist beliefs, rules and legislation and that they would have recognized Chinese people as equal partners in the country they were helping to build. It was not to be.

Most Chinese navvies came to Canada expecting to save enough money to return to China. Despite extremely frugal living, most were only able to save approximately forty dollars a year. Nearly five thousand workers decided either out of choice or necessity to remain in Canada. Many found jobs in the growing lumber companies and coal mines. Many others moved to towns and cities to find work and start new lives in what financial necessity had rendered their adopted home.

The white inhabitants of those towns were presented with a problem. It had been tacitly agreed by railway officials and the federal and British Columbia governments that the Chinese workers would be exploited then forced to leave Canada as soon as the railway was done. Macdonald had stated that intention in the House in 1882.[34] The promised expulsion of the Chinese railway workers was demanded by newspapers across the province.

Preparations had long been under way for the day the "coolies" repaired from the field. In 1883, the British Columbia legislature passed several bills meant to deal with what was becoming popularly known as the "yellow peril." An Act to Prevent Chinese from Acquiring Crown Land was declared *ultra vires* by the B.C. Supreme Court. The Chinese Regulation Act, which sought to expedite Chinese deportations, suffered a similar fate. An Act to Prevent

Chinese Immigration was disallowed by the federal government, for it too was beyond the limits of the province's constitutional jurisdiction. Frustration mounted quickly.

In reaction to unconstitutional provincial and municipal laws that were appearing with increasing alacrity, Sir John, whose nickname was Old Tomorrow, resorted again to that most Canadian of tactics, the Royal Commission. The Royal Commission on Chinese Immigration was comprised of Dr. Joseph Adolphe Chapleau, the federal Secretary of State, and Dr. John Hamilton Grey, a B.C. Supreme Court judge. The reaction to Grey's appointment was almost unanimously negative in B.C., Grey had, after all, just declared several anti-Chinese pieces of legislation illegal. Victoria's Mayor Shakespeare boycotted the proceedings to great publicity. In an article that attacked Grey while betraying the popularity of the racism of the day, the *British Colonist* published an article stating, "He can in no sense be regarded as a representative of anti-Chinese elements in the province or as a representative of public opinion on the Chinese question."[35]

The Royal Commission met in Victoria, New Westminster and Yale. It heard from fifty-one witnesses, but only two were Chinese and both were from the Chinese consulate in San Francisco. Much of the testimony was startling in its revelation of the depth of racial hatred among the province's power elite. For example, a representative of the Victoria Lodge of the Noble and Holy Order of the Knights of Labour, comprised of labour, business and church leaders, testified that

> Vice, including prostitution and gambling is abundant in those [Chinese] quarters…. They are a non-assimilating race. Their vices are disgusting. They turn their sick out into the streets, and their lepers to fill our prisons. They control the labour market in the city. They are of no benefit to this country…. The Chinese are a disgrace to a civilised community, and we beg that steps may be taken to stop the influx of Chinese to our shore.[36]

The economic benefit of Chinese labour and the cleanliness of Chinese places of business have already been noted. Add to these the fact that there were no cases of leprosy anywhere in British Columbia at that time. Add too that there were only 160 Chinese women in the entire province and it is clear that the accusations, like many other statements made during the hearings, were built on a foundation of racist lies, half-truths and innuendo.

The Royal Commission afforded publicity and a cloak of legitimacy to the racist blustering of the witnesses and thereby helped inflame racist hatred. Its report admitted that Chinese people were doing a great deal to help the province's economic development. The commission's recommendations, however, were predictable when one reads its mandate: "The object of the Commission is to obtain proof that the principle of restricting Chinese immigration is proper and in the best interests of the Province and the Dominion."[37] It did what it was told, ignored its own findings, and concluded that "the worst of Chinese immigrants," such as the poor, women, and children, should not be allowed to enter. It recommended that a ten-dollar head tax be imposed on all Chinese immigrants to reduce the numbers and weed out those undesirables.

The head tax easily passed through the legislative process in Ottawa and became law. The B.C. legislature was outraged. It had wanted complete exclusion and deportations. It reacted by again passing the previously disallowed Chinese Immigration Act that completely barred Chinese entry into the province. A ship filled with over two hundred Chinese immigrants was turned away from the Victoria harbour under the auspices of the law. Macdonald disallowed the law again, not because its intentions were wrong but because immigration remained a federal responsibility.

In an effort to assuage the anger spurred by the return of the Chinese navvies, the reduced but continuing Chinese immigration, and the disallowances, Macdonald introduced an amendment to the Franchise Act. The amendment rendered it illegal for any person of Chinese extraction to vote in a federal election. The restriction even applied to naturalized Canadian citizens of Chinese descent. The prime minister showed his willingness to exploit Chinese workers while allowing them none of the benefits of citizenship when be rose in the House to explain the new law. He said,

> The Chinaman...has no common interest with us, and while he gives us his labour and is paid for it, and it is valuable, the same as a threshing machine or any other

agricultural implement which we may borrow from the United States on hire and return it to the owner on the south side of the line; a Chinaman gives us his labour and gets his money, but takes it with him and returns to China; and if he cannot, his executors or his friends send his body back to the flowery land. But he has no British instinct or British feelings or aspirations, and therefore ought not to have a vote.[38]

If a person could not vote in a federal election he could also not vote in provincial or municipal elections. All three levels of government had thereby conspired to rob Chinese people of the franchise. To restrict the right to vote according to race in a democratic state is systemic racism at its ugliest. Chinese-Canadian citizens were not able to vote in a federal election until after the Second World War.

Meanwhile business and labour leaders were taking action of their own. There were concerted moves made to implement stricter economic segregation. Unions played a leadership role in this effort. Unions do not exist to protect the rights of workers. They protect only the rights of their members. B.C. laws and the rules of nearly every B.C. union barred Chinese workers from union membership. Smaller all-white unions were seen as preferable to larger, and more powerful, inclusive unions. Locking union hall doors to Chinese workers allowed union leaders to portray them as enemies competing for their members' jobs. The competition was more imagined than real. In most cases, Chinese workers took jobs that white workers would not accept. Further, their labour allowed business expansion which created more jobs. Racism, however, prefers folk myth to fact.

One of the first and most powerful labour organizations in British Columbia was the Knights of Labour. In the fall of 1886, the Vancouver chapter undertook a campaign to restrict Chinese labour and business by boycotting white businesses that employed Chinese workers or patronized businesses owned by Chinese entrepreneurs. Those ignoring the boycott found a large white X painted on the sidewalk outside their establishment, and people were encouraged not to cross it. The campaign was relatively successful. Many Chinese workers were fired and many contracts with Chinese business people were cancelled.

Newspapers supported the boycott, and their articles and editorials indicated widespread support among the white population.

In November 1886, for example, a column in the *British Colonist* stated,

> The Knights of Labour are still relentlessly pursuing the war against Chinese labour which they inaugurated…. By this means Vancouver will be ridden of the plague to white labour which threatened to invade the city in great force before the knights made a move in opposition to it. No Chinaman need apply at Vancouver. They run the risk of a cool reception and a warm send off.[39]

The *Vancouver World* reported on April 2, 1886 that the sale of two building lots to Chinese men was a "violent wrench to public sentiment."[40] The *Vancouver Morning News* supposedly spoke for many Vancouver citizens when it wrote on June 2, 1886 that the Chinese must be kept out of the city to spare the citizens the "evil which has cursed all Pacific coast towns."[41] That Chinese people were helping to build the province and fulfil Canada's national dream did not seem to matter.

In the eye of this hurricane of hatred, a contractor named John McDougal made either a brave or stupid but certainly interesting decision. McDougal hired Chinese labourers to clear 350 acres of a five-hundred-acre parcel of land near Vancouver called the Brighouse Estate. At that time it was approximately two miles from the city, separated by swamp and forest and joined by the most rudimentary of roads. McDougal later explained that he was able to win the tender because he planned to save fifty percent of labour costs through hiring cheap Chinese workers. He stood to make a profit of $21,000.

The large anti-Chinese element of the city was outraged. The day after 250 Chinese workers arrived and were surreptitiously moved to the estate, a meeting was held at city hall. It was chaired by R.D. Pitt, who was an official with the Knights of Labour. Other leaders present that night were Vancouver mayor M.A. MacLean, three city councillors, a local magistrate and representatives from the clergy. The meeting inaugurated a group called the Vancouver Vigilance Committee. The committee's expressed purpose was to force the Chinese Brighouse Estate workers out of Vancouver.

January 8, 1887 offered a cool and clear Sunday evening. Seventy-five members of the Vigilance Committee and 250 local supporters traversed the rough trail to the estate. With jeers, shouts and threats of violence, nineteen Chinese workers were coerced into leaving. They were escorted to the harbour and their fares to Victoria paid. Several hundred dollars worth of their personal property was left behind. They were not compensated. A crowd of six hundred watched the spectacle and cheered as the small craft vanished into the mist. In the days that followed, more Chinese workers were similarly persuaded to leave. Each time, an ever-growing crowd applauded their departure.

Few things breed boldness as surely as a hint of success. New meetings of the Vancouver Vigilance Committee were convened at city hall. The people of Vancouver woke up one morning to find the following bill pasted on fences, buildings and poles, and a shortened version in their newspapers:

Due notice is hereby given to warn all Chinamen to move with all their chattels from within the corporation of the city of Vancouver on or before the 15th day of January 1887, failing which all Chinamen found in the city after the above date shall be forcibly expelled therefrom and their goods and household effects shall be consigned to either Coal Harbour or False Creek as convenience may propose. And furthermore, the authorities of the town are kindly cautioned not to risk their lives in trying to rescue the Mongolians, or giving themselves any unnecessary trouble as the undersigned are in terrible earnest.[42]

The deadline passed without incident but the Vigilance Committee's intentions had been made frighteningly apparent. Letters were written to prominent white people asking them to stop patronizing Chinese businesses. More white Xs were painted in front of shops that employed or did business with Chinese people. A number of well-attended public meetings roused more support for the committee's goals and tactics.

On January 20, a rumour spread that hundreds of Chinese immigrants were arriving at the harbour. Three hundred angry, club-wielding men sped to the docks to greet them. The rumour was false but the incident foreshadowed what was to come.

The committee's activities grew in popularity. As the campaign gathered momentum it grew beyond the ability of the Vigilance

Committee to control it. Pitt convened a meeting on February 2 at city hall. The meeting saw the formation of a new group with the blunt moniker The Anti-Chinese League. Its organizing committee was comprised of prominent business, labour and church leaders. Although the mayor and city council knew the league was being formed in their chambers they were not part of it. Neither did they act to stop it.

After two more weeks of boycotts, the anti-Chinese movement again became violent. On February 24, for some reason believing that the tense period of the previous month had passed, John McDougal moved Chinese workers back from Victoria to the Brighouse Estate. Upon hearing the news, Pitt quickly arranged another city hall meeting. A large crowd gathered outside and heard speaker after speaker demanding the immediate and total expulsion of Chinese people from the city. When whipped to a fever pitch, the crowd turned to the estate. They boomed "John Brown's Body" into the cold night as they marched.

A mob of three to four hundred descended upon the makeshift cabins that housed the estate's Chinese workers. The shocked young men were pulled from their beds and beaten. The camp was demolished and a huge fire engulfed the cabins. The men's personal belongings were tossed into the inferno.

With the victims beaten and cowed and the fires dying, the mob began to disperse. It was only then that Vancouver police chief Stewart and a few constables arrived. A police officer had been present at the city hall meeting, had heard the speeches and had watched the departure for the Brighouse Estate, but the police had done nothing to interfere. Stewart ordered the remaining members of the mob to return to their homes. The Chinese workers were gathered and placed in a roofless shed. They listened as the flames destroyed the last of their property and the impassioned crowd chanted "Who says the Chinese must go?" followed by a loud "Aye!" and then "Who says the police must go home?" followed by another "Aye!" The chants continued as the stragglers finally left the estate.

The night, however, was not yet over. As the mob re-entered Vancouver it made its way to Chinatown. Drunk with rage, the rioters rampaged down Carrall Street and among the shanties at False Creek. They looted Chinese businesses, smashed windows and burned homes. As men, women and children fled to save themselves from the mob and the fires they were beaten, kicked and stoned. Many were chased into the nearby bush. Others were driven into the cold water of the harbour and pelted with rocks. About eighty-six Chinese men were torn from their families, placed in small boats and shipped to New Westminster.

Burned-out buildings, shards of broken glass, and the eyes of desperate, homeless people met the dawn. Rather than grieve for or sympathize with the victims, the Vancouver city council met that morning to issue an order that all Chinese residents living in the False Creek area should immediately leave the city.

There was no public outcry against the racial violence or the expulsions. While grudgingly critical of the means employed, all local newspapers supported the expulsion of Chinese people. The *New Westminster Columbian* reported, "The country would no doubt be better rid of the Chinaman but it must get rid of them by legal means even if it takes time to do so."[43] A *Victoria Colonist* article stated,

> While sympathising with the residents of Vancouver in their desire to become a city free from the Chinese element, yet all well wishers and good citizens of the new town cannot but think that the policy they have pursued in order to attain the end sought is far greater evil than the presence of a few Chinese among them.[44]

The provincial government in Victoria expressed disapproval of the race riot. On February 28, the legislature dispatched thirty-five provincial constables to Vancouver to restore and maintain order. It was explained that the Vancouver police and city officials could no longer be trusted since "the parties charged with the police protection of the city were not only afraid to enforce the law but were in sympathy with the agitation."[45] Many Vancouver citizens were outraged that the "Victoria Specials" were being sent to their city. Newspapers reported that the people of Vancouver were far more upset about the cavalier attitude of Victoria than by the riot that had just torn through their midst.[46]

On March 8, the provincial police escorted one hundred Chinese workers back to the Brighouse Estate through a cordon of angry, shouting city residents. By the fifteenth, work resumed. In mid-July it stopped. The Vancouver city council passed a by-law

Last Steps to Freedom: The Evolution of Canadian Racism

prohibiting the clearing of land in hot, dry weather. With no work to do, the Chinese workers on the estate dwindled in number to three servants. The law had quietly accomplished what the rioters could not.

•

Anti-Chinese mass violence subsided after the riot. Perhaps people can remain in a state of agitation for only short periods of time before returning to everyday pursuits. The break in the violence lasted from the late 1880s to the late 1890s and was perhaps due more to demographics than anything else. In those years, Chinese immigration slowed while white immigration from the East increased significantly. The province's white population had grown from 54,000 in 1880 to 135,000 in 1890. Chinese immigration began rising again in the 1890s, but the ratio of whites to Chinese was such that Chinese people were growing somewhat less conspicuous.

Meanwhile, quieter, more insidious, systemic racism remained and grew more deeply entrenched. Anti-Chinese newspaper articles reinforcing negative stereotypes remained common. Nearly all theatres, restaurants, hotels and other public places remained segregated or barred Chinese entry completely. Canadian citizens of Chinese extraction could still not vote or hold public office. The British Columbia legislature continued to struggle with legislation to further restrict Chinese immigration.

By 1896, the long depression under which Canada and the world had suffered was grinding to an end. A young, handsome, charismatic Quebecer named Wilfrid Laurier was leading the Liberal Party. Laurier won votes in Ontario and Quebec by promising a compromise solution to the contentious racial and religious issue of separate schools for Manitoba. He won votes in British Columbia by promising to support that province's desire to restrict Chinese immigration. In 1896, Laurier became the prime minister of Canada.

Once in office, Laurier sifted through the anti-Oriental laws that had been passed by the British Columbia legislature and racist proposals being pressed upon him by British Columbians in his caucus. The B.C. legislature requested that the federal government stop Chinese immigration by raising the head tax on Chinese immigrants to five hundred dollars. Laurier made no secret of his thoughts on the matter. In an April 1899 letter to Reverend A.

Carmen the prime minister wrote, "For my part, I have very little hope of any good coming to this country from Asiatic immigration of any kind."[47] He worried, however, about acceding to British Columbia's demands.

Laurier's caution was spurred mostly by his realization that Canada and the British Empire had established good and economically valuable relations with Japan. He did not treasure the notion of jeopardizing that relationship by supporting measures that would insult Japan or harm Japanese people in Canada. Nonetheless, the pressure from B.C. needed attention. Laurier compromised by negotiating a gentleman's agreement whereby the government of Japan voluntarily restricted emigration to Canada. Since the Chinese government was still in turmoil and had no relationship with either Canada or the Empire, no such caution was necessary with respect to Chinese immigration. Laurier raised the head tax on Chinese immigrants to one hundred dollars effective January 1, 1901.

This action was not good enough for the B.C. legislature. To address the unabated pressure and criticism, Laurier created a Royal Commission. It was led by Toronto lawyer R.C. Clute. Other commissioners were New Westminster canning-factory owner D.J. Dunn and B.C. labour leader Christopher Foley. Its 1902 report stated that while Chinese people helped some industries their overall impact was negative. It said that, according to testimony, the Chinese people were dirty, untrustworthy, poor, dangers to the peace, unfit for full citizenship, generally obnoxious, and did not pay their share of taxes.[48] It recommended that the entry tax be raised to five hundred dollars. Laurier accepted the report's recommendations and the head tax was raised to five hundred dollars effective January 1, 1904. The number of Chinese immigrants went from 4,019 in 1903 to eight in 1904.

Life remained difficult for Oriental people suffering the barbs and restrictions of a racist society. There were futile attempts by some Japanese and Chinese people to end the discriminatory laws under which they toiled. For example, Tomey Hamma, Canadian-born but of Japanese descent, took the B.C. Elections Act of 1895 to court, arguing that as a Canadian citizen he had the right to vote. He won in the lower courts but the provincial government appealed. The case went to the Judicial Committee of the Privy Council in London, where it was overturned. Oriental Canadian citizens could not vote in Canada.

Schools remained segregated. In the 1880s and 1890s a few Chinese children had attended missionary schools. Others attended Chinese separate schools formed by community organizations such as the Empire Reform Association and the Chinese Consolidated Benevolent Association. Most parents wanted their children to learn English and British ways and tried to enrol them in public schools. In 1901, a movement began in Victoria to have Chinese children excluded from public schools. The spokesperson of the local Trades and Labour Council, T.H. Twiggs, said that Oriental children were injurious to the moral tone of the schools. He said,

> It is regrettable indeed that it should be found necessary to separate at the public schools the children of one portion of the inhabitants from the other for the preservation of the Anglo-Saxon standard of moral and ethical culture. [But it is necessary due to] the aptness of Chinese to use words, without knowing their meaning, and disregard for decency in giving expression in English to their lascivious thoughts.[49]

The Victoria school superintendent created a new school district in the Chinese section of the city, and all Chinese students were legally obliged to attend. The de facto segregation occurred despite the fact that not a single teacher who spoke at any of the board meetings dealing with the issue claimed that Chinese students were disruptive or bad influences on white students. At that time there were only twenty Chinese students attending the city's five white schools. Victoria's racial segregation policy remained until 1908. In that year, the British Columbia Department of Education racially segregated all of the province's schools.

The break in overt racist violence ended in the summer of 1905. Violent acts against Chinese people suddenly increased in number and intensity. Chinese workers were beaten and forced to leave Salmo. The homes of Chinese residents were burned and people beaten and whipped in Penticton. A new Vigilance Committee was formed in Vancouver, and at a well-attended meeting it was again decided that all Chinese people would be driven from the city. The next day dozens of Chinese people were accosted and some were put on boats and sent into the bay.

The reason most often cited for the renewed violence was a surge in non-white immigration. In 1906, the Japanese government temporarily eased the restrictions of its gentleman's agreement and allowed more emigration to Canada, while growing numbers of Japanese people began arriving from Hawaii. In July 1907 alone, twenty-three hundred Japanese immigrants arrived. At the same time, forty-seven hundred Sikhs arrived from India and, despite the fact that they were British citizens, received a welcome as inviting as did the Japanese.

Newspapers reflected and stirred the agitation caused by the new arrivals. On September 9, 1907, for example, the *Vancouver Daily Province* editorial stated,

> We are all of the opinion that this province must be a white man's country.... We do not wish to look forward to a day when our descendants will be dominated by Japanese, or Chinese, or any colour but their own.[50]

Tension rose quickly. Governor General Earl Grey visited British Columbia in the spring of 1906 and was appalled by what he saw. He wrote to Laurier that the troubles between the races were more acute than those he had seen in South Africa.[51] Grey also indicated how little things had changed since the 1860s when he said in another letter to Laurier that "No political figure could hope at this time for support in British Columbia unless he stood for exclusion of Asiatic immigrants."[52]

Contributing to the volcanic atmosphere was labour unrest. There were 138 strikes in 1906. Much of the trouble had been attributed to the growing radicalization of American organized labour. The International Workers of the World, commonly called the Wobblies, had been making inroads into British Columbia's labour organizations. To this mix was added the racism that had united workers in B.C. for years. Every union manifesto in the province denounced Oriental labour and demanded an end to Oriental immigration.

In 1907, the British Columbia legislature passed the Natal Act. It was patterned and named after laws enacted to separate the races in South Africa. Versions of the Natal Act had been passed before but disallowed in 1899 and 1903. The new act stated that prospective immigrants had to be able to write a European language to be admitted, and it barred businesses from employing anyone who could not write a European language.

On September 7, Lieutenant-Governor James Dunsmuir announced his refusal to sign the Natal Act. It was as *ultra vires* as all the other provincial laws that addressed immigration. That night, two thousand people showed their hatred of Chinese people, anger with Dunsmuir and disdain for constitutional law by marching down Vancouver's Cambie Street beneath banners stating "Stand For A White Canada." By the time they reached Hastings Street five thousand were marching. By city hall eight thousand angry, chanting people had gathered. Dunsmuir was burned in effigy. Reverend H.W. Fraser was one of two clergymen who spoke. He said, "It was pure Anglo-Saxon blood that made the Empire and it would never have been made with a mixture of the Asiatic blood.... Let us have a White Canada."[53]

The violence began on Carrall Street. As it had twenty years before, the mob burned and pillaged homes and businesses. Innocent people were beaten. Frank Uyerhara was a child at the time. He later described the riot from his perspective, hidden in the basement of his parents' home:

> When word came that the crowd was nearing, those along Powell Street got their first taste of a blackout; lights were turned off. All was dark and still. A deadly hush reigned. It was broken by a distant murmur which quickly filled the night air. Soon the tramp, tramp, tramp, of many feet and the sound of many voices became audible. Mothers clutched their children closer in the darkened back rooms of their homes. Not a word was spoken. At last, a mass of marching men swung around Main heading up Powell picking up crushed rocks from the semi-paved street and hurling them at the windows.... A child's shrill cry split the dark silence of one of the houses. It was followed by another, and another. A bedlam of wailing broke loose.[54]

The rioters tore through the Chinese area and then headed to the adjacent Japanese neighbourhood, but some of the Japanese people had guns. Shots were fired, the mob dispersed, and the violence subsided. At that point the police arrived.

Amid bandaging wounds and cleaning up the next day, a number of Japanese and Chinese people purchased weapons. The two-thousand-member Oriental Exclusion League hung banners inscribed "White Canada" across a number of city steets. A number of pedestrians accepted and wore "White Canada" ribbons that were distributed downtown. Except for sporadic acts of violence and an ill-fated attempt to burn a Chinese school, however, the next night was calm.

Laurier sent a letter with Minister of Labour Rodolphe Lemieux to Tokyo to apologize. No letter or representative was sent to China. Deputy labour minister and future prime minister William Lyon Mackenzie King was dispatched to B.C. to investigate the riot. King awarded $9,000 in compensation to Japanese and $26,000 to Chinese riot victims.

The violence subsided but the demands for an absolute end to the Oriental presence in B.C. intensified. Lemieux supported these demands. Like labour and business leaders, he made it clear that his prime motive in doing so was not economic but racial. He said,

> British Columbians object to a vast alien Colony, exclusive, inscrutable, unassimilative, with fewer wants and a lower standard of living than themselves, maintaining intact their peculiar customs and characteristics.... They have to safeguard the future and the distinctiveness of their race and civilisation, and in their passionate and unalterable conviction, they cannot be protected unless the free ingress of orientals is restricted and regulated.[55]

Under growing pressure to exclude non-white immigrants, Laurier altered the immigration laws to stop Sikhs and Japanese immigrants from arriving in Canada through a third country.

The Liberal immigration policy became the most important issue for most British Columbia voters in the next federal election. Conservative leader Robert Borden campaigned in British Columbia under the slogan "White Canada." A telegram from Borden to the people of British Columbia that appeared in newspapers during the campaign stated, "The Conservative party stands for a white Canada, the protection of white labour, and the absolute exclusion of Asiatics."[56] The Conservatives had won none of British Columbia's seven seats in the previous election. Under its blatantly racist platform it won five. Borden became prime minister.

•

The First World War diverted attention from anti-Chinese activities. The war's end refocussed that attention. Chinese people were again attacked from many fronts. Newspapers maintained a constant racist commentary. The March 11, 1914 *Vancouver Sun* editorial, for example, stated that there was among the people of Vancouver an

> instinctive repugnance among the white races to marriage with Orientals.... All experience goes to show that it would take generations to break down the social and family barriers between the Japs and the Chinese and the whites, if indeed it could ever be effected.... If British Columbia is to be a white man's country, the whites must have a fair chance.... It is a matter of race preservation.[57]

Twelve years later the *Nanaimo Herald*'s May 10, 1922 editorial stated,

> It is bad enough that good Canadians are unable to find employment while Orientals are at work, it is worse when Orientals become employers themselves, engage in trade and business and even settle on the land. These settlers can never become Canadians. There can never be any blending of the two races, and the Canadians cannot live in competition with the Oriental in any line of business.[58]

While it is difficult to measure, one must assume that the editorial stands taken by newspapers over the decades reflected the views of many of their readers. Further, as is the wont of editorial writers, they also instructed those readers.

Farmers did not seem concerned about white settlers establishing new farms and orchards. They showed a paranoiac panic, however, about Chinese people buying land. In 1913, a number of Okanagan Valley residents met and agreed not to sell land to Orientals for five years. They then asked the provincial government to enact legislation to restrict Orientals from moving to the area.

A similar meeting was held in Kelowna in January 1920. It was resolved that "the ownership of land in B.C. by Japanese and Chinese is continually increasing, and constitutes a peril to our ideal of a white British Columbia, as it is impossible for Japanese and Chinese to become assimilated as Canadian citizens."[59] A motion was passed whereby it was agreed that no land would be sold to Oriental people from that day forward. At that point Chinese and Japanese people owned only 112 acres in the entire Okanagan Valley and just twenty-two square miles of farmland in the entire province.

That these meetings were more than isolated incidents is seen in the fact that the racist intent of the land restriction idea was reflected in statements made on behalf of all the province's farmers by farmers' publications and organizations. In 1919, for example, the February issue of *B.C. Fruit and Farm* magazine stated, "The proportion of Orientals to whites in B.C. is too great, but only in one sense, and that is in owing to the fact that they are in business for themselves and are not, as they should be, working for white men."[60] The United Farmers of British Columbia held annual conventions, with farmers from throughout the province in attendance. At its 1925 convention it was moved that a "monogamous and not a dual population is in the best interests of Canada both for the strength of the nation and its institutions in peace."[61] The motion passed.

In 1919, the British Columbia Federation of Labour dropped its anti-Oriental ideas in its adoption of socialist ideas of brotherhood. This act, however, was an exception. Labour leaders remained at the forefront of anti-Chinese organizations. W.J. Bartlett and Percy Bengough, for example, were leaders in the Knights of Labour and at the same time the Asiatic Exclusion League, which claimed as its goal, "to keep the Province and the Dominion for the white man by stopping any further Oriental immigration."[62] That its leaders reflected the racism of the membership was seen at the 1890 annual meeting of the British Columbia Trades and Labour Congress when a motion was passed to continue to exclude all Chinese workers from union membership. A similar motion was passed at every such meeting for the next fifty years.

Further evidence that racism remained a dominating force in organized labour was seen in 1928. Motions were brought before the Vancouver and New Westminster Trades and Labour Councils asking for support in restoring the franchise to Chinese people in British Columbia. Both motions were rejected. Rather than expand their membership and power by having Chinese and other non-white workers as members, nearly all B.C. unions remained racially segregated. As King concluded in a 1907 letter to Laurier, "I believe it is no longer merely a labour, but has become a race agitation."[63]

The business people of the 1920s still felt threatened by Chinese competition. Like their predecessors they found it easier to resort to racism than to meet the challenge as they would if the competitors were white. The B.C. Sugar Refining Company, for example, ran an advertisement that said white people should avoid using Chinese sugar because it was "refined by semi-naked, unwashed, steaming, smelling coolies [and] has a fine chance to become inoculated with all the unpleasant things which such conditions are likely to produce."[64]

In 1922, the B.C. Board of the Retail Merchants of Canada wrote a letter to Prime Minister King that expressed the white business community's feelings. Over the signature of chair George S. Hougham, the letter demanded an end to Oriental immigration and suggested forced repatriation of all Oriental people presently in Canada. It went on, "To us it is not merely a question of competitive merchandising.... It is in fact a struggle of a far deeper significance in which home, family and citizenship consideration outweigh mercenary motives."[65]

The Christian churches of British Columbia continued to either explicitly support or refuse to oppose the racist beliefs and activities that swirled around them. The Methodist superintendent of Oriental Missions in B.C., Rev. G.E. Hartwell, wrote in 1913 that Chinatown was "...the carcass to attract the foul birds of western vices, the dumping ground of those evils which the white man wishes removed from his door."[66] On July 20, 1921, the Anglican Bishop of New Westminster was quoted in the *Vancouver Daily World* as stating, "We should have a province that will be white; that will be British and that will be Christian."[67] In his January 1922 *Report to the General Ministerial Association of Vancouver* for the minister of the interior, Rev. N.L. Ward continued the consistently racist line taken by church leaders when he wrote,

Unless the Christian Churches of British Columbia rise up in earnest to convert these Oriental people in their midst the history of the North African church will be repeated and Christianity will be wiped out by an Oriental wave of theosophic Buddhist thought...."[68]

Meanwhile, racism continued to be either enthusiastically supported or shamelessly exploited by political leaders who either wrote, strengthened, or refused to overturn racist laws. Laws restricting access to public services, housing and jobs, limiting the franchise and controlling immigration were kept in place and built upon in the 1920s. Federal leaders continued to disallow racist provincial legislation when it violated the B.N.A. Act by intruding into federal jurisdiction but proved themselves willing to endorse racist legislation if it was constitutionally sound.

The laws that moved the state up the racist ladder were enacted by people who reflected and represented the views of their constituents and felt secure in publicly proclaiming those views. Consider their words. Liberal advertisements for the 1921 British Columbia provincial election stated, "Liberal candidates are pledged to a white British Columbia." The Liberals won. In a speech to the Ottawa Rotary Club in November 1927, Premier J.D. McLean stated that the British Columbians had "no complaint against the individual Oriental, who was, as a rule, honest, industrious and thrifty but it was a question of preserving the British white race."[69] In 1928, Premier Simon Fraser Tolmie said, "We are anxious to keep this a British country. We want British Columbia British and nothing else."[70]

Prime ministers echoed premiers' messages. Macdonald said, "It is not advantageous to the country that the Chinese should come and settle in Canada, producing a mongrel race."[71] Laurier said, "The dominion can get along very well without Chinese labour and Chinese parsimony."[72] Borden said that British Columbia should forever be a "British and Canadian province, inhabited and dominated by men in whose veins runs the blood of those great pioneering races which built up and developed not only western Canada but eastern Canada."[73] King wrote, "that Canada should remain a white man's country is believed to be not only desirable for economic and social reasons but highly necessary on political and national grounds."[74]

The systemic racism against which Chinese Canadians struggled had one more step to take. The five-hundred-dollar head tax had failed to stop Chinese immigration completely. To remedy the situation, the British Columbia legislature passed the British Columbia Immigration Act in 1922. It inflicted devilishly stringent entry guidelines upon prospective Chinese immigrants. Its stated purpose was to "totally restrict the immigration of Asiatics into the province, keeping in view the wishes of the people of British Columbia that this province should be reserved for the people of the European race."[75] The law was obviously *ultra vires*.

Rather than disallow it, however, the federal government devised one of its own and passed the Chinese Immigration Act. It became popularly known as the Chinese Exclusion Act, for it applied only to Chinese people and simply banned their entry into Canada. Exceptions were made only for students, who had to leave once their studies were completed, merchants who came with sufficient money and contacts, Chinese children born in Canada, or members of the Chinese government. It came into effect in 1923. Ironically, it was at that time that thousands of European immigrants were being welcomed to Canada.

The Chinese Immigration Act was a natural step. It confirmed Canada's place upon the exclusion and expulsion rung high upon the racist ladder. The act remained in effect until 1947. Only a handful of Chinese people came to Canada. It bespoke a state tolerant of hatred where racism was a part of, or supported by, all social institutions. For a generation, the door of compassion, tolerance and understanding was clamped shut.

2

Ukrainian Canadians 1896–1915
A Case of Mistaken Identity

Prison is prison, no matter where.
—Phillip Yasnowsky

Phillip Yasnowsky had been working as a miner for two years when he was suddenly fired. The quality of his work had been fine. He had always been on time and got along well with his supervisors and fellow workers. Phillip Yasnowsky was fired because he was Ukrainian.

Yasnowsky travelled to North Bay then to Toronto looking for another job. No one would hire him. He made his way to St. Catharines, where he planned an escape to the United States. One morning, while he was quietly finishing breakfast at a small restaurant, a policeman noticed his non-Anglo-Saxon features and asked to see his pass. Unable to produce the internal passport, which according to federal law all Ukrainians had to carry, he was arrested. All of his money, some two hundred dollars, was taken.

He was detained without charge, without trial and without legal representation, in Toronto's Stanley Barracks. Along with other Ukrainians sharing the ordeal, he slept on cold, concrete floors. Meals consisted of bread, a thin slice of old meat, raw cabbage and weak tea. The outdoor courtyard was surrounded by barbed wire and monitored by guards carrying rifles with fixed bayonets.

After several weeks in Toronto, Yasnowsky and the Ukrainian prisoners were taken by train to a detention camp at Kapuskasing. The camp was run by the Canadian militia. The prisoners cleared

55

roads, dug ditches, cut trees and performed many other back-breaking jobs. They worked when the air was thick with black flies, through blistering heat and through the ruthless cold of northern Ontario winters. Their forced labour was carefully supervised by the ever-present armed guards.

Phillip Yasnowsky's ordeal was not rare. That is the sad part of his story. He was one of thirteen hundred men in the Kapuskasing detention camp. Two-thirds were Ukrainians and the rest were Poles, Croats, Hungarians, Turks and Germans. The Kapuskasing camp was also not rare. During the First World War, twenty-four detention camps held 8,579 men. The majority, some six thousand, were Ukrainian. Their crime, and the crime of nearly all who were were torn from their families and forced to live under brutal conditions, was that they were Ukrainian.

•

Yasnowsky's story, like those of the other prisoners, really began nearly fifty years earlier. In July 1867, there were fireworks in Ottawa to celebrate the formation of a new dominion, but Sir John A. Macdonald was no fool. He knew that Canada existed for the most part in name only, for if Ottawa did not exercise sovereignty from the Atlantic to the Pacific then the expansionist Americans would soon move north. Macdonald dreamed of a British country truly living up to its motto of stretching from sea to sea.

As steel rails slowly crept along the prairie, his dream remained hollow. It was useless without people. In 1872 Macdonald created the Dominion Land Act, which offered a quarter section, 160 acres, of land free to anyone who would settle upon it. The CPR publicized the offer in Eastern Canada and Britain, knowing that it would benefit in the short run by transporting the settlers and in the long run if a prairie economy evolved. The federal government spent a half million dollars advertising and administering the new act. Twenty-six companies were created as entrepreneurs raced to cash in on the potential bonanza.

Ten years later only 1,242 permanent European settlers were in the West. It is believed that even that number may be inflated since many used Canada only to get to the warmer and more prosperous United States. Throughout the 1880s, more people left Canada than arrived. The Dominion Land Act's failure was due mostly to the economic depression that gripped the industrialized world at that time. Debt, bankruptcies, bank failures and farm foreclosures created an economic climate that left few people willing to risk all they had on a prairie adventure. Macdonald died in 1891 knowing he had only begun his work.

In 1896, Wilfrid Laurier led the Liberal Party to power. He shared Macdonald's opinion that the West must be filled both to stave off American expansion and to enable Canada to fulfil its potential. Laurier appointed a former Manitoba cabinet minister, the brash and hard-working Clifford Sifton, as his minister of the interior. Sifton would settle the West.

Some of the structural and bureaucratic changes necessary to make the government's work in immigration more efficient had already been done when Sifton took his post. The Department of the Interior had been severed from the Department of Agriculture, where it had languished under-funded and unappreciated. Sifton enlivened the new department. He forced railway companies to release thousands of acres of land, that they had been holding as part of a long-term tax dodge, for settlement. Immigration centres were built in one hundred western towns. A Commission of Immigration was established and housed in Winnipeg. The North Atlantic Trading Company (NATC) was formed, and it quickly dispatched agents throughout northern Europe selling transport tickets to Canada.

An enormous advertising campaign was launched. Posters were printed in several languages, extolling the virtues of life in Canada. They cried of the democratic government, the invigorating climate and, most seductively of all, the free land. Primary-school readers were donated to English and Scottish school boards, through which children were indoctrinated regarding the glories of Canadian life. Even Queen Victoria could not escape Sifton's reach. During her diamond jubilee in 1897, her royal procession passed beneath a huge banner proclaiming the opportunities for settlers in Canada.

Sifton made it clear to the agents in his department's employ that despite the dire need for immigrants, and the enormous amount of energy and money being spent to attract them, the government would adhere to a strict policy of racial exclusion. Africans, Orientals and those from southern Europe were not to be among the chosen. Sifton decided that the immigrants best suited to Canada's needs were white, Slavic peasant farmers. He told NATC officials that when choosing the people to entice to come to Canada they should look over the prospects in the hope that "there might be one or two stout, hardy peasants in sheepskin coats. Obviously the peasants are the men who are wanted here."[1] Sifton later repeated the argument in the House of Commons, stating,

> I think the stalwart peasant in a sheepskin coat, born on the soil, whose forefathers have been farmers for ten genera-tions, with a stout wife and a half-dozen children is good quality.... These men are workers. They have been bred for generations to work from daylight to dark. They have never done anything else and they never expect to do anything else.[2]

The peasants in sheepskin coats to whom Sifton referred were for the most part Ukrainians. The Ukrainian people have survived a long and troubled history. The Ukrainian ancestral home encom-passes what is now the Ukraine, southern Poland, Romania and parts of Austria and Slovakia. Ukrainian history can be traced to Vladimir the Great, who ruled much of the area in the years around the turn of the first century A.D. During that time, and for centuries afterward, the region was torn by nearly constant warfare. Borders were drawn and redrawn, with scant attention paid to ethnicity or self-determination.

The Ukrainian culture and language were forced to evolve under the scrutiny of often unsympathetic political and religious leaders. Culture and language held the Ukrainian people together, allowing a sense of self-worth and identity from generation to generation through the tumultuous years of rebellion and up-heaval. Culture did for the Ukrainians what it does for us all: it provided a sanctuary against the winds of change.

By the 1840s, the Austria-Hungary Empire had gathered an unnatural patchwork quilt of ethnic groups within its borders. Nearly 3.5 million Ukrainians lived in the eastern province of Galicia and around 300,000 in the northern province of Bukovyna. Polish nobility held much of the political power and Romanians most of the economic power. Ukrainians had little of either. Ninety percent of Ukrainians were serfs living as slaves on land owned by ruthless landlords. Permission was required for a serf to improve his land or educate his children, or for his children to be married. Lords were police, judges, juries and very often executioners.

Serfdom was abolished in 1843 by King Ferdinand I. The Vienna government compensated the lords for the loss of their serfs with money and land, then increased the taxes on the newly freed peasants to pay the bill. Peasants were burdened by debt incurred to pay the crushingly high taxes. Interest rates averaged seventy-six percent. Ukrainian farms became increasingly tiny as land was sectioned and sold to pay debts, then divided again to provide land for children. By the 1870s, over 500,000 Ukrainians had lost their land in Galicia alone. Nature then frowned on the peasants. A series of famines from the 1840s to the 1870s led to mass starvation. A cholera epidemic in 1873 killed ninety thousand Galicians. Throughout the 1880s, around one thousand Galician peasants a week died from hunger and hunger-related diseases.

Adding to the crises was a concerted attack on the Ukrainian culture. Ukrainian schools were banned, cultural centres were closed, and in many towns it became illegal to speak Ukrainian. The church offered little in the way of help. Most Greek Orthodox priests augmented their piddling salaries by charging exorbitant rates for weddings, funerals and christenings.

Ukrainian leaders responded to the cultural crisis by creating reading clubs. Ukrainian poets and authors became essential links to a cultural past that had become dangerous to embrace. Poet Tara Shevchenko became a folk hero, and his poems, speaking of resistance to oppression, became rallying cries to politically minded Ukrainians. The reading clubs led to the establishment of peasant cooperatives, theatre groups and lecture series. They became increasingly political. Reading club organizers were often the only literate people in town and were thus dubbed intellectuals. It was to them that most peasants turned for redress against unfair treatment by church or local government officials.

Despite the efforts to retain their cultural identity, by the 1890s most Ukrainians had by necessity stopped publicly referring to themselves as Ukrainian. Cruel poverty ground them down. As church leaders became more benevolent, many people became more closely tied to their churches. Most Galicians had become Greek Catholics and had begun calling themselves Ruthenians. They were distinguished from Orthodox Catholics who lived mostly in Bukovyna. Reading club members struggled to protect the

Ukrainian language and culture in the face of this splintering.

With no end to the poverty and oppression in sight, many Ukrainians began to look further afield for better places to raise their children. Many men left their families to find work in Germany and Prussia and even Pennsylvania coal mines. The Brazilian government sent agents to Galicia seeking labourers for their burgeoning coffee plantations, and nearly 200,000 desperate but hopeful Slavic people, including many Ukrainians, went to Brazil. Letters soon returned telling of slave conditions on malaria-infested plantations. The Brazil adventure left people sceptical of immigration agents and foreign government claims.

Ivan Pylypiw and Vasyl Eleniak were two young Ukrainian men working in Germany when they heard of the offer of free land in Canada. After asking where the country was, they promised their wives they would return after investigating it. In September 1891, they landed in Montreal. A month later, and flat broke, they arrived in Winnipeg. They were greeted by a German-speaking land agent who helped them to find work on a Mennonite farm. Pylypiw wrote to his wife, "Our people never live like that, except at a celebration. My own eyes could not believe that a plain farmer could live like a lord."[3] With the support of the Canadian government Pylypiw returned home and soon persuaded twelve Ukrainian families to undertake the adventure. They settled near Gretna, Manitoba.

Ukrainian men had fought in the British army in Canada in the War of 1812. Other Ukrainians had been part of Lord Selkirk's force at Red River in 1817.[4] These Ukrainians, however, had surrendered thoughts of returning home, of bringing their families to Canada or of maintaining their Ukrainian identity. Ivan Pylypiw and Vasyl Eleniak are generally accepted as the first Ukrainian settlers in Canada.[5]

Letters home from the Manitoba settlers created excitement in Ukrainian villages. Questions the letters raised were answered by Dr. Joseph Oleskiw. Oleskiw was a Galician and a professor at Lviv University with a Ph.D. in agriculture. He collected a great deal of information on a number of prospective countries that he felt could save his people from their misery. In July 1895, Dr. Oleskiw travelled to Canada and met with several government officials and convinced them to open an immigration office in Galicia. Upon his return, Oleskiw published a number of pamphlets, the two most important of which were *About Free Lands* and *About Emigration*.

Reading societies ensured wide distribution, and even the illiterate were made aware of their contents. The advice was accurate, homey and practical. Oleskiw sold Canada as the best alternative for prospective Ukrainian emigrants.

On a crisp April morning in 1896, a group of 107 Ukrainian immigrants, led by Dr. Oleskiw's brother Volodymyr, peered through the mist at Quebec City. They were concrete evidence of the marriage of Canada's needs with the needs of the Ukrainian people. There was no romance in leaving home. One Ukrainian woman wrote, "The people of the whole village assembled in our yard to say farewell to us, and when the church bells started to ring, all the people started to cry as if it were a funeral."[6] Many took small packets of Ukrainian soil to spread on their new land.

Most families were forced to sell everything they owned to afford the trip to Lviv or Antwerp or Hamburg, then the ship to Quebec City and the train to the West. Unscrupulous agents and con men strewn along the line robbed trusting people of what little they had left. The same ships transported grain and cattle to Europe and people back to Canada. The immigrants were crammed into steerage compartments where they shared quarters with the rats, lice and stench left by the previous cargo. The twelve- to twenty-eight-day journeys were filled with seasickness, bad food and boredom. Sleep was difficult in noisy quarters upon seaweed mattresses.

Arrival in Canada presented a string of immigration officials. Doctors were notorious for demanding bribes for bills of health. Many people were deported due to sickness contracted en route. Some were deported for maladies as simple as varicose veins. Many families were split as sick children were returned to Europe alone, leaving their families in Canada without enough money to accompany them.

Special immigrant trains whisked the families to the West in relative comfort. There were stoves for heat and cooking and comfortable wooden bunks. Occasionally an interpreter accompanied a group to the West, but this was the exception rather than the rule.

Nearly all immigrants eventually arrived at Winnipeg's Immigration Hall. The cavernous building was a former locomotive repair depot with offices in the centre. Along the walls were rough-hewn bunks. There were stoves, installed by Doukhobour immigrants, and a central pump. While many slept inside the large drafty building many others slept outside in makeshift tents.

Men reported to the immigration officials and presented ten dollars to secure a land claim. Local farmers, working for the government, made daily trips to pick up the men who had been processed and take them to choose their new land. After trips lasting days and sometimes weeks, the men would return for their families. Greatly inflated prices were paid for flour, tools and other essentials before long journeys to a new life began.

The law stated that to retain the land settlers had three years in which to erect a house and buildings for livestock and to clear and plough thirty acres. Settlers faced two problems. First, the journey and the crooks relieved them of almost all money. Fifty percent of Ukrainian settlers were nearly penniless by the time they made it to their land. Second, the best land was gone. Railroads, churches, and British, German and American settlers had secured it years before the Ukrainians arrived. The available land was spread like a checkerboard across the desolate prairie, leaving families forced to make do with substandard land far from neighbours, towns or railway lines.

The first houses were almost always mud hovels dug out of the prairie sod and usually only ten by fourteen feet in size. They were damp and cold and invited sickness. Until small gardens could provide food, most families survived on berries, rabbits, gophers and an ersatz soup made of prairie grass and fungus. Men were forced to leave to find work so that essential farming implements could be purchased. Work was usually found with mines and railways. Meanwhile, women and children harnessed themselves to ploughs and cut the virgin soil. There are many cases of women walking fifty or more miles to the closest town to trade for a sack of flour or some other foodstuff. Women bore the brunt of the hard times.

By the turn of the century, the homesteading era was ending and a few years of good crops and high prices enabled many to build proper houses and barns. Over seventy percent of Ukrainian men were able to work on their farms on a fulltime basis. A report written by the Alberta Department of Education in 1900 spoke of the prosperous appearance of most of the Ukrainian farmsteads. It stated,

I was impressed with the prosperous appearance of most of the farms. ...in spite of the apparently unfertile nature of the soil, the little homesteads are surrounded by patches of wheat, rye and hemp and invariably a good vegetable garden. Most of the houses are small but with their thatched roofs and heavy overhanging eaves on plastered walls they are picturesque.[7]

From 1896 to 1900, approximately twenty-five thousand Ukrainians had settled in Canada. The majority, around seventeen thousand, were in Manitoba. They were the largest immigrant group to arrive in the Sifton flood. As more and more Ukrainian families began to move beyond survival and subsistence farming, they began to look outward. Their numbers afforded them a measure of confidence. They were used to fighting for survival and they struggled again to protect, and seek protection within, their culture.

The first Ukrainian schools were established in Alberta by Reverend Tymkevych. Manitoba created a number of schools in which Ukrainian children were taught in both Ukrainian and English. In Alberta and Saskatchewan schools, a period of time each afternoon was set aside for Ukrainian-language instruction where numbers warranted. The first bilingual training school for Ukrainian teachers was established in Winnipeg in 1905. The teachers quickly organized themselves into a vibrant force for social change called the Ukrainian Teachers Organization. They helped establish reading halls and night classes to address adult illiteracy and to teach English as a second language. Similar activities took place in Saskatchewan.

In 1903, the first Ukrainian-language newspaper, called the *Kanadiysky* (Canadian) *Farmer,* began publication in Winnipeg. The paper joined the Ukrainian daily called *Svoboda* (Liberty) which had been published in New Jersey and made available in Canada since 1893. A number of other Ukrainian-language newspapers appeared including *The Morning* in 1905, *The Red Banner* in 1907, *The Ukrainian Voice* in 1907 and the *Canadian Ruthenian* in 1911. The newspapers were instrumental in unifying and fortifying the Ukrainian people and communities.

The concern for education, literacy and culture was seen in the establishment of reading societies. Tara Shevchenko's portrait often graced the meeting places, and his poems were taught to the young. In 1906, Canada's first Shevchenko Concert was held in Winnipeg. Concerts, plays, operas and poetry readings filled Logan Avenue's Manitoba Hall and similar establishments across the West.

Those who had arrived as children had by the first decades of the twentieth century begun to enter the workforce. Some stayed on farms but many did not. They were joined by thousands of Ukrainian immigrants still arriving from Europe but settling increasingly in eastern cities. By 1907, forty-three percent of Ukrainian Canadians worked not as farmers but as urban labourers, where they followed the pattern of nearly all recently arrived ethnic groups and took the lowest-paying, lowest-skilled jobs. They worked in textile mills in Montreal, lumber mills in Ottawa and steel plants in Hamilton.[8] The government created a railway labour shortage in 1906 when it banned Oriental workers. Nearly ten thousand Ukrainians were hired to fill the gap, allowing railway construction to continue.

Ukrainian workers were often involved in the creation of unions. Sometimes these activities took the form of radical unionism. Such was the case in Winnipeg with the formation of the Ukrainian Socialist Democratic Party, which played a leading role in the organization of the July 1917 construction workers' strike in Winnipeg.

Politics at that time was nearly exclusively controlled by British, French, and in the West, German men. By 1914, a few Ukrainian activists had begun to chip away at these walls. In Franklin, Manitoba, for example, the Ukrainian community tired of being ignored by the British-dominated town council and, led by Theodosy Wachna, became legally separated from Franklin and formed their own municipality which they called Stuartburn. Within a year, the new town boasted improved roads, three Ukrainian-language schools and a post office. Similar actions took place in Gimli, Kreuzberg, Brokenhead, Mossy River, Dauphin and Chatfield, Manitoba, and in Two Hills, Mundare and Smoky Lake, Alberta. The town councils held meetings beneath the Union Jack but in both English and Ukrainian. In 1911, Ukrainian Theodore Stefanyk became a Winnipeg city councillor. He was supported by a combination of Ukrainians, Germans and Poles. Stefanyk worked hard to ensure that Ukrainians and other ethnic minorities were hired by the city for public works projects and paid the equivalent of their English counterparts.

By 1914, it should have been clear to all that the Ukrainian people had overcome incredible hardship both in leaving their native land and then in establishing themselves in Canada. It should also have been clear that their cultural, political and economic contributions were enriching the dominion. Historian Myrna Kostash has stated that "Without the men and women in sheepskin coats there would have been no prairie economy outside the Hudson's Bay Company, native hunters and trappers, and the NWMP in their forts."[9] Whether Kostash is overstating the case can be argued. It nonetheless remains certain that Ukrainians, along with the other Slavic immigrants, were the flesh and blood upon the young country's bones.

Ukrainian immigrants believed that they were entering a promised land where they could turn their backs on oppression. They soon realized, however, that a great many Canadians, the press, business and labour leaders and even the government that had worked so diligently to draw them to Canada held them in contempt. They could not have predicted the oppression with which they would be forced to deal.

•

The failure of leadership and the ascent up the racist ladder began with the arrival of the first Ukrainian immigrants to the prairies. There are many examples of individuals betraying prejudice. An English-speaking teacher in Edmonton admonished her class for having dirty fingernails by saying that they were as bad as "a bunch of stupid Ukrainians."[10] Many of Winnipeg's upper-class British ladies spoke of the benefits of hiring Ukrainian girls as maids and domestic help, for "they" were hard workers.[11]

A great many prejudiced people perpetrated discriminatory acts. In Brokenhead, Manitoba, English settlers sold their farms for less than market value and moved when news arrived that Ukrainians had bought land close by. A Ukrainian woman walked for miles one freezing winter day to mail a letter. She was forced to wait outside a post office in sub-zero cold because the interior was for British customers only. In 1897, an official at Winnipeg's Immigration Hall was fired after months of verbally abusing Ukrainian immigrants with racist slurs and for using a whip to move immigrant women and children from one place to another.

Anti-Ukrainian sentiments were spread and often created by newspapers which, through encouraging negative stereotypes and prejudice, supported a chauvinist desire to maintain an all-white, all-British West. A couple of examples illustrate the point. S.A. Thompson wrote in *Review of Reviews* in November 1893 that filling the West with good British stock would allow Canada to "advance that Anglo-Saxon civilisation which seems destined to dominate the world."[12] In February 1899, the *Winnipeg Telegram* warned readers that if Ukrainian immigration continued, "our boasted British institutions will become a mere simulacrum, in the name of which the most odious tyranny and misrule will be practised."[13]

Many newspapers were simply political mouthpieces of their owners. This fact led to quite different views on Ukrainian people. The *Manitoba Free Press*, for example, was a Liberal paper. In fact, in 1898 it was purchased by Clifford Sifton. From 1896 to 1905 its editorials about Ukrainians were sixty-one percent positive, thirty-six percent neutral and only five percent negative. The *Winnipeg Telegram*, on the other hand, was a Conservative paper. Its editorials that mentioned Ukrainians in the same years were two percent positive, three percent neutral and an overwhelming ninety-five percent negative.[14] Ideological beliefs and a predominance of anti-Liberal and, therefore, anti-immigration owners and editors resulted in Canadian newspapers nearly unanimously attacking Ukrainian people. Stories were often reprinted across the country, resulting in people who had never met or even seen a Ukrainian being introduced through ugly stereotypes. Again, a few examples tell the tale.

The *Quebec Mercury* reported on March 22, 1899 that Ukrainians were "bestial in their habits, dirty and unkempt, poor in pocket and criminal in the antecedents."[15] The *Halifax Herald*'s March 18, 1899 editorial stated,

> The Galicians, they of the sheepskin coats, the filth and the vermin, do not make splendid material for the building of a great nation. One look at the disgusting creatures as they pass through over the C.P.R. on their way west has caused many to marvel that beings bearing the human form could have sunk to such a bestial level.[16]

The *Winnipeg Telegram*'s March 7, 1899 editorial stated,

Not only are they poor and filthy, but their moral character is disgraceful.... Not only do they hold robbery and murder in very light estimation, but they are inveterate and unscrupulous perjurers.... All the time evidence is being furnished as to their disgustingly low moral standard. ...there are very few white women who sink so low as to become the mistresses of Chinamen yet the Galician women have no scruples against so doing.[17]

A number of popular books joined newspapers in popularizing anti-Ukrainian stereotypes. Among the most important of these was a novel entitled *Call the Foreigner: A Tale of Saskatchewan*, published in 1909 and written by a Presbyterian minister from Winnipeg named Charles Gorden under the pseudonym Ralph Conner. It became a bestseller in Canada, Britain and Europe. The novel pitted good against evil. Good was the masculine, pious and virtuous Anglo-Canadian, and evil was the terrible Ukrainian in the guise of a pitiful character named Margaret Ketrel. Ketrel was saved in the end by abandoning her family, her culture, her language and slovenly Ukrainian ways to join the church and adopt an Anglo-Saxon way of life. In 1922, Gorden was promoted and became the moderator of the Presbyterian Church in Canada.

Another very popular book was James S. Woodsworth's *Strangers Within Our Gates*, also published in 1909. Woodsworth was a Methodist minister and superintendent of the All People's Mission in Winnipeg. The book's thesis was that Anglo-Saxon Canadians had a responsibility to their church and their country to "educate and elevate" immigrants to save Canada from being dragged down to the culturally and morally depraved levels of non-British people. Woodsworth dehumanized the Ukrainian people while perpetuating and further popularizing negative stereotypes. He wrote of "a physical endurance bred of centuries of peasant life and an indifference to hardships that seems 'characteristic of the Slav.'"[18] Later he argued, "Centuries of poverty and oppression have, to some extent, animalised him. Drunk, he is quarrelsome and dangerous. The flowers of courtesy and refinement are not abundant in the first generation of immigrants."[19] J.S. Woodsworth was later the driving force behind, and the first leader of, the Cooperative Commonwealth Federation.

Influential politicians took the stereotypes as given and reflected or exploited the growing acceptance of prejudiced beliefs and discriminatory acts. They helped hoist Canada up the racist ladder by decrying the dangers Ukrainians presented to the country. First, it was argued that Ukrainians would not or could not assimilate. Among those presenting the argument was Victoria member of Parliament E.G. Prior, who had already made himself known as an opponent of Oriental immigration. In an 1899 House of Commons speech he turned his sights on the Ukrainians, asking rhetorically,

> How can we expect Canadians to welcome these people? We have nothing in common with them. They cannot assimilate with us in any way, and the settlers around them say they do not wish their young people to have any communication with them whatever. Are such people likely to make good citizens and contribute to the building up of the British Empire?[20]

Prior's arguments, and those of the MPs who rose to support his fear, were widely reported in the press. Prior later admitted that he had never met a Ukrainian person, seen a Ukrainian community or even visited the prairies other than to pass through by train. He nonetheless stood by his assessment of the nature of the Ukrainian people, explaining, "I have heard a great deal about them."[21]

The second fear was the flip side of the first; that is, that Canada and Anglo-Saxon Canadians would be in trouble if Ukrainians did assimilate. The fear was based on a realization of the potential political and economic power of a large and completely integrated Ukrainian population. The concern was expressed by Edmonton MP Frank Oliver, who rose in the House on April 12, 1901 to criticise Sifton's support of what he called the "sheepskins." Oliver said,

> I have heard hon. members say that these strange people, these slavs, will assimilate with other people. Do you know what that word "assimilate" means? ...Do you know that it means that if you settle on a farm on the prairies amongst them in the neighbourhood you must depend for the schooling of your children on the tax-paying willingness and power of people who neither know nor care anything about schools? Do you know that it means the intermarriage of

your sons and daughters with those who are of an alien race and of alien ideas?[22]

Oliver also stated in the House that Ukrainians "are not fit for the free institutions of this country and the time will soon come when they will hold the balance of political power here unless a damper is put on them very soon, and when they become our legislators, God help us."[23]

Finally, many expressed the old bugaboo that Ukrainians would weaken the Anglo-Saxon race. The most prominent among political leaders who espoused this idea was Manitoba Conservative Party leader Hugh Macdonald. Sir John's son shared his father's concern with racial purity and even borrowed a phrase his dad had used against Chinese people. On September 23, 1899, he said, "I will do everything I possibly can to prevent the influx of an alien race. We do not wish to see in this province a mongrel race, and if we can do anything to prevent it we are going to see it."[24]

It was recognized at the time that much of the racist ranting in which many politicians were engaged was motivated by partisan interests. The *Toronto Mail and Empire*, for example, reported in 1898 that "A great deal of prejudice has been excited against the Galicians, partly through the efforts of ignorant writers...partly also through the deliberate misrepresentation of party organs."[25] Did the political leaders truly believe the ugly ideas they spouted or were they merely exploiting them in the belief that the notions were sufficiently popular among their constituents to win electoral support for them and their party? Either alternative is discomforting. As the West developed, support for racist ideas became a major ingredient in electoral success.

Many individuals and groups fought the negative stereotypes, prejudice and discrimination. Not surprisingly, Clifford Sifton was among the Ukrainians' most ardent supporters. He argued against the racism that fuelled the criticism levelled against the Ukrainians by promising that they would soon be assimilated. He also spoke repeatedly and persuasively of the economic benefits of having the stalwart peasants on the prairies. He once pleaded for empathy and support, stating in the House,

they are people who have lived in poverty. That is no crime on their part.... I venture to say that the ancestors of many prominent citizens of Canada were poor in that country whence they came, and nobody thinks less of them on that account.[26]

Some church leaders also officially supported Ukrainian immigration and sought to publicize a more accurate picture of Ukrainian people since, after all, Ukrainians had been Christian since Vladimir the Great brought the religion to Kiev in 988. Upon the arrival of Ukrainian immigrants in the Canadian West, Protestant and Catholic church leaders competed to win them as adherents. Many schools, reading societies and Ukrainian-language newspapers were created with church help.

While their churches struggled to help and win the support of Ukrainian settlers, however, many ministers and priests betrayed personal racist beliefs. Many of these were stated in the pulpit and others were published. In 1913, for example, a Presbyterian minister wrote of the Ukrainians that "The close relations into which we are brought with these people who are degraded and vicious are out to force us to do them good in self-defence. Either we must raise them or they will lower us."[27] The prejudiced individuals within the church led many Ukrainians to doubt the sincerity of church efforts on their behalf. The Ukrainian people had few friends in the land that had worked so hard to attract them.

With racist suspicion and fear aroused, and the first halting moves up the racist ladder taken, the step to officially sanctioned discrimination was a small and simple one. Organized discriminatory activities were seen first in the workplace. In 1907, a typical year, there were approximately ten thousand full- and part-time Ukrainian railway workers. Despite the fact that the Ukrainian labourers worked well and lived frugally, they were terribly mistreated. They were paid $1.35 for each ten-hour day, which was half of a British or French worker's pay. English- or French-speaking foremen performed like chain gang guards. There were many cases of brutality. Ely Culbertson, who worked as a bridge expert for the CPR in those years, wrote that

There was a never-ending stream of new serfs, shanghaied by the mass procurement agencies of the East.... The Ukrainians were held in check by the small Anglo-Saxon element present in every camp who, being decently treated, were always ready to put down with fists, clubs and even guns any outbreak of the 'Bohunks'.[28]

Ukrainians of the Greek Orthodox church traditionally celebrate Christmas on January 7. On January 7, 1901, one hundred Ukrainian CPR workers took the day off to observe their holiday. All were fired. They were not paid for the previous week's work. They were left to walk twenty miles through the snow and sub-zero temperature back to Fort William.

In the summer of 1901, CNR maintenance workers staged a strike. Although they did not support the strike, nearly one hundred Ukrainian labourers found themselves without work or lodging. They were the only strikers separated from the whole and summarily fired. Unwelcome in nearby Medicine Hat, the tired, hungry men walked to Edmonton. They found themselves equally unwelcome there and were reduced to living in caves outside the city, which locals laughingly dubbed the Galician Hotel. The men sneaked into town at night, seeking jobs and food. The city council was informed of their plight but did nothing. By the time the strike ended, nearly all had left the area. They left with a clear understanding of the railway's, the municipal government's and the public's opinion of them and their presence in Canada.

Organized labour could have worked against discriminatory hiring practices. Prior to the 1920s, however, nearly all unions were craft unions, leaving unskilled labourers largely without protection. Since nearly all Ukrainian workers were unskilled, they were vulnerable to the whims of employers. This was at a time when the Ontario inspector of mines E.T. Corkhill estimated that thirty-three percent of all mining accidents happened as a result of employers' practices and that there was an unusually high accident rate among immigrant workers.

While their practices and policies discriminated against all immigrant labour, many Canadian unions acted specifically against certain groups, one of which was the Ukrainians. In 1909, the Trades and Labour Congress of Canada undertook a door-to-door campaign in a number of Canadian cities in an attempt to have the government limit Ukrainian immigration and to try to persuade employers to refrain from hiring Ukrainian workers.

The widespread discriminatory hiring practises led many Ukrainian Canadians to hide their cultural uniqueness and ethnic origins. Many Ukrainian people changed their names to get work. A young Ukrainian woman named Winarsky applied to the Edmonton Public School Board and was rejected. She changed her name to Wilson and reapplied with no more qualifications than before. She got the job.

Various levels of government could have passed legislation to discourage the racist practices of employers and unions. Instead, the federal government and a number of provincial governments reinforced them with discriminatory laws. Federal legislation extended the time one had to live in Canada before applying for naturalized citizenship from three to five years. The law affected thousands of Ukrainian people by denying them the franchise for an additional two years. Without the right to vote one could not be on the voters' list. Without inclusion on that list one could not own land or secure a business licence.

Many provincial governments aimed racist legislation specifically at the Ukrainian people. The most blatant of these actions was in Manitoba. In the 1899 provincial election, Conservative Party candidates argued that Sifton put Ukrainians in Manitoba only to secure Liberal votes. To save Manitoba from the Ukrainians, the Conservative Party proposed a means test to screen those qualified to vote. Conservatives contended that Ukrainian people without adequate knowledge of English should not be registered and those already registered should be disenfranchised. Party leader Hugh Macdonald argued that it was democratically responsible to deny the franchise to "an ignorant boss-ridden Galician, brought up in serfdom, and without the slightest conception of the issues he is voting on."[29] It is interesting to note that Macdonald was advocating the removal of the franchise from many people who had been in Canada for nearly ten years, who were property owners and, most importantly, Canadian citizens. It is also interesting that there was no attempt to remove the franchise from all immigrants. On July 27, 1899 the *Manitoba Free Press* reported that Macdonald

did not wish to have a mongrel breed in this part of Canada. He wanted good men of the same race as ourselves. He would add to the next franchise act, an education clause cutting out anyone who cannot sign his name and cannot read in English. He would not, however, cut out the Mennonites.[30]

In a letter to an Icelandic newspaper called the *Heimskringla*, Macdonald again made the point that his policy proposals were aimed only at Ukrainians. He wrote, "This clause is only intended to debar large flocks of Slavs, who have come here these last years, and who, on account of their numbers are becoming dangerous to the free institutions of the country...."[31]

Before the election there were thirty-two Liberal seats in the Manitoba legislature. Partly due to the Liberal platform of racial tolerance, the election reduced them to fifteen. The Conservative Party's racist, anti-Ukrainian campaign raised their number of seats from five to twenty-three.

A spate of racist legislation followed. Ukrainians in Manitoba had to be in Canada for seven rather than three years to own land or stand for public office. All non-British immigrants, no matter how long they had been in Canada and regardless of whether they were naturalized Canadian citizens or not, had to pass a literacy test to vote in municipal or provincial elections. The literacy tests were administered in the person's choice of English, French, Danish, German, Swedish or Icelandic. It was illegal to administer the test in Ukrainian. Thousands of Ukrainians, many of whom were Canadian citizens, were thereby robbed of their democratic right to vote.

It is clear, therefore, that after answering Canada's call to immigrate, the Ukrainian people were being taunted in public places, denied work, denied union membership, harassed by unions, insulted in the press, disenfranchized, and attacked and abandoned by their governments. As bad as all of this was, however, it was nothing compared to what followed. Another step up the ladder was about to be taken.

•

In August, 1914 a squabble between several of Queen Victoria's relatives tumbled unintentionally into the First World War. Before the senseless slaughter ended, nearly ten million people were dead. The triple entente of France, Russia and Britain was lined up against Germany and its allies, the most important of which was Austria-Hungary. With Britain's declaration of war, Canada was automatically at war. Prime Minister Borden's cry of "Ready Aye Ready" sent thousands of young Canadians to slog it out in the mud of France and Belgium.

Borden had a problem. For eighteen years the Canadian government had been bribing and cajoling thousands of German and Austrian people to immigrate to Canada. What was he to do with them now that their countries of origin were suddenly Canada's enemies?

To understand the government's solution, and how that solution affected Ukrainian people, one must consider two factors. First, the war was not called the First World War until the Second began and we cynically began to number them. It was referred to as the Great War to end war forever. It would be quick and glorious and the boys would be home by Christmas. It was very popular. Further, although at the outset of the war only around fifty-five percent of the Canadian population was of British extraction, most positions of political and economic power were held by people of that shrinking majority. Consequently, British imperialism, which manifested itself as the need to rush to England's side in her time of need, was effectively publicized as the only proper Canadian attitude toward the war.

The combination of the zeal for a popular war and the imperialist fervour gave rise to nativism. Nativism always results in people of visible minorities being subjected to sudden onslaughts of verbal abuse, vandalism and violence. In 1914, anything or anyone seen as non-British was considered dangerous, unpatriotic and possibly treasonous. This belief led the citizens of Berlin, Ontario, for instance, to change their city's name to Kitchener and to throw their statue of the kaiser into the Grand River. In ballparks across the country, frankfurters were renamed "hot dogs." Mixing war frenzy with nativism and pouring that ugly combination into the already boiling vat of racism caused an explosive reaction.

The second factor to be considered in understanding Borden's solution was the confusion over the Ukrainian people's ethnic origin. As has already been noted, Europe's constantly shifting borders resulted in Ukrainian people living in Romania, Poland, Russia and Austria-Hungary, with most who immigrated to Canada from the temporarily Austro-Hungarian provinces of Galicia and Bukovyna. Immigration officials knew at the outset that there was confusion as to the Ukrainians' nationality and recognized that the arrivals were not really Austrians. An immigration official in Quebec City reported in 1896 that "a number of settlers from Austria called Ruthenians, have come out recently...they appear to be

closely allied with the Galicians [but] they speak a language difficult to interpret, very few strangers having heard it."[32] German-
speaking interpreters who had been pressed into service to deal
with German-speaking Austrians threw up their hands.

The problem of properly classifying the Ukrainian was also
recognized by Ukrainian leaders at the time. Kyrylo Genik wrote
for *Svoboda* and later the *Kanadiysky Farmer*. In articles published
around the turn of the century he argued that the Ukrainians were
willing to call themselves anything to escape to the New World.
Immigrants were advised to remain quiet and be Austrian. Genik
argued that remaining quiet was relatively easy for most since for
years it had been illegal or unwise for Ukrainians to claim their true
nationality when completing forms or speaking with government
officials. Further, he argued that since the Ukraine was not recognized as a nation-state, many felt a desire to claim any recognized
country as their own to avoid feeling nationless. Austria would do.

Genik urged Ukrainians to feel proud of their Ukrainian heritage and declare themselves Ukrainian. As far back as 1902 he had
written, "We must rid ourselves of this lack of nomenclature and
our responsibility is to do this as soon as possible."[33] Unfortunately,
the confusion regarding the true nationality of the Ukrainian people remained rife in 1914.

Two incidents brought the growing nativism and ethnic confusion together with the long-festering anti-Ukrainian prejudice and
discrimination. The first involved the Austrian vice-consul in Ottawa. In July 1914, before the declaration of war, he stated that there
were approximately 150,000 "Austrians" in Canada. He ordered all
to return and fight in the Austrian army. Advertisements were
placed in English- and Ukrainian-language newspapers promising
that the emperor would pay the expenses of any Austrian national
who chose to go. Not a single person took up the offer.

The second, and more widely publicized, incident involved
Greek Catholic bishop Budka. He had been in Canada for two and
a half years, and had often expressed his love for Austria and
Austrian culture, having lived and trained there as a young man.
On July 27, 1914, Bishop Budka issued a pastoral letter from his
Winnipeg office. The letter made it clear that Ukrainian people were
spread across many European countries. The first paragraph spoke
of "the demoralisation of our brethren in Galicia and in Hungary."[34]
The letter differentiated between Ukrainians and Austrians again

in discussing the assassination of Austrian Archduke Franz Ferdinand. It stated, "The enemies of Austria, especially the enemies of the Ruthenian-Ukrainians, do not disguise their joy in the wake of this tragedy."[35] The letter then suggested that, despite these ethnic differences and problems, Ukrainians should return and fight for the Austro-Hungarian army. It stated,

> Perhaps we will have to defend Galicia from seizure by Russia with its appetite for Ruthenians; maybe we will have to defend our parents, wives, children, brothers and our entire land before the insatiable enemy.... In any event, all Austrian subjects should be at home in a position ready to defend our native land, our dear brothers and sisters, our nation.[36]

Bishop Budka's letter was dutifully read in churches in Manitoba and in many other Greek Orthodox churches across Canada. Many English- and Ukrainian-language newspapers ran excerpts. Despite Budka's widely publicized plea, and despite the fact that it came only days after the Austrian vice-consul's similar request, again not a single Ukrainian Canadian volunteered to fight for Austria.

Only a few weeks later Canada declared war. Budka immediately issued a retraction stating that the declaration changed everything. He wrote that all Ukrainians should fight for Canada and the British Empire. He said,

> So at this time when England turns to us as its faithful subjects with the call that we stand under its flag—when the British state requires our assistance—as loyal sons of the British state, we Canadian Ukrainians have a great and holy duty to stand under the flag of our new homeland, under the flag of the British state, and sacrifice, if necessary, our property and our blood.[37]

Like his first letter, Budka's retraction was read in many Greek Orthodox churches. Like most retractions or corrections, however, it did not receive the same press coverage as his first letter. The damage was done.

A number of nativist-racist stories and editorials damned

"Austrians" in Canada as dangerous and disloyal. Facts no longer seemed to matter. A public meeting took place in Winnipeg on August 18, 1914. An *Edmonton Bulletin* story entitled "Ruthenian Orator Talks High Treason" stated that at the Ukrainian Hall a speaker named Paul Turneuko spoke in Ukrainian urging people against enlistment in the Canadian army. The report was wrong. The speaker was named Paul Krat. Krat's speech criticized Budka's first letter and recommended that the audience not enlist in the Austrian army. He admonished the crowd to join the Canadian forces to defend the way of life they had chosen for themselves and their children.

A few days later, the *Bulletin* criticized Krat for supporting the establishment of a Ukrainian state within Western Canada. Krat had said no such thing. He had advocated the creation of an independent Ukrainian state to be carved from parts of Austria, Poland, Romania and Russia. Krat wrote to the editor correcting the story but the correction did not help. The *Bulletin* accused him of treason for suggesting that part of Russia, Canada's loyal ally, should be taken.

Some newspapers were fairer. The *Manitoba Free Press*, for example, reprinted both of Budka's letters. Editor J.W. Dafoe's August 11, 1914 editorial stated, "there has never at any time been any question as to the loyalty of the majority of the Slav settlers of Manitoba and Canada. They will be faithful sons of their adopted country."[38] Unfortunately for the Ukrainians, the more accurate and reasoned reporting was lost in the war whoops. Like Budka's original letter, the anti-Ukrainian stories, no matter how inaccurate or dubious their source, were afforded much wider distribution and received much wider acceptance.

On September 3, 1914 the Canadian government invoked the War Measures Act. The act suspended the civil rights of Canadians and allowed a temporary dictatorship by cabinet, allowing cabinet decisions, through Orders in Council, to automatically have the force of law. An Order in Council passed that day stated that all German and Austrian people who had arrived in Canada since 1902 were enemy aliens. The mislabelled Ukrainian people of Canada were suddenly enemies of the land they were helping to build and willing to defend.

On October 28, another Order in Council stated that all German and Austrian people had to register at specified offices administered by the RCMP in the east, and by the North West Mounted Police in the West. They would be kept under close surveillance. They had to surrender all firearms. The police could enter and search their homes at any time. Those with jobs could keep them but had to report to police headquarters on a monthly basis. Those without jobs would be interned as prisoners of war. Prison camp construction began.

The government's Orders in Council legitimized the newspapers' reports of the disloyalty of the German and "Austrian" Canadians. Employers reacted quickly. Thousands of Ukrainian workers across the country were fired because they were Ukrainian. The suddenly unemployed people were interned.

Unions that for years had promoted anti-Ukrainian discrimination reacted as well by encouraging employers to fire Ukrainian workers. Many supported Anglo-Saxon workers who refused to work with Ukrainians. In 1915, for example, miners in Hillcrest, Alberta, went on strike, refusing to work with Ukrainians or to return to work until the Ukrainians were fired and interned. The Ukrainian miners were taken away. The Trades and Labour Congress suggested that all Ukrainians should be placed on forty-acre plots of rocky land in northern Ontario and left to fend for themselves.

In the war's first year, 2,009 enemy aliens were investigated and 396 interned. Of those, 310 were Ukrainian. In the war's first winter, the internment camps housed four thousand men. Approximately three-quarters of the prisoners listed as Austrian are believed to have been Ukrainian.

The internment camps were organized by a new branch of the Justice Department called the Internment Operations Branch, with sixty-nine-year-old retired major-general William Otter in charge. Internment camps were established near Halifax, Quebec City, Montreal, Toronto, Kingston, Petawawa, Spirit Lake, Kapuskasing, Brandon, Lethbridge, Vernon, Nanaimo, Port Arthur and Amherst. The largest were the Vernon and Kapuskasing camps. The camps were all quite similar. Most were located in desolate places far from the closest town or city. They were surrounded by high fences and barbed wire and patrolled by armed guards with specially trained dogs. Most barracks were hastily constructed wooden buildings that generally welcomed the wind and elements. They were sweatboxes in the summer and intolerably cold in the winter.

The camps were segregated according to race, occupation, and previous military service. German prisoners reportedly received better treatment and food than their Ukrainian counterparts. The small number of German prisoners of war who were transported from Europe received the best treatment of all. Prisoners were forced to dig ditches, clear road paths, shovel snow and perform many other menial tasks. Unions were promised that prisoners' work would not steal jobs away from English- or French-speaking Canadians. Many jobs were dangerous, tedious, and back-breaking. Prisoners received no money, instead earning thirty coupons a month which could be traded for oranges, tobacco or other goods. Camp black markets thrived.

A Ukrainian-Canadian prisoner named Phillip Marchuk had escaped to the United States and found a job. He was caught on May 16, 1916, sneaking back to gather his family. Marchuk had two small children, and his wife Maria was pregnant with a third. Maria was left to tend the family farm and raise their children alone until Phillip's release in April 1919.

Wasyl Cinga of Glace Bay, Nova Scotia, was threatened with internment when the RCMP discovered that he had sent six dollars to his sister in Bukovyna. He avoided the camp by convincing police that his sister's village was only three miles from the Russian border and that she was really more loyal to Russia than Austria.

Maftey Rotri was able to escape the camps by keeping his job as a carpenter. In 1916, however, the authorities at the Spirit Lake, Quebec, camp announced a need for carpenters. Rotri was arrested, interned at Spirit Lake and forced to work on the camp expansion project. When his work at Spirit Lake was done he was transferred to Kapuskasing where he remained interned until the war's end.

In many camps, Ukrainian men sang traditional Ukrainian folk songs at night. They occasionally staged plays. Stories were told and Tara Shevchenko's poems were recited. They wrote letters to loved ones, but all were mercilessly censored. Few letters were delivered to the prisoners and visits were limited to ten minutes once a month, but few families had the means to make the long journeys to the camps.

There were a number of escape attempts. Guards were ordered to shoot those trying to escape. Andrew Gropko was eighteen years old when he was shot and killed attempting to escape from the Brandon camp in June 1915. Later, seventeen men escaped from the camp.

There were several camp protests and revolts. The best known occurred in Ontario in 1916. Phillip Yasnowsky was one of the thirteen hundred prisoners at the Kapuskasing camp. Long after his internment ended he recalled a day when approximately six hundred new Ukrainian prisoners arrived. They were emaciated, had been beaten, and spoke in faltering voices of not having eaten in three days. They explained that after slaving for months at the Petawawa camp they had announced their intention to refuse work on the upcoming Ukrainian holy day celebrating the Feast of Annunciation. The guards cut their food rations but the prisoners refused to change their plans. Straw was removed from their bunks and winter clothing was taken. Floggings began in the prison courtyard. They were forced to carry fifty-pound sacks of sand on thirty-mile hikes through the snow. They refused to give in. Finally, they were reduced to bread and water. The "revolt" leaders were then shipped to Kapuskasing.

They were given the night to sleep, and their new prison mates helped as they could. The next morning they were hauled from their bunks and punched and kicked into lines. Other Ukrainian prisoners were lined up to watch the abuse, but after only a few minutes they rushed the guards. One prisoner was struck with the blunt end of a revolver. Shots were fired. The major in charge rallied his three hundred troops, who fixed bayonets, turned, and rushed the sixteen hundred unarmed prisoners. The prisoners fled to their barracks, leaving nine seriously wounded men.

One hundred and seven men died in the internment camps. Some were killed in escape attempts and some from illness. Others died due to merciless mistreatment. Camp Commander Korpus bragged in a report to Ottawa that he maintained discipline by ordering men to roll call several times a day and having them stand at attention for long periods of time. He wrote, "A few hesitated, but an automatic six shooter pointed at their faces made them step lively. They stood up like sheep and answered their names."[39] Many prisoners carried psychological scars for the rest of their lives. An internee wrote,

> My wife's brother went nuts in one of their camps. He was taken away and when he finally got back he was never the same again. They had broken his spirit up there in northern Ontario. He could never get over the injustice of his treatment, the falseness of his hope in this new world.[40]

Meanwhile, the Ukrainian people who were not interned tried to carry on. They mailed letters and Christmas presents to those in the camps. They continued to register with the RCMP and suffer the indignities of surprise searches and questioning. Many Ukrainian people had their property taken, their homes and churches vandalized, and their children harassed and beaten. They grew used to finding their mail opened, read and censored, and goods stolen before delivery.

Many organized to try to end the internments and mistreatment. The Ukrainian Canadian Citizens Committee, the Ukrainian National Council and the Ukrainian Social Democratic Party all sent delegations to Ottawa. All spoke of the unfairness of the registrations and internment camps and of being Ukrainians and loyal Canadian citizens and not Austrians at all. It was to no avail.

Ukrainian editors and political and religious leaders organized to lobby the government. One group comprised of Bishop Budka, Manitoba MLA Tara Ferley, and the editors of the *Kanadiysky Farmer*, *The Ranok* and *The Sprinkler* met with the minister of the interior and with Borden but could not effect change.

A group of wives and mothers of internment camp prisoners met with the prime minister on March 5, 1918. According to the *Vegreville Observer*, Borden assured the women that Ukrainians were interned not because they were Austrians but "as an act of mercy as many employers through a mistaken idea of patriotism had discharged their men leaving them in a helpless and destitute condition, so that internment seemed to be the best way of dealing with the matter."[41] He assured them that no Canadian citizens were among those in the camps. It is not known whether the prime minister sincerely believed the lies he told the women that day.

The bilingual school system fell under attack in 1915. The Manitoba government decided that it was inappropriate to allow the teaching of Ukrainian in schools while Austrians were enemy aliens. Ukrainian-language instruction was banned. When the decision was announced, Ukrainian people and others sympathetic to the cause organized a rally outside the legislative building. Liberal MLA D.A. Ross berated the crowd, screaming over the din, "If you don't stop this agitation I'll run you all into Brandon."[42] Premier Norris was asked to comment on Ross' statement. The premier supported Ross, saying, "any man speaking against the British institutions or saying anything openly against the best interests of the country should be rounded up."[43] Borden said nothing. By the end of 1916, bilingual education and Ukrainian-language classes had been banned in all three prairie provinces. It became illegal to teach Ukrainian in any school. In Manitoba, all copies of the widely used *Ruthenian Bilingual Reader* were collected and ceremoniously burned.

In February 1917, another wrinkle was added to the international situation when Czar Nicholas was overthrown in Russia. In October, the group that ousted the czar was itself overthrown by the Bolshevik party led by the charismatic Vladimir Lenin promising bread and peace. Shortly after assuming power, Lenin delivered on half of his pledge by pulling Russia out of the war.

The Russian Revolution precipitated a Red scare in Canada and the United States. Everything remotely connected to Russia, communism or socialism became suspect. A new Order in Council declared that all Russian people in Canada were enemy aliens. Another declared that all Slavic socialist parties and organizations were banned. The list specifically mentioned fourteen organizations including the Ukrainian Revolutionary Group and the Ukrainian Social Democratic Party. Like obedient guard dogs the Canadian people were turned and pointed toward a new enemy.

The anti-socialist hysteria grew quickly. Much of the wrath of those feeding the hysteria was aimed at Ukrainians since they led Canada's biggest socialist party. A large delegation marched to the Manitoba legislative building and demanded that all remaining free Ukrainians be rounded up, interned, then deported, as they were preparing a revolt to overthrow the government of Canada. An MLA was appointed to investigate the imminent revolution. He travelled to Springfield, which had been purported to be the hotbed of Ukrainian revolutionary activities. He spent a pleasant afternoon with a number of farmers who were as bewildered as he about the fuss.

The bannings did not stop at political organizations. An October 25, 1918 Order in Council banned newspapers in fourteen languages, rendering all Ukrainian-language newspapers illegal. It became illegal to hold public meetings in any of the fourteen languages. Since churches were considered public places, it was suddenly illegal to conduct Ukrainian church services. Local Ukrainian literary societies, for so long a mainstay in preserving and promoting Ukrainian culture, were banned. Plays could not be performed and songs could not be publicly sung in Ukrainian. This was the final assault on the Ukrainian people. No longer just Ukrainian people but now the Ukrainian language and culture were deemed dangerous and illegal. The new bannings illustrated the ruthless, totalitarian nature of the wartime Canadian government as it sought to control not only what a group of its people did but what they thought. The racist ladder's final rung had been reached.

The grim irony of the racist laws that were levelled at Ukrainian people was not lost on reasonable observers at the time. Rev. J. Shaver of the United Church wrote,

> The Government spent more money advertising among the Ukrainians and other south-east Europeans to bring them here than among the people of the British Isles and then, when they had come, did little or nothing to give them a proper perspective of the difference between this country and that from which they came.... [Many] are now living in fear and trembling lest they are to be bundled into trains and shipped back to their European countries.[44]

•

The First World War ended on November 11, 1918. Every artillery gunner on both sides of the line apparently fired at precisely eleven o'clock, then claimed the last shot of the war. It was a silly end to a stupid war. The Canadian government was not yet through firing upon the Ukrainian people.

By the war's end, eight thousand enemy aliens had been registered and 8,579 had been interned. Of those interned, six thousand were registered as "Austrians." They were by far the largest ethnic group interned. It had cost about $1.5 million per year to maintain the camps. In April 1919, the war had been over for six months but 2,117 people remained interned. Nearly all were Germans but four hundred Ukrainians were among the prisoners.

The other Ukrainian prisoners had been slowly released beginning in 1916. They had been released not because of the injustice of their imprisonment or because they were deemed no longer dangerous but to address the labour shortages that had hampered the ability of several industries to maintain war production. Ukrainian prisoners were seconded to locations specified by business leaders and government officials. They worked for little or no pay and lived in abominable conditions with inadequate clothing and food and under armed guard.

One of the many slave labour camps was in Haliburton, Ontario, where Ukrainian men worked on railway construction. A letter from one of the young men illustrates the anguish of those confused, exploited, barely bilingual men:

> we cannot stand any longer to stay in the bush, we are sick from hard work, we have friends and families at Oshawa and we can work with them in the same factories so good as our friends and rapport [sic] to the police every month.... We beg send us our parole cards or tell us who kept [sic] them for us. We think that our employer Frank Austin have them only he not want to return them to us.[45]

They worked at mines, lumber camps, farms and railway construction sites. Many were held in forced labour camps for months.

Even after the last people had been released from the internment and labour camps, Ukrainian people continued to be subjected to mean-spirited racist violence. The worst of the attacks occurred in Winnipeg, Port Arthur, Calgary, Drumheller and Sudbury. In none of the cases did local police attempt to arrest the perpetrators. Manitoba premier Norris, in fact, created an Alien Investigation Board in response to the attacks. Its purpose was to organize the distribution of registration cards to "loyal" aliens, which would allow them to work. Those without cards could not work. The cost of bribing officials to obtain a card quickly rose.

Officially sanctioned discrimination continued unabated. Many unions announced that they supported the dismissal of foreign workers to create jobs for returning soldiers. Among them were the British Columbia Employers' Association and the British Columbia Loggers Association, a number of mining companies and the CPR. CPR vice-president D.C. Coleman explained, "The aliens who had been on the land when the war broke out and who went to work in the cities and the towns, taking the jobs of the men who went to the front [should] go back to their old jobs on the land."[46] Coleman, and those who either believed or pretended to believe in what he espoused, ignored several facts. They ignored the fact that all soldiers in the Canadian army were not of British or French origin. They also ignored the fact that thousands of Ukrainians had been driven from their land during the war. Restrictions on citizenship and democratic rights had rendered it nearly impossible for new-comers to purchase land or for established farmers to buy more. Many Ukrainian farms had been lost when the principal breadwin-ner was interned or banished to a work camp and families about to lose farms were unable to find work or secure loans to save them. Coleman, and the many others who made similar arguments, displayed the typically short and selective memories of minds poisoned by racism.

The federal government slowly moved down the racist ladder and lifted many of the restrictions imposed by the various Orders in Council after the war. In 1919, however, the Borden government passed the Dominion Act, depriving Ukrainians of the ability to obtain naturalized citizenship for ten years. Three years later the act was repealed.

In 1919, a group billing itself as "peaceful law-abiding and loyal Ukrainian citizens" met in Vegreville, Alberta. They repeated the same loyalty oaths to Canada that their fellow Ukrainians had been swearing for years and issued a document entitled "An Appeal to Legislative and Executive Bodies and to Our Fellow Citizens of Canada." It was sent to the prime minister and all nine premiers. The document outlined a brief history of the arrival of Ukrainian settlers in Canada and the substantial economic contribution they had made. It mentioned that ten thousand Ukrainian Canadians had claimed to be of Russian descent and then fought in the Canadian military in the Great War. It noted that in 1917, King George V presented the coveted Victoria Cross to Ukrainian-Cana-dian soldier Filip Konoval. The document then reviewed the man-ner in which Ukrainians were treated before and during the war despite the fact that not one Ukrainian Canadian had volunteered to fight for Austria or had been found guilty of a single treasonous or seditious act. It then outlined the numerous ways in which employers, unions, and federal and provincial laws continued to discriminate against Ukrainian people. The document received no response.

Meanwhile, many Ukrainians continued to thrive despite the continuation of discriminatory laws and practices. Language and some traditions were slowly forgotten, and many proud Ukrainian names were Anglicized by those willing to surrender part of their heritage to evade racist roadblocks. In 1965, Lester Pearson's government appointed the Royal Commission on Bilingualism and Biculturalism. The fourth book of the Bi and Bi Commission's report addressed the histories and contributions of ethnic groups other than British and French. It spoke highly of the economic and cultural contribution of the Ukrainian people and acknowledged that there had been "some resistance" to the large numbers of Ukrainian immigrants shortly after their arrival in the 1890s. Its authors did not, however, acknowledge any discriminatory actions directed against Ukrainian Canadians. It stated that discrimination against the Ukrainians is impossible to prove because it was not seen in laws. In a confusing and clearly incorrect argument, the authors concluded that "One reason that there has been little discriminatory legislation in Canada has been the discriminatory nature of our immigration."[46] The report briefly mentioned wartime racist discrimination. It noted the mistreatment of Japanese and Italian Canadians in World War II and of German Canadians in both world wars. It did not mention the Ukrainians. The officially sanctioned state racism meted against Ukrainian Canadians before, during and after the war was washed from the record. Perhaps it is easier to mythologize the past than face harsh truths.

3

Jewish Canadians 1738–1948
The Devil's Accomplice

Hitler: Patron Father, how can I so confuse, exasperate and implicate the righteous nations that I may conquer and rule them in your name?
Lucifer: Offer them the Chosen People.
—From the play *Lovebound* by Adele Wiseman

There were 917 men, women and children aboard the *St. Louis*. It had been a luxury liner, and many of the remnants of its rich appointments were still evident. The passengers who steamed from Hamburg that day, however, saw the *St. Louis* not as a holiday cruise ship but as their last ticket to freedom. It was to whisk them from certain death.

Those aboard the *St. Louis* were part of Adolf Hitler's attempt to rid the Third Reich of Jewish people. Jews could leave if they wanted to leave. All they needed was a place to go. The *St. Louis'* passengers held expensive Cuban visas, but upon arrival they were informed that Cuban officials had changed their minds. The refugees could not enter the country. After days of arguing and pleading the legality and morality of their case they were forced to leave. They tried Panama, Uruguay, Paraguay and Argentina but met hostility at every port. The Americans responded with two coast guard gunships that escorted the *St. Louis* north along the seaboard to ensure it did not dock. Finally, in July 1939, the *St. Louis* found itself at Halifax. The captain petitioned the Canadian government to afford refuge for his tired, frightened and desperate passengers.

Canadians were well aware of the *St. Louis'* plight, for

newspapers had been filled with heart-wrenching stories of the sad tale. The request for sanctuary reached the floor of the House of Commons and the federal cabinet table. The announcement of the government's decision was left to the deputy minister of immigration, Frederick Blair. The people would not be rescued. Blair explained that Canada could not save all the Jews of Europe and that "the line must be drawn somewhere."[1]

The ship left for Europe. Through ingenious moves by the captain, the passengers were relocated in Britain and a number of northern European countries. After the Nazi army swept through those countries two hundred of the original *St. Louis* passengers were captured and later met their deaths in extermination camps. We could have saved them. We chose not to do so. The Canadian government's decision was tragic but consistent with the exclusionist immigration policies directed against Chinese immigrants. It was also consistent with the myriad of racist laws, regulations and practices created, enforced or at least tolerated by nearly all those in positions of power.

•

The first Jewish man in Canada was a woman. Twenty-year-old Esther Brandeau smuggled herself into Quebec in 1738 aboard a ship called the *Saint-Michel*. She had disguised herself as a boy and had fooled the ship's authorities for four years as she sailed around the world variously acting as cook, tailor, baker and ship hand. She was born in Bayonne, France, the daughter of Jewish parents who had fled the Portuguese inquisition, which had seen the murder of thousands of Jewish people by Catholic leaders intent on converting Jews to Catholicism. The ship's captain was not amused by Brandeau's deception. He sent her ashore at Quebec City and sailed away. Quebec government officials informed Brandeau that according to French and Quebec law, Jewish people were not allowed in the colony. Church and government officials tried to persuade her to convert to Catholicism, but, invoking the name of her brave and persecuted parents, she refused. Finally, on the order of Louis XVI, she was shipped back to France at the government's expense.

The exclusionist laws of New France had been established years before Brandeau's arrival. Cardinal Richelieu had created the Company of New France in 1627 and had stated in its charter that the colony was for Catholics only. Later, the 1685 Black Code was sanctioned by both the French king and the Pope. It decreed that all French officials both in France and in its colonies must expel all Jews as enemies of the state and of Christ. Despite the racist wall, a small number of Jewish people found their way into New France. Almost all were escaping European inquisitions. The most common ploy was to publicly convert to Catholicism while continuing to privately practise Jewish customs and traditions.

The first Jewish people in Canada who were allowed to remain Jewish settled in Nova Scotia in the 1740s. They were British soldiers who elected to stay in Halifax after the completion of their tour of duty. Samuel Hart became the first Jewish Canadian to hold public office when, in 1793, he won a seat in the Nova Scotia assembly.

It took the Conquest to change things in Quebec. With the British in charge, the laws restricting Jews in the colony were lifted, but anti-Semitism remained alive. It was seen in the destroyed career of Ezekiel Hart. Hart was born in Trois-Rivières in 1770. His father, Aaron Hart, had been part of the British force that had taken Montreal in 1760. He stayed after the campaign and built a very successful fur-trading business, becoming the largest landowner in Lower Canada. His son was more interested in law and public service than business. Young Ezekiel was advised by his father to forget such ambitions in Lower Canada, for anti-Semitism was so deeply rooted in the colony that Jewish people had no chance in Quebec public life. Ezekiel showed the arrogance of youth and pursued his dream.

After working to establish himself as a well-spoken and sincere advocate of the needs of the people of Trois-Rivières, Ezekiel Hart was elected in 1807 to the Lower Canada legislative assembly and, according to tradition, asked to swear allegiance to the King with one hand on the New Testament. Hart refused. He explained that the oath would be meaningless for him but that he would swear the oath upon the Torah with his head covered in keeping with Jewish tradition. The oath was administered and Hart took his place the next day. Lower Canada's Attorney General Jonathan Sewell rose in the House that day and introduced a resolution demanding that Hart be ejected, for he had not properly sworn his oath. Hart was ejected on a vote of twenty-one to five. The resolution stated, "Anyone professing the Jewish religion cannot take a seat nor sit nor vote in the House."[2]

Hart asked Chief Justice James Reid about his right to take his seat and was told that there was no legal statute that prevented him from doing so. Hart cited this opinion as well as English precedents stating that Jewish people could swear legally binding oaths while omitting references to Christianity. The House did not budge. A by-election was held and Hart easily won. This time he took the oath on a Christian copy of the Old Testament and with his head uncovered. A new resolution ejected Hart again. The British government was petitioned by sympathetic governor James Craig, but to no avail. There would not be a Jewish representative in the Quebec legislature until the 1920s.

Many Jewish people refused to accept Lower Canada's anti-Semitic laws. They were inspired by Hart's courageous but doomed struggle for full citizenship. In the late 1820s, petitions were organized by prominent Jewish citizens asking the Lower Canada legislature to officially recognize the Jewish religion. Such recognition would have allowed courts to accept and support Jewish contracts, land claims, inheritances, and birth, death and marriage records, among other things. The petitions discussed fairness, morality and the liberal doctrines of the French and American revolutions. They noted the economic contributions of Jewish business people and the military contributions of Jewish soldiers in the War of 1812. After months of negotiations a bill was introduced. Its ponderous name was; "An Act To Declare Persons Professing The Jewish Religion Entitled To All The Rights And Privileges Of The Other Subjects Of His Majesty In This Province." It won royal assent in 1832 and was considered Canadian Jews' Magna Carta. Unfortunately, what is true now was true then. Laws can be altered, but society's attitudes must shift for real and permanent change to occur.

The late 1800s witnessed a resurgence of anti-Semitism in Europe. It came from three main directions. First, in 1864, Pope Pius IX issued a syllabus proclaiming that all religions were not equal. It ordered Catholics to fight the forces of indifference, sanctioning religious intolerance and the hatred of non-Christians. Second, a number of brutally anti-Semitic books were published in the 1870s. Most important among these were Wilhelm Marr's *Der Sieg des Judenthums unter dem Germanenthum* and Pastor Adolf Stocker's *Christichsoziale Arbeitspartei*. Both were translated from German into a number of languages. Both rekindled pejorative Jewish stereotypes and recreated the myths of a Jewish desire to control the world's press and economy. The third direction from which the new wave of hatred came was a series of dramatic, internationally famous court cases involving Jewish people framed for crimes they did not commit. The most significant were those involving Beilis, who was charged in Russia with murdering Christian children and using their blood for Jewish rituals, and Dreyfus, who was found guilty in France of selling war secrets to Germany.

The return of church- and state-sanctioned anti-Semitism had its most tragic manifestation in Russia and the Ukraine. Pogroms began in Yelisavetrad in April 1881. In town after town, Jewish people were beaten and their houses burned, and many were killed. Survivors fled with the possessions they could carry and family they could find. The army and police allowed some pogroms to occur and organized others themselves. By 1919, twelve hundred pogroms had taken place, resulting in the deaths of over fifty thousand Jewish people.

Officials in many world capitals rose above suspicions of Jewish people and sought ways to help the thousands of refugees scrambling to escape the madness. As Canada's high commissioner in London, Alexander Galt persuaded the Canadian government to offer sanctuary to pogrom victims. Prime Minister Sir John A. Macdonald was at first cool to the idea of Jewish immigrants but was later persuaded that their numbers would help the flagging immigration campaign. A note to Galt revealed that he had accepted the stereotypes attached to Jewish people. Macdonald wrote, "A sprinkling of Jews in the North-West would be good. They would at once go in for peddling and politicking, and be of as much use in the new country as cheap jacks and chapmen."[3] Jewish refugees began arriving in May 1882.

While a few of the refugees settled in the West, most found their way to the country's growing urban centres. By the turn of the century, Montreal had the greatest Jewish population, followed by Victoria, then Toronto. By 1921 there were 126,200 Jewish people in Canada, with nearly three-quarters in Quebec and Ontario. About seventy percent were skilled workers, compared to about twenty percent among all other immigrant groups. More literate than many of their counterparts, many Jewish immigrants left a wealth of letters, articles and books. Many spoke of the relief they felt at finally being free from fear and want. A. Asovsky expressed thoughts typical of many. He wrote,

But I shall never forget that early period in Winnipeg. Quite often as I sit at my table, where, thank God, nothing is wanting, I remember that first meal and it seems to me that I still see those hungry, wearied faces staring at the food before them.[4]

By the 1800s, anti-Jewish stereotypes were firmly established in Canada and anti-Semitic laws and practices already had a hundred-year history. The arrival of great numbers of Jewish immigrants and the upsurge in European anti-Semitism, coupled with the existing wildly popular and systemic intolerance of all minority racial groups, created a situation in which Jewish Canadians would be sure to suffer. And suffer they did.

•

As in Europe, anti-Semitism in Canada was nurtured by intellectuals and religious leaders. The most important intellectual in late nineteenth- and early twentieth-century English Canada was Goldwin Smith. Smith was born in England to a wealthy family and was educated at Eton and Oxford. A prolific writer with a razor-sharp wit and keen intellect, he became the Regium Chair in Modern History at Oxford and later a professor of English history at Stanford. In 1871, Smith moved to Toronto, where he married the widow of Henry Boulton and moved to The Grange, one of the city's finest houses. He entertained Canada's academic, political, religious and business elite and wrote a number of widely read and very influential articles for *The Canadian Monthly*, *National Review*, *The Week* and other periodicals. His stature as an internationally respected intellectual lent his articles and dinner conversations considerable weight. His views helped shape Canadian liberalism and the thoughts of many of the country's most influential people. Vincent Massey wrote of being in awe of the great man. A young William Lyon Mackenzie King spoke in glowing terms of Smith and his ideas, and it was with a letter of introduction from Smith that he travelled to Harvard in 1897.

Goldwin Smith was a virulent anti-Semite. He wrote that Jews controlled the international press and even a number of Christian religious journals. He claimed they had infiltrated a number of governments at the highest levels. British prime minister Disraeli was, for Smith, an example of this infiltration. Disraeli could not be trusted because he was a Jew, and it was as a Jew that he had dragged the British Empire to war in South Africa in 1899. Smith wrote that the Boer War was little more than, "a war waged with British blood to uphold the objects of Jewish sympathy, or to avenge Jewish wrongs."[5]

Smith helped to popularize and, because of his stature and reputation, legitimize negative Jewish stereotypes in Canada. He consistently expressed the opinion that Jewish people were parasites who added nothing to the countries in which they lived, while exploiting opportunities to enrich themselves. He wrote that Jews were "encamping in all other nations, absorbing their wealth by financial skill...and bringing pogroms upon themselves by their exclusiveness."[6] They could not be trusted because they felt no allegiance to their "host" country but only to themselves and their race. He wrote, "A Jew is not an Englishman or Frenchman, with a special deity for his own race. The rest of mankind are to him not merely people holding a different creed, but aliens in blood."[7]

Smith suggested an end to Jewish immigration. He wrote that "Few greater calamities perhaps have ever befallen mankind than the transportation of the negro and the dispersion of the Jew."[8] He wrote, "The Chinaman, though he may be vicious himself, is not a corrupter of the community...whereas the Polish Jew unhappily is."[9] Smith supported the idea of creating a Jewish homeland in Palestine as a way of ridding all countries of the Jewish menace.

Smith was the most prominent English-Canadian intellectual to popularize anti-Semitism. There were many others in government and universities. Another who deserves mention is Major Clifford Douglas. To understand Douglas, and indeed part of the reason for the growth of anti-Semitism in Canada, one must understand the power of *The Protocols of the Elders of Zion*.

The Protocols of the Elders of Zion was a propaganda tract written in Russia in 1903 by Czar Nicholas II's secret police. Its purpose was to split opposition by having groups turn against Jewish people instead of the state. The book purported to be the work of a committee of Jewish people speaking on behalf of all Jewish people. *The Protocols* suggested that Jewish people participated in ritual murder ceremonies involving blood taken from murdered Christian babies, and other similarly warped lies. It also suggested that Jewish people were involved in an international conspiracy to control the world's economy. Their strategy, it said, was to infiltrate industrialized countries and take control of large businesses and banks until the economy of the entire world was eventually in their hands. A series of university studies showed *The Protocols* to be propaganda tripe with huge sections lifted directly from a French anti-Semitic tract. After the Russian Revolution, the *Protocols* were republished, with new editions appearing in a number of languages around the world. Again they were exposed as a hoax, but many people still believed the lies.

Clifford Douglas was either duped by or willing to exploit the *Protocols*. Douglas was a Scottish army engineer who had immigrated to Alberta. He often lied about his past, falsely claiming to have graduated from Cambridge and to have been a Westinghouse Company engineer. Douglas espoused the creation of a new economic order beginning with the elimination of Jews. In 1922, he wrote,

> We have a good many more Jews in important positions in this country than we deserve.... ideas which can be traced through the propaganda of Collectivism to the idea of the Supreme, impersonal State, to which every individual must bow—seem to derive a great deal of their most active, intelligent support from Jewish sources, while at the same time a grim struggle is proceeding in the great financial groups, many of which are purely Jewish, for the acquisition of key positions from which to control the World State when formed.[10]

In 1924, Douglas wrote an important book called *Social Credit*. The book outlined his political and economic theories in detail. It detailed his hatred of Jewish people and his sincere belief in an international conspiracy. He wrote, "it is the Jews as a group, and not as individuals, who are on trial, and the remedy, if one is required, is to break up the group activity."[11] To rid the country of Jews would return control of the economy to "real" Canadians, and the financial problems of the state could be solved.

The book became the ideological basis for the formation of the Social Credit Party of Alberta. The party was led by William Aberhart, who had made his mark as a Christian fundamentalist preacher nicknamed Bible Bill. He once said on his popular radio program that Jewish people must someday accept Jesus as the son of God and until they do, "they must expect the curses of the world and can not expect the Blessings of God."[12] Aberhart accepted and promoted Douglas' ideas of an international economic conspiracy and spoke of the need to break it. He never publicly supported Douglas' belief that Jewish people were at the heart of the conspiracy, but many in his party did. The most important of these was L.D. Byrne, who acted as Aberhart's adviser and party policy consultant for many years. Byrne once wrote, "There is a close connection between the *Protocols* and the appalling state of the world today and [the] attempt to enslave mankind which is being made by those in control of finance."[13]

The Social Credit Party formed the government of Alberta in 1935. It was often forced to answer accusations of anti-Semitism. Aberhart, for instance, was asked to explain why Douglas had written to Adolf Hitler in 1938 praising the Nazi leader's Jewish policies. Delegates to the 1947 party convention passed a motion supporting Douglas' economic ideas but denouncing his anti-Semitism. It is odd indeed to support a man's ideas but not the very basis of those ideas. The Social Credit Party continued to win Alberta elections until 1971.

The most important francophone-Canadian intellectuals have always been Quebec nationalists. Nationalism is more than a love of one's country. It suggests suspicion of other countries, peoples and cultures and is by definition xenophobic, ethnocentric and exclusionist. Further, Quebec nationalism is not a civic nationalism in which all citizens are considered equal members of the nation but an ethnic nationalism which argues that only those of the ethnic majority deserve membership. As stated by Michael Ignatieff, "It is the national community that defines the individual, not the individuals who define the national community."[14] Those not of French-Catholic heritage, so-called "pure wool," are not real Quebecers.

One of the most important Quebec nationalists was Henri Bourassa. Bourassa was a sharp-tongued, ruthless debater. He was proud to be the grandson of Louis-Joseph Papineau, who had led the 1837 Lower Canada Rebellion. Bourassa's varied and celebrated career included becoming the mayor of Montebello at age twenty-two, a member of parliament for twenty-one years, and a member of the Quebec National Assembly for five. He also founded and, from 1910 to 1929, edited Quebec's most influential newspaper—*Le Devoir*.

Bourassa called Goldwin Smith "the most profound liberal thinker of the day."[15] Like Smith, Bourassa believed and promoted the myths and stereotypes that had been foisted upon Jewish people. He argued that east-European Jews had brought pogroms upon themselves by their actions and their refusal to assimilate. He stated in the House of Commons that "Russian peasants have been sucked for centuries by Jewish usurers…it is not surprising they are now acting terribly in dealing with them."[16] Later, also in the House, he said, "The Jews are the most undesirable class of people any country can have …. They are vampires on a community instead of being contributors to the general welfare of the people."[17] In a 1906 newspaper article, Bourassa repeated the argument, calling Jews "the class which sucked the most from other people. They live as vampires on the people…. Parasites who oppress the poor."[18]

Bourassa experienced a conversion in 1926. Some say it was a long trip abroad and a private audience with the Pope that inspired the change. Whatever the cause, Bourassa suddenly renounced anti-Semitism and publicly apologized to all Canadian Jews through Member of Parliament S.W. Jacobs. He began to argue that those who are not French and Catholic could be loyal Quebecers. These views alienated him from his nationalist followers.

French-speaking Quebecers had long realized that they existed precariously as a religious and linguistic minority in North America. The Catholic church was seen as a bastion against forces that could rob Quebecers of their identity, culture and dignity. Until the end of the Duplessis era in 1959, very few major political decisions were made without consulting church leaders.

Quebec's most powerful religious leader was Abbé Lionel-Adolphe Groulx. Groulx was born in the small Quebec town of Vaudreuil. After his ordination he taught college history, then completed his education in France. His influence went far beyond the church, for he was a historian, lecturer, poet and philosopher. Even more than Henri Bourassa, Groulx provided the intellectual basis for Quebec nationalism. Former Quebec Liberal leader Claude Ryan called him the "spiritual leader of modern Quebec."[19] Former Parti Québécois leader René Levesque called him "one of the heroes and fathers of modern Quebec."[20] Schools, streets, a Montreal subway station, a college and even a mountain now bear his name.

Groulx believed that the presence of Jewish people in Quebec hurt the province because they felt loyalty only to themselves. He proposed that they be banished. He said that the Jewish person

> finds himself involved in all revolutions, when he is not
> their principal agent.... He will do anything for money so
> we find him at the bottom of every shady affair, at all
> pornographic works, books, cinema, theatre, etc. He shows
> no moral scruples in business.... What solutions can we
> bring to the Jewish problem? Here, too, there is no easy
> answer. Strong peoples may be able to absorb or assimilate
> the Jew at not too great a cost. Is this also true of little
> peoples like our own, still so poorly equipped in economics?[21]

From 1920 to 1928, Groulx edited a monthly periodical called
L'Action Française. He also created *L'Action Catholique* and later
L'Action Nationale. His periodicals echoed his anti-Semitic views.
L'Action Catholique editor Abbé Edouard Valdore Lavagne wrote a
number of articles that portrayed Jews as Satan-worshippers whose
goal was not only the economic control of all nations but also the
destruction of the Christian religion. He argued that Jews were
destroying Catholicism by controlling the international press and,
in so doing, were "active in preventing the establishment of sincere
Catholic publications."[22]

More important than the relatively small circulation of his
periodicals was the support his ideas received from the much larger
French-language dailies such as *Le Devoir*. It reprinted many of
L'Action Nationale's columns verbatim. Groulx wrote many of the
articles, often under the pseudonym Jacques Brassier. It was under
this name that he also wrote the anti-Semitic novel entitled *L'Appel
de la Race*.

With English- and French-speaking intellectuals shaping,
legitimizing and helping to popularize anti-Semitic stereotypes,
institutional leaders moved to increase and entrench segregationist
laws and regulations. Their actions were consistent with, and
augmented, those directed against Chinese and Ukrainian
Canadians. Among the many forms that anti-Semitic discrimination
took in Quebec was the economic segregationist movement called
achat chez nous. It began in 1907. Its leaders were the Catholic church,
French business people, the press and the provincial and municipal
governments. The idea behind *achat chez nous* was that Quebec's
economy was threatened by all those who were not French Catholics.

The solution was to persuade francophone Quebecers to boycott all non-"pure wool" businesses. Jewish businesses were specifically targeted. In 1907, political activist Paul Tardivel revealed the anti-Semitic hatred at the heart of the movement when he wrote, "Our compatriots can use this means very effectively to defend their interests and to prevent the Jewish invasion."[23]

Achat chez nous meetings were held in communities throughout the province. Nearly all were held in Catholic churches, and parish priests often played pivotal roles in organizing local movements. Abbé Groulx actively supported *achat chez nous*. He wrote of the movement's ultimate goal in *L'Action Nationale*,

> Do not buy from the Jews. We need only say to our French Canadian customers, "Do what everybody is doing. Buy from your own people." ...within six months, within a year, the Jewish problems would be resolved, not only in Montreal but from one end of the province to the other. There would remain only the Jews who can subsist from each other. The rest would be forced to disperse, to seek their livelihood in occupations other than trade.[24]

The movement soon turned violent. In a number of cities and towns, Jewish-owned shops were smashed, looted and burned. In March 1910, a well-known journalist named Joseph Edouard Plamondon delivered a sordidly anti-Semitic speech at a meeting of the Association Canadian de la Jeunesse Catholique in Quebec City. He said, "Thieves of our property, corrupters of our women, murderers of Christian children, the Jew is also the fomenter of revolutions where he finds full scope to exercise his habitual perfidies."[25]

His audience then marched to the Jewish section of town and began looting Jewish shops and homes and mercilessly beating any who tried to stop them. The police did nothing. Charges were brought against some of the rioters but were later dropped. The business and personal property losses were not compensated.

Benjamin Ortenberg was among those who suffered in the riot. He filed suit against Plamondon. In an odd twist, the lies contained in *The Protocols of the Elders of Zion* were soon on trial. Plamondon claimed that he was not slandering Jewish people in his speech but merely speaking the truth. Ortenberg won the case but the judge was quick to point out that only Ortenberg himself, and not all the city's Jews, had been harmed. Jewish people were on their own. The trial afforded Plamondon's anti-Semitic ideas even wider publicity. The court's refusal, or legal inability, to refute them as lies and propaganda helped fuel the anti-Semitic hatred that the *achat chez nous* movement had brought to the surface.

Nearly all local governments supported the movement. Many took the opportunity to move against their Jewish citizens. In Trois-Rivières, for instance, city council and the Jewish community had been arguing for years over land used for a Jewish cemetery. In 1910, the city settled the matter by simply expropriating the land and, in the middle of the night, exhuming the bodies and moving them out of the city. No warning was issued and no compensation was paid. Meanwhile, the Montreal city council upheld a request to ban appearances by internationally known actress Sarah Bernhardt on the grounds that she was Jewish. The council then withdrew all support to Jewish charitable organizations because, as one councillor explained "all Jews are rich, and if there are any poor Jews they too would soon be rich."[26]

The majority of the Quebec press endorsed *achat chez nous,* with *L'Action Catholique, Le Patriote* and *Le Devoir* leading the charge. Most saw the movement against Jewish people as merely a natural extension of Quebec nationalism. *Le Patriote,* for instance, reported, "This is not anti-Semitism. It is simply legitimate defence. It is not to bully or to persecute the Jewish merchant. What can be more natural and normal."[27] Groulx's *L'Action Catholique* repeated the movement's barely disguised goal: "If we do not buy from them, then they will leave."[28]

Many newspapers, including *Le Nord, L'Action Française, Progress de Villeray* and others, supported *achat chez nous* by refusing to accept advertising from Jewish businesses. Many francophone business people appealed to growing anti-Semitism in their advertising. An advertisement in *Le Devoir* from Parc Lafontaine, a Montreal grocer, was typical of this tactic. The ad copy stated,

> We remind you again that 75% of the chain stores are managed by Jews. If you follow the papers you will also see that these people are brought before the courts for dishonest practices. Don't be attracted by their low prices, for their intentions are to sell at higher prices.[29]

Jewish merchants noted a significant drop in sales. Many told an investigating committee of the Canadian Jewish Congress that customers would enter stores, ask if the proprietors were Jewish, then leave if the answer was yes. Others suffered the indignity and expense of having anti-Semitic slogans painted on their windows or attached to bricks and thrown through them. Jewish children were beaten up and adults harassed. Many spoke of the pain of being rejected by the province that had been their home for generations.

The First World War presented Jewish Canadians with a dilemma. How could they support Canada when Canada was not only blatantly anti-Semitic but also allied with the Russians who had been encouraging pogroms against Jewish people for nearly three decades? Although there were arguments within many families, five thousand Canadian Jews voted with their feet and joined the Canadian armed services. Another three hundred volunteered for the British regiment called the Jewish Legion. An incredible thirty-eight percent of all Jewish males of military age served in the Canadian forces. That was a higher percentage than any other ethnic group in Canada, including British Canadians. The percentage of Jewish soldiers winning medals in the war was also higher than any other ethnic group.

Despite the demonstrations of loyalty, the *achat chez nous* movement gained momentum throughout the war and the decade that followed, and grew into areas not envisioned, but no doubt welcomed, by its founders. Racial segregation became commonplace. Signs appeared at hotels, restaurants, parks, beaches and elsewhere barring Jewish patrons. The front door of the prestigious Laurentian Hotel, for instance, was adorned with a large red and white sign proclaiming, "No Dogs Or Jews Allowed." As bad as things were, they would get worse.

•

The 1933 German election created a mess. The tangle of parties elected resulted in political deadlock. Germany's aging president, the World War I hero Hindenberg, was persuaded by business and military advisers to allow Adolf Hitler and his Nazi party to form a government.

Hitler had made his plans painfully clear in *Mein Kampf*, which he wrote in 1923 while in prison for treason. *Mein Kampf*, which means "my struggle," argued that the Germanic, or so-called Aryan race was superior to all others. Its superiority granted it the right, in fact the obligation, to expand itself and create a superior society. The establishment of this society required the purging of all inferior races. Jews were among those to be eliminated.

Once in power, Hitler moved quickly to ban then destroy all opposition and establish a totalitarian dictatorship. He then began to systematically carry out the plans he had outlined a decade before. There were three distinct stages in the elimination of the Jews. First, Jews were told they could not live among the Germans as Jews. Laws were passed outlawing the Jewish religion and banning Jewish businesses. Second, Jews were told they could not live among the Germans. Ghettos were created, into which Jewish people were herded and then subjected to inhuman conditions of filth and overcrowding in the hope that they would either die or kill one another. Third was the final solution. Jews were told they could not live. They were tricked into leaving the ghettos and taken to camps where they were worked to death, used in cruel and inhuman "medical" experiments, or simply murdered upon arrival. Six million European Jews, one million of whom were children, perished. Several million gypsies, Slavs, communists, Jehovah's Witness adherents and homosexuals were also slaughtered in the death camps.

News of Nazi atrocities was readily available in Canada throughout the 1930s. The front pages of Canadian newspapers told of the ghettos, the burning of synagogues and the millions of disappearances. Assumptions about the death camps later became confirmed reports. Until the war began in 1939, Hitler had encouraged Jews to leave Germany, and many did. The *St. Louis* voyage was one such attempt. The refugees added credence to the stories of horror that were already well known. Some apologists, trying to justify the absence of an effective international response to the plight of the Jews in Germany and Europe, have tried to argue that no one knew what was going on until the liberation of the death camps in 1945. Those people are wrong. We knew.

An important factor in Hitler's popularity in Germany was the depression that was ravaging the economies of every industrial state. Economic downturns are notorious for inviting people to seek simple explanations for complex problems, and villains to blame. In

Canada, as in Germany, Jews provided a perfect scapegoat for all of society's ills, as they were already believed by many to be in control of the world's economy so they naturally had to be responsible for the depression. As increasing numbers of Canadians began to be more public in their vilification of Jews, the popularity of Hitler and his fascist, racist ideas grew.

The trend was seen in Toronto. A couple of incidents illustrate the trend well. The first occurred at a baseball game. In 1930s Toronto, sports leagues were organized according to race. There were Jewish, Italian, Greek and Anglo-Saxon teams. The depression made the free baseball games very popular. April 16, 1933, saw a Jewish team playing an Anglo-Saxon team at Willowdale Park. A group of Anglo-Saxon spectators waved a large Nazi flag, shouted anti-Semitic abuse and painted swastikas on park buildings. The shouting, chanting young men soon left and the game resumed.

Two evenings later the two teams returned, along with a huge crowd and a resumption of the racist abuse. A fight broke out in the stands and quickly spilled onto the field, then into the street. Truck- and carloads of Jewish youths appeared on the scene. Lead pipes, rocks, baseball bats and other makeshift weapons entered the fray. Within an hour thousands of people were involved in a wide-ranging and violent riot. The maelstrom continued for six hours until, at two o'clock in the morning, it finally subsided. Hundreds were injured and dozens of mostly Jewish homes and businesses were smashed. Newspapers dubbed it the "Christie Pitts riot."

Chief of Police Draper was criticized by the press, city council and many of his own officers for not acting on a tip that the riot was being planned and would take place that evening. The police claimed that one of the city's pro-Nazi swastika clubs had been responsible for the riot. Toronto city council announced plans to act against swastika clubs and to arrest those brandishing swastikas in public. Nothing of consequence came of the council's well-intentioned huffings. Only two of those who began the riot were arrested, and both were later released without charges.

Newspapers attacked the city council's suggestion that swastika club activity be curtailed, arguing that restrictions would be a violation of freedom of speech. The *Toronto Telegram* blamed Jewish people for the riot. It suggested that Jewish groups were importing gangsters from the United States to violently attack Gentiles. The *Star* and the *Globe and Mail* both reported that the Christie Pitts riot was an isolated incident and argued that anti-Semitism did not exist in Toronto. Jewish people were advised to forget it.

A second incident that illustrated the growing anti-Semitism in Toronto involved swimmers at Balmy Beach in the warm summer of 1933. Balmy Beach was a short streetcar ride from the predominately Jewish districts of Spadina Avenue and the Ward. Trouble started when Balmy Beach locals began complaining about the number of Jewish people who frequented the beach and that Jewish mothers nursed babies and changed their children into bathing suits in the back seats of cars.

In August, the Balmy Beach Swastika Club was formed, comprised mostly of unemployed youths who frequented the beach. Members swore allegiance to Hitler and wore swastikas as their club symbol. Jews were harassed and some were beaten up. Soon, the club moved beyond the beach and began verbally and physically assaulting Jewish people on their way to the beach. Club members, and others who supported their ideas, drove through Jewish neighbourhoods at night and flung garbage on lawns and front porches, and rocks through windows. Swastikas appeared on fences, buildings and sidewalks. The police did nothing.

On one particularly warm August evening, the swastika club prepared to enjoy a dance it had organized on the beach. Large black swastikas adorned the dance hall. Jewish youths, who had had enough of seeing their family members insulted and threatened, gathered and moved toward the building but fell into the arms of waiting police officers. As they were peacefully turned away and escorted home they were surrounded by club members singing to the tune of "Home on the Range":

Oh give me a home where the Gentiles may roam
Where the Jews are not rampant all day
Where seldom is heard a loud Yiddish word
And the Gentiles are free all the day. [30]

Toronto mayor Stewart condemned the swastika club. He called its actions un-British and un-Canadian. Newspapers, however, were more tolerant. Both the *Globe and Mail* and the *Toronto Star* said that race hatred was unfortunate but that the swastika club members were perfectly within their rights to express their feelings. The police stepped up patrols on Balmy Beach the next weekend. It did not matter. A large brawl erupted on nearby Kew Beach when a large group of Anglo-Saxon swimmers roughly removed a number of Jewish families from the beach and nearby picnic sites. They were told not to return, for the beach was no longer open to Jews. There were no arrests. The police did nothing to address the ban.

The beach incidents and the Christie Pitts riot could be dismissed as the actions of a few hotheads if they did not betray the fact that something far more insidious was going on. They represent only two of many violent incidents that occurred in Toronto and a number of other Ontario communities throughout the 1930s, and they represent the refusal of police or municipal leaders to recognize or acknowledge a systemic problem. The violence was itself just a symptom of a climate of anti-Semitism that had infiltrated the province at many levels.

As in Quebec, racial segregation was the norm throughout Ontario, as hundreds of golf and tennis clubs, campsites, playgrounds, beaches, restaurants, bars, motels, summer camps and picnic areas were posted with "Gentile Only" signs. Some Ontario universities had quotas to restrict the number of Jewish students and another set of rules to control the number of Jews who could study law, medicine or engineering. A number of insurance companies charged Jewish customers double or triple regular premium rates. Many landlords refused to rent to Jews. A number of Jewish families were told by real estate agents about neighbourhoods in which they could simply not consider purchasing a home. Very few of Toronto's banks and insurance or trust companies would knowingly hire Jews, and most other businesses restricted employment and advancement opportunities. Many boards of education refused to hire Jewish teachers.

The career of Jean Tissot illustrates the degree to which systemic anti-Semitism had grown. In 1935, Tissot was one of two long-standing members of the Ottawa Police Department found to have been distributing anti-Semitic literature supporting increased school segregation while on duty and in uniform. They were asked to stop and received mild reprimands. Tissot had been a regular contributor of *Le Patriote* and *Le Devoir* letters to the editor. In one *Le Devoir* letter he had written that Jewish people were "the most destructive parasite in creation [who participate in] arson, fraudulent bankruptcy, usury, smuggling and traffic in vice."[31]

Tissot contested the Ottawa-West seat in the 1935 federal election

under the banner of H.H. Stevens' extreme right-wing Recon-
struction Party. During the campaign, Tissot was found guilty of
printing libelous, anti-Semitic material directed at A.J. Freiman,
who owned Ottawa's largest department store. He was fined fifty
dollars, and he continued to campaign and spread his anti-Jewish
beliefs. Tissot lost the election but won twenty percent of the twenty
thousand votes cast. At least four thousand Ottawa voters thereby
expressed support for his anti-Semitic beliefs and activities.

Tissot left the Ottawa Police Department after the election and
applied to become chief of police at Rouyn, Quebec. His anti-
Semitism had become well known, as he had received a great deal
of publicity through his widely published letters, his trial and his
strong finish in the election. He got the job. While chief of police, he
regularly wrote anti-Semitic letters to newspapers, continued his
activity in the anti-Semitic Canadian National Party and helped
organize the distribution of anti-Semitic pamphlets across Canada.
In 1938, a newly elected city council fired him. Within days he was
appointed to a provincial government post on the Quebec Liquor
Commission. He was also placed in charge of gun permits for the
city of Montreal. Meanwhile, he continued to write, attend rallies
and work on behalf of anti-Semitic groups in the city. One is left to
consider the nature of governments that hired and placed in positions of responsibility people who actively and publicly promoted
race hatred.

Many individuals and groups spoke against anti-Semitism.
Many pondered the irony of Canada's condemnation of fascism
while condoning similar attitudes at home. The *Ottawa Journal*, for
example, published an editorial on March 21, 1935 that was inaccurate but at least recognized the paradox at play:

> Racial prejudice is foreign to the Canadian tradition and
> abhorrent to all instincts of fairness and decency. [Anti-
> Semitic] attacks do represent a deplorable attempt to dupli-
> cate in this country bitterness and enmities that have their
> origin in other lands and they should be suppressed sternly.[32]

The voices of reason were few. Maurice Eisendrath, Rabbi of
Holy Blossom, warned, "In Quebec anti-Semitism is a way of life. In
the rest of Canada it is more an after thought. Here it is much more
subtle. There it is widespread and demonic."[33] Many people warned

of what could happen if the anti-Semitism continued to escalate. A Jewish MPP warned the Ontario legislature that "Unless something is done quickly the Jewish people may well meet the same fate in Canada that the Jews are meeting in Germany."[34] He exaggerated only a little.

•

Adrien Arcand was a thirty-year-old failed journalist and McGill University drop-out when he came to the public's attention in 1930. He was a self-styled Quebec nationalist who believed that all non-French non-Catholics should be kicked out of the province. He edited three weekly newspapers called *Le Goglu*, *Le Miroir* and *Le Chameau*. All three supported the *achat chez nous* and all three were unashamedly anti-Semitic.

Arcand's reputation and power were built on the Jewish school question. The churches controlled education in Quebec. According to an 1831 law, Jewish parents sent their children to Protestant schools. By 1930, Jewish children comprised over forty percent of the Protestant school population, but despite this fact, laws prohibited Jews from becoming teachers or school board trustees. Jewish parents began asking for more influence over curriculum decisions. A bill, presented in the Quebec National Assembly by MNA Athanese David, proposed the creation of a separate Jewish school board. The Catholic clergy, from the archbishop to parish priests, spoke against the bill. They were concerned that it would allow too much money to be directed to non-Christian activities. Other than the church there was little organized opposition to the bill, but with the church involved the issue grew.

Arcand then entered the fray. Arcand attacked the David bill in his newspapers, arguing that it was a Jewish ploy to undermine the power of Christianity in Quebec. The April 4, 1930 *Le Chameau* editorial stated,

> Since Jews only seek parliamentary favour when a country is corrupt, there had to be extended decadence in Quebec before they could come to demand recognition as an official minority by means of the David Bill. The province must be sufficiently dominated by money, dance, jazz, cinema, fashion, literature, and Jewish prestige before Jews would dare

demand what they never saw fit to demand in any other country.[35]

Arcand printed flyers, posters and banners and organized a number of well-attended rallies. The combined attack by Arcand and the church effectively changed the wider public's perception of Jewish parents from concerned citizens to ruthless power-mongers intent on destroying all that Quebec held sacred. The notion was a relatively easy sell in the midst of the propaganda surrounding the *achat chez nous* movement. Many Quebecers recognized the anti-Semitic campaign for what it was and spoke against it. Premier Taschereau and Henri Bourassa were among their numbers. Taschereau was nonetheless forced by overwhelming public pressure to withdraw the David bill.

Arcand and his growing number of anti-Semitic followers were charged with the adrenaline of victory. Arcand began to read more of Hitler and Mussolini. In 1929, he had founded the Patriotic Order of the Goglum. In 1931, he reorganized the order into independent cells according to an idea gleaned from Mussolini. Anti-Semitic Quebecers were thereby given an organization to join where their views could be legitimized by others who shared them.

Arcand's newspaper attacks against Jews became more scathing. He wrote in *Le Miroir* in November 1930,

Jews are like cockroaches and bugs. When you see one, you can be sure there are a dozen around. And when you see a few around, in all cities and on all their streets, don't be fooled. There are many around. It is too bad we cannot exterminate them with insecticides, but we can count on the good sense of our country-men.[36]

Arcand could be dismissed as a crank if not for the newspapers that provided him a province-wide audience, his blossoming popularity, and the people and groups that allied themselves with his cause. By 1935, his Order boasted fifty thousand members organized into fifteen zones. Frederick Edwards wrote in *Maclean's* magazine in 1935, "Merely to call Arcand a windbag and his movement a chimera is not quite good enough...to deny that he had a following, and that the number of that following are increasing weekly, is plainly unintelligent."[37]

Arcand enjoyed the enthusiastic support of Quebec's omnipotent Catholic church. Meetings of the Patriotic Order of the Goglum were nearly all held in Catholic churches, which seldom asked for the regularly charged rental fees. Parish priests were nearly always among those either in attendance or actively organizing the meetings. Fathers Dion and O'Neill recognized the growing anti-Semitism among priests in the 1930s in a 1956 article that stated, "the literature which arouses the enthusiasms of young Arcand disciples has penetrated presbyteries and has guided the consciences of more priests than we dare imagine."[38]

The anti-Semitic beliefs and actions of parish priests were supported and, in many cases, encouraged by church leaders. Mgr. Gauthier, Archbishop of Montreal, met with Arcand shortly after the David education bill was announced and personally asked Arcand to lead the struggle against it. The archbishop met Arcand several times during the campaign and later publicly thanked him for his efforts. Abbé Groulx also supported Arcand and his activities. His L'Action Nationale published many glowing articles about Arcand's new Order. Groulx's growing admiration for and support of Arcand and his fascist ideas were expressed in a 1934 article in which he referred to Arcand and wrote,

> Who will prove to be a de Valera, a Mussolini, whose policies be disputed but who, over a ten year period made a new Ireland and a new Italy.... Let us with our humble hearts, ask Providence for this leader without whom no people can forge their destiny.[39]

Camillien Houde felt Arcand's power and the depth of Quebec's hatred for Jews. Houde was the mayor of Montreal and the leader of Quebec's Conservative Party. Both the party and Houde personally had regularly contributed money to Arcand and his newspapers.[40] Houde and Arcand later had a falling-out when the mayor supported the David bill. While Houde saw it as a chance to segregate Jewish children, he was attacked as caving in to Jewish pressure. Two Le Chameau editorials in March 1932 were entitled "When Will the Conservative Party Rid Itself of the Pro Jewish Houde?" and "Houde's Bonds with Jewry Have Disheartened the Citizenry."[41] Although the effect of Arcand's slanders upon Houde's political fortunes cannot be accurately measured, the mayor's popularity plummeted shortly after the assaults began. Partly as a result of his clash with Arcand, Houde lost the next election.

As Arcand's power continued to grow he won the support of the federal government. Richard Bedford Bennett had become the federal Conservative Party leader in 1927. The wealthy, rotund bachelor was a man whose sensitivity was seldom betrayed by a cold, aloof manner. He was known for his dictatorial style of running his party and government. A Parliament Hill joke had a woman asking the identity of a man walking alone and muttering to himself. Her husband responded that it was Prime Minister Bennett conducting a cabinet meeting. Precious little happened in the party or government without his direct knowledge and approval.

In 1930, Bennett led his party against the King Liberals and understood that the Canadian electoral system was such that he could not win the government without doing well in Quebec. Conservative Party officials approached Adrien Arcand with a promise to support his cash-strapped newspapers in return for his endorsement. The deal was sweetened with a promise of a contribution from the party to the Patriotic Order of the Goglum. Bennett met with Arcand in June and they cemented the deal. The Conservative Party paid Arcand $27,000.[42]

Arcand's papers began to write glowing accounts of Bennett and the Conservatives and ferocious reviews of King and Liberal candidates. Arcand packed Conservative meetings with cheering enthusiasts and Liberal meetings with merciless hecklers. He lent his growing celebrity to Conservative rallies, interrupting his anti-Semitic diatribes to heap effusive praise on Bennett and Conservative candidates. Bennett took twenty-four Quebec seats—more than had ever been won by the Conservatives. The party was swept into power with a majority government.

Only two years later, Arcand's papers were again experiencing financial difficulties due in large part to a spate of libel suits brought against Arcand and the papers by Jewish merchants whose businesses and reputations had suffered at the hands of his anti-Semitic rallies and articles. He wrote to Bennett asking for another contribution. Bennett did not immediately respond, leading Conservative politicians to rally to Arcand's side. Leslie Bell, Conservative MP for St. Antoine, explained in a letter to the prime minister that Arcand and his people were staunch Conservatives who had helped win the last election and would be needed to win the next.[43] Deputy Speaker Arcand Lavargne and Speaker of the Senate P.E. Blondin also wrote to Bennett on Arcand's behalf. Conservative MP John A. Sullivan wrote to the prime minister stating, "Mr. Arcand is without exception the best French-Canadian writer, and his paper is making great headway. It would be a pity to see it fall, and you alone can help it in the present circumstances."[44] Bennett's responses to the letters are not known. It is known, however, that no more Conservative money was forwarded to Arcand. In March 1933, coincidentally the very month that Hitler became the chancellor, all three of Arcand's newspapers folded.

The loss of his newspapers freed Arcand to spend more time with his Order and other anti-Semitic activities. He was a vocal supporter of fourteen Notre Dame Hospital interns who walked off their jobs in protest of the fact that a Jewish intern, Samuel Rabinovich, had joined their staff. Interns from Montreal's five other hospitals joined the protest. Spokespeople argued that it was wrong to force Québécois interns to work with a Jew. *Le Devoir* sympathized and asked rhetorically, "Who can blame them?"[45] Editorials and letters to editors offered unqualified support, many stating that it would be disgusting to be touched by a Jewish intern. The St. Jean Baptiste Society, the Catholic church and many others also supported the segregationist action. Rabinovich was forced to resign.

The year 1935 brought the next federal election. The Conservative Party needed a person to organize the Quebec campaign. Bennett appointed Adrien Arcand to be his Quebec publicity director. In addition to his duties in this regard, Arcand again made a series of campaign appearances, pledging his support and the support of all his followers to Bennett and the Conservative Party.

Politics is notorious for creating odd alliances. No doubt many of those in the Conservative Party who courted Arcand's favour, then enthusiastically supported him, did so because Arcand was so effectively attacking both Liberals and the socialism of the Cooperative Commonwealth Federation. One is left to ponder, however, whether partisan gains have ever been worth the cost of aligning oneself, one's party and a nation's government with a man and a movement whose ideas are openly racist.

•

While Canadian anti-Semitism was becoming more deeply engrained, European Jews were being crushed. Families were being ripped apart, lives were being destroyed, and other lives were being snuffed out by a cold, efficient killing machine. Canada was seen by many European Jews as a utopia, far away and free from the madness around them. At Auschwitz, there was a barracks for the storage of clothing, jewellery and other valuables that were stolen from the prisoners. It was considered an oasis of wealth and security amid the hell of the camp. The doomed prisoners called the barracks "Canada."

Perhaps they would have chosen another name had they been aware of Canadian policies toward those who had yet to reach the camp gates. In 1920, the Jewish War Orphans Committee of Canada had been formed to address the news that thousands of Jewish orphans were dying in the Ukraine as a result of war, poverty and civil strife. Despite its long-standing exclusionist immigration policies, the government allowed two hundred of the orphans to come to Canada. Unfortunately, the entry guidelines were so stringent that only 146 of the eight thousand sallow-faced children who passed before the committee were issued Canadian visas.

Two years later, the newly formed Jewish Colonisation Committee pressured the prime minister into trying to rescue some of the thousands of Jewish families that had fled the Ukrainian pogroms and were suffering in squalid Romanian refugee camps. Strict rules were again outlined and permission granted for the rescue of five thousand. Again, the rules were such that the full quota was not met.

New immigration regulations were introduced through a number of Orders in Council beginning in 1927. Since the Laurier-Sifton era, immigrants had been allowed into Canada with only a few exceptions. The new rules turned this maxim on its head. Suddenly, no immigrants were allowed except under special circumstances. Section 82 of the new immigration act stated that rules regarding immigration could be amended at any time by an Order in Council without consulting parliament. Section 4 stated that the minister in charge of immigration could approve or disapprove of any individual seeking to immigrate to Canada. These sections of the act meant that the minister, and ultimately the prime minister, could pretty much do as they pleased with respect to immigration.

The new rules were used specifically to bar particular races, including Blacks, Chinese and Jews. A deal was made between the immigration department and steamship and railway companies whereby they could select the people who met the new criteria as preferred immigrants. Jews were placed in a separate category. Jews could only be allowed into Canada under a special permit issued personally by the minister. Each case was addressed individually. Foreign governments were told of the new regulations so that they could advise Jewish citizens contemplating immigration to Canada. A letter from the immigration ministry to the Dutch government, in response to an inquiry as to whether a Jewish man could join his family in Canada, said, "The chief criterion for admission to Canada is race.... It is a fact that Jews, having once obtained permission for their families to join them, if only temporarily, are exceedingly difficult to get rid of again."[46] The request was refused.

Any Jewish people who slipped through the first net were caught by a second. Jewish immigrants endured medical and other means tests that had standards far higher than those administered to other perspective immigrants. Some of the tests would be funny if they were not so sad. An immigration department doctor in Halifax, for example, forced Jewish immigration applicants to run around his office as quickly as they could for as long as they could and then rejected them for having faint hearts.

Unfortunately for the Jews of Europe, the Jews of Canada were not well organized. This fact is understandable when one considers that they were originally from various countries and, except for concentrations in a few cities, were scattered throughout Canada. They were also splintered in that they were upper-, middle-, and lower-class, Zionist and non-Zionist, Yiddish and non-Yiddish, and Orthodox and non-Orthodox. Perhaps more importantly, most wanted little more than to retain their religion while assimilating quietly into the Canadian culture. The Canadian Jewish Congress had formed in 1919, but it had little authority. Like other ethnic groups, Canadian Jews spoke with many voices. The most significant spokespeople for Canadian Jews were Jewish members of Parliament Samuel Jacobs from Montreal, Sam Factor from Toronto and A.A. Heaps from Winnipeg. It was this fractured Jewish community that rose to meet Hitler's challenge.

A number of concerned Jewish citizens from Montreal formed the Jewish Immigration Aid Society (JIAS). Its goals were to persuade the government to relax its exclusionist, anti-Jewish immigration policies and to help those few Jewish immigrants who managed to get into Canada to leap through the final hoops of the process and settle in new homes. The JIAS blew the whistle on the inequity of the medical tests in a 1928 report to the government. The report stated, "Hundreds of Jews who have been permitted in the past to come to this country are now being rejected for various reasons which, for the most part, are suggestive of a policy that tends to exclude Jewish immigration to Canada."[47]

The Canadian Jewish Congress appointed a committee in the spring of 1934 to see the prime minister about saving some of Europe's Jews. Government officials ignored the fact that many of the immigration restrictions on Jews and others were imposed in the prosperous 1920s and were quick to use the depression as an excuse to maintain the strict rules. Committee representatives Lazarus Phillips and H.M. Caiserman were told that a mass rescue operation was out of the question due to the tattered state of the Canadian economy. In a small concession, Prime Minister Bennett agreed to consider rescuing European Jewish professionals who could help Canada's economy. A list was drawn up, consisting of seventy-six European Jewish engineers, doctors, chemists and other highly educated and skilled people. Short biographies detailing their achievements were included with each name. Bennett received the list without acknowledgement, then made no decision for months. Finally, in the spring of 1935, in a terse note to the Canadian Jewish Congress he announced that none of those on the list would be admitted. No reason was given.

William Lyon Mackenzie King became the prime minister of Canada again in 1935. It is polite to call him eccentric. Some have called him strange due to his toying with the occult, his construction of a phony ruins on his estate, the importance he seemed to place on dreams and visions, and other odd personal habits. He was prime minister longer than any other person. His style of leadership was to determine where the parade was going, then jump out in front. It was as deputy minister of labour that King had been introduced to racism when he investigated the 1907 Vancouver riot. He reflected a popular belief of his day when he wrote that Canada should forever remain a "white man's country."[48] The prime minister had already made his views on Jewish people well known. Just before the 1930 federal election, a skilled politician and political organizer named Bernard Rose, a Jewish man from Toronto, had been recommended to King as the new Liberal Party organizer in Ontario. The prime minister wrote,

> I do not know anyone who is better able to interpret Liberal principles and policies to the electorate. His services ought to be utilised in connection with campaign work. [But] I suppose it would hardly do to have one of Jewish extraction in charge of Party organization.[49]

Rose did not get the job.

The prime minister's naive views on fascism and bigoted views on race are revealed in a diary entry in which he wrote,

> Hitler and Mussolini, while dictators, have really sought to give the masses of the people some opportunity for enjoyment, taste of art and the like.... the dictatorship method may have been necessary to wrest this opportunity from the privileged interests that have previously monopolised it.... Hitler might come to be thought of as one of the saviours of the world.... his ends, [were] the well-being of his fellow man; not all fellow-men, but those of his own race.[50]

Unlike Bennett, King ruled by consensus. Cabinet ministers were afforded considerable latitude in running their departments, and many, perhaps most famously C.D. Howe, became very powerful. The minister of mines and resources was Thomas Crerar. King liked Crerar and respected his opinions and leadership to such a degree that he appointed him to the post of deputy prime minister. The immigration department fell within his ministry, but Crerar was busy and had little interest in immigration. He left nearly all day-to-day operations to Deputy Minister of Immigration Frederick Charles Blair. Blair was a long-time civil servant who had risen through the ranks through his officious nature and fastidious attention to detail. He effectively controlled immigration in Canada from 1935 to 1949.

Blair demonstrated his anti-Jewish prejudice in nearly all he said and did. He wrote, "I often think that instead of persecution it would be far better if we more often told them frankly why many of them are unpopular. If they would divest themselves of certain of their habits I am sure they could be just as popular in Canada as our Scandinavians."[51] Blair took the barring of Jews from Canada as his personal mission. He later boasted of his success, writing, "Pressure on the part of Jewish people to get into Canada has never been greater than it is now and I am glad to be able to add, after 35 years experience here, that it was never so well controlled."[52]

Blair ordered that he would personally consider every Jewish immigrant. Memos to agents around the world made his policy on Jewish immigration clear. In 1935, a Jewish railway engineer named Hans Heinemann applied to immigrate to Canada and was told by the Canadian agent in charge that "No Jews were being allowed into Canada."[53]

King was under pressure to adopt a less restrictive Jewish immigration policy. The Canadian Jewish Congress continued to write letters, present petitions and send delegations to Ottawa. In March 1938, American president Franklin Roosevelt added to the pressure on the King government by organizing an international conference to address the Jewish refugee question. Canada was the last country to agree to attend. The conference was held in Evian, France. Nothing of consequence was decided. It had been a public relations ploy.

Soon after the Evian conference Blair showed the government's refusal to bend to international pressure by making its restrictions even tighter. Blair increased the amount of money needed by Jewish people to apply for entry into Canada from $10,000 to $15,000. King and Blair both expressed publicly that it was a shame that Jewish people were dying but that it was really not Canada's problem. King wrote in his diary on March 29, 1938, "We must seek to keep this part of the Continent free from unrest and from too great an intermixture of foreign strains of blood."[54]

The government's anti-Semitic policies enjoyed enormous support. In 1994, Pope John Paul publicly apologized for the Catholic church's actions in the 1930s and 1940s which tacitly supported the Holocaust. In Canada, support for anti-Semitism and the government's refusal to rescue European Jews was far from tacit among many church leaders and spokespeople. At a Social Credit meeting in Montreal, for example, a parish priest delivered an anti-Semitic tirade ending with the demand that no Jews should be allowed into the country. An observer was disturbed by the speech and wrote to Cardinal Villeneuve protesting the inappropriateness of the priest's remarks. Villeneuve did nothing. A Catholic newsletter printed in September 1937 expressed the church's beliefs:

> All countries are unanimous in recognising that we have no greater enemy than the Jews. They are the source of all great cataclysms. They participated in the French Revolution and the Russian Revolution. They are the most fervent leaders of Freemasonry, the promoters of discord, the agitators of strikes, and finally they are the propagandists of Communism.[55]

Few in King's government publicly criticized his anti-Semitic policies. Many departments implemented policies that were as anti-Semitic as those of the immigration department. The Department of Indian Affairs, for example, was in charge of granting licences for certain clubs and bars. On May 25, 1936, the department replied to an application for a club licence with a letter that stated, "If this club is Jewish, we have no space available. If not, there would be a charge of $5 per week for the privilege."[56]

Ernest Lapointe was King's Quebec lieutenant and minister of justice. He was outraged when it was announced that Samuel Jacobs was to represent Quebec at the coronation of the King in 1937. Lapointe did not care that Jacobs was a respected member of Parliament and the choice of the Empire Parliamentary Association. Lapointe fired a letter to the Speaker of the House stating that he "objected to a Jew being named as Quebec's representative at the coronation of the King."[57] The prime minister was asked by reporters to comment on Lapointe's objection and replied in typical King style that he saw nothing wrong with either Jacobs' appointment or Lapointe's letter.

Meanwhile, the anti-Semitic, exclusionist immigration policies and practices continued. King's Liberal caucus colleagues Wilfrid Lacroix, C.H. Leclerc and H.E. Brunelle led the anti-Jewish movement in the House of Commons. Lacroix tabled a petition containing 128,000 signatures from the St. Jean Baptiste Society demanding even broader restrictions on Jewish immigration. King accepted the document, bowed, but said nothing.

The prime minister received little criticism from across the floor of the House of Commons, for Robert Manion, who had succeeded Bennett as leader of the Conservative Party, fully supported all exclusionist immigration policies. At party fund-raisers in Ontario and Quebec he maintained the myth that the racist immigration policies were a product of the depression, arguing that Jews should not be allowed into Canada "So long as one Canadian remained unemployed."[58]

Some premiers also publicly supported the federal government's anti-Semitic policies. British Columbia premier T.D. Pattulo wrote to King stating that his province was opposed to allowing any more Jewish immigrants into Canada.[59] Pattulo, of course, was speaking on behalf of a province that had for nearly a century been supporting policies to bar Oriental immigration.

In Quebec, disgruntled Liberals and Conservatives had joined forces to form the Union Nationale. In 1936, it formed the government and Maurice Duplessis became premier. Duplessis was not above using Quebec's anti-Semitism to score political points. In a 1933 speech in Montreal, he had stated that the federal government and the Liberal government of Quebec were planning to bring 100,000 Jewish immigrants to Quebec and that only he could stop the invasion. It was a complete fabrication but Duplessis knew the proper buttons to push with voters.[60]

The Union Nationale's semi-official tabloid was *l'Illustration Nouvelle*. The paper was edited by Adrien Arcand. Arcand completed this work for the Quebec government while continuing his active participation in fascist, anti-Semitic rallies and while serving as the president of the anti-Semitic National Social Christian Party. In 1937, a viciously anti-Semitic pamphlet entitled *The Key to the Mystery*, written by Dr. Gabriel Lamert, who was one of Arcand's lieutenants in the National Social Christian Party, was distributed throughout Canada. It was printed using Union Nationale presses and paper.

Duplessis' minister of colonization was H.L. Auger. While a Montreal alderman, he had proposed a motion demanding a total ban on Jewish immigration to Canada. The resolution was debated and defeated, but not before Auger's anti-Semitic views became front-page news in the city. Auger hired Joseph Manard, who had helped finance Arcand's newspapers, to act as deputy minister of colonization. Manard continued to publish the cruelly anti-Semitic *Le Patriote* while acting as a Quebec government civil servant.

The Canadian press was largely neutral or in support of racist government policies. In Quebec, the French-language press was enthusiastic in its endorsement of the anti-Jewish immigration rules. *Le Devoir* was typical. It maintained its anti-Semitic stance under the editorship of Georges Pelletier. *Le Devoir*'s April 17, 1937 editorial applauded King's Jewish immigration restrictions and hinted that Jews currently in Canada should be deported. It also attempted to perpetuate the lies of *The Protocols of the Elders of Zion* in stating, "What above all worries non-Jews is the feeling of harbouring portions of another people, who are unassimilable, from a nation which aims at the domination of the world and of whom several members foment revolutions."[61]

There were many who publicly opposed anti-Semitism and tried to persuade King to save European Jews. Henri Bourassa spoke against the hatred. The governments of Ontario and Saskatchewan passed laws that sought to curb anti-Semitic hate literature and segregationist practices. Vincent Massey was the Canadian high commissioner in London. He recommended to the government that it relax its regulations in order to save as many European Jews as possible. These voices, and some others, were added to the continuing efforts of the Canadian Jewish Congress and other Jewish organizations. The protests, however, were of little avail.

•

Kristallnacht tested the consciences of the most fervent anti-Semites. It occurred on November 9, 1938 and was called the night of broken glass, for in a carefully coordinated attack Nazi soldiers smashed and burned every synagogue and nearly every Jewish shop in Germany. It was the beginning of the Holocaust's second stage. It was front-page news around the world.

The Canadian Jewish Congress organized a national day of mourning for November 20. Some Canadian newspapers began to swing in favour of allowing increased Jewish immigration. The *Windsor Star*, *Winnipeg Free Press*, *Toronto Star* and even some French-language papers joined a new chorus of protest against King's restrictive policies. King was moved to write in his diary that although he predicted opposition from his cabinet and caucus, and especially from Quebec, he would do something to help more Jews escape into Canada. He wrote that it would be the "right and just, and Christian thing to do."[62] In the House of Commons, however, the ever-cautious prime minister announced that the whole matter needed more study.

Frederick Blair was stoic in the face of the Holocaust's mounting violence and Hitler's aggression in Austria and Czechoslovakia. In the summer of 1939, Blair was still turning down Jewish applicants who had more than the required amount of money and exceeded all other entry standards. He declared that all Jewish immigrants had to be farmers, then stated that he did not believe that there were any Jewish farmers so all who claimed they were must be lying and should be rejected.[63]

Hitler's blitzkrieg poured over the Polish border on the morning of September 1, 1939. By the third of the month, Britain was at war, and by the tenth Canada had joined her. The children of those who had been cannon-fodder in the war to end all wars signed up to do it all again.

The war added a new wrinkle to the question of Jewish immigration. Many Jews were suddenly citizens of an enemy country. An interesting case was that of twenty-five hundred German Jews who had escaped the Holocaust just before the war began and were housed in temporary shelters in Britain awaiting passage to any country that would have them. After the fall of Dunkirk, they were reclassified as enemy aliens. Since the Canadian government had already agreed to accept prisoners of war from Britain, the British government shipped the bewildered people to Canada, where they were imprisoned and guarded like any other prisoners of war. They were allowed gifts and visits from Canadian Jewish organizations. Many formally asked to be allowed to join the Canadian army to return to Europe to fight Hitler. All requests were denied. Finally, in 1941, a labour shortage persuaded the government that they were not dangerous after all, and they were released on the condition that they resume their education or take a job in Canadian industry. Sixty people under the age of twenty-one entered universities under the sponsorship of Canadian Jewish patrons. All others quickly found jobs. Only in October 1945 did Order in Council 6687 grant them official landed-immigrant status and end the prisoner-of-war classification.

Meanwhile, King and Blair maintained their anti-Semitic immigration policy, ignoring changing circumstances and growing opposition. Vincent Massey wrote to Blair in 1940 explaining that 150 Polish Boy Scouts were in Romania and could be rescued if the government acted quickly. He assured Blair that only around ten percent were Jewish. Blair was dubious. In discussing the matter with King, he suggested that Massey was prone to exaggeration and that the number of Jewish boys was probably closer to eighty percent. Blair rejected the request and suggested the boys be sent to the Congo.

A few months later Blair passed up a chance to save more children. After the conquest of France, Hitler had placed Nazi puppet Pierre Laval in charge of Vichy. Jews were rounded up and adults transported to their deaths in eastern Europe. Children as young as two were left to fend for themselves in squalid camps. American Jewish groups were shocked when Laval agreed to release the children for emigration, demanding only that they be taken immediately.

Saul Hayes, director of the Canadian Jewish Congress, desperately attempted to contact Crerar or Blair, but they neither accepted nor returned his calls. After days of frustration, the matter was brought before the minister, and cabinet was briefed on the situation's urgency. Samuel Bronfman, who had become a leader in the Canadian Jewish Congress, promised to finance the rescue operation personally. Blair wrote a briefing paper to Crerar expressing his belief that the children were only a smokescreen. He believed the Canadian Jewish Congress was merely trying to break the government's anti-Jewish policy by getting a few children into Canada, then using them to ask later that their parents be allowed to follow. Blair advised that it had been difficult to shut the door on Jews and that it should not be opened for the sake of a few children.

Three months after Laval's offer, the American government pledged to accept five thousand children. The British government, still struggling to rebuild after the blitz, agreed to accept all children who could prove they had even a distant British relative. The Canadian government announced that it would take only five hundred but that even they would be accepted only if they remained foster children and were not adopted by any Canadian family, for after the war they would all be returned to France. None of their parents, if ever found, would be allowed to join them.

In September 1943, Frederick Blair retired. He was awarded a medallion for meritorious service to the country. His successor was the more liberal-minded A.L. Jolliffe. While Jolliffe did not share Blair's anti-Semitic fervour, he was a loyal civil servant dedicated to carrying out the policies of his government. Consequently, Blair's ghost haunted those working to end racist immigration policies.

Pressure on the government to punch holes in the racist wall surrounding Canada continued to mount. International pressure came from new conferences such as the 1943 Bermuda Conference in which all participants except Canada agreed to substantially increase their quotas of Jewish refugees. It became the policy of the C.C.F. and even the Conservative Party to move down the ladder and alter exclusionary immigration laws. R.B. Bennett's farewell speech to the House of Commons included a plea that the government act to save some of Europe's Jews. King began to face regular and accusing questions about his anti-Semitic policies in the House. English-language newspapers became nearly unanimously critical. The *Winnipeg Free Press*, for example, stated in its April 3, 1943 editorial that

> It would be encouraging, indeed, to hear some day very soon that the Canadian government was taking active steps to open our country's doors to the victims of the murderous Nazi persecution.... It would be a permanent blot and shame upon us, if the chance, being offered, we rejected it [but] Anti-Semitism, shameful though it must be to admit it, has far too large a footing among Canadians.[64]

Despite the pressure from critics, and undeniable evidence of the death camps, King remained unmoved. At the war's conclusion, the government proudly announced statistics the prime minister believed would quiet his critics. It was stated that the government had allowed thirty-nine thousand refugees into Canada during the war. A breakdown of the number, however, indicated that twenty-five thousand were prisoners of war and that eight thousand were British nationals. More telling were numbers of Jewish refugees that had been saved by other countries. A partial list includes: the United States, 200,000; Britain, seventy thousand; Argentina, fifty thousand; Brazil, twenty-seven thousand; China, twenty-five thousand; Bolivia, fourteen thousand; and Chile, fourteen thousand. Canada rescued only five thousand.

George Vanier visited the Buchenwald concentration camp in April 1945 as Canada's ambassador to France and wrote to King about the sickening sights he beheld. He also expressed his disgust not only at the Nazis but also at the Canadian government for doing so little to save those whom it could have rescued so easily. His letter ended, "How deaf we were."[65]

By 1948, Blair was dead and King had retired. The war was over and a prosperity that was breaking economic records was transforming the country into one of the wealthiest on the planet. Canada's immigration policies were changed to reflect new political and ideological trends and to meet the needs of a changing economy. A labour shortage swung the door of immigration open, and some Chinese and Jewish immigrants were allowed through. A stipulation stated that for every Jew at least one non-Jew had to be admitted.

Canada had officially stepped down a rung on the racist ladder, but the anti-Semitism that the nation's leaders had created and supported remained. Many signs barring Jews stayed in place. Many golf, tennis, yachting and social clubs continued to bar Jewish members. Some universities, including the University of Toronto, maintained quotas on Jewish students. In 1954, Prime Minister St. Laurent refused to appoint Louis Raminsky as the governor of the Bank of Canada because he was Jewish. The Holocaust's horror, however, rendered it in decidedly poor taste to be too open about one's dislike of Jewish people. The state had stepped down but not off the racist ladder. The emotions stirred by two centuries of official anti-Semitic hatred and reinforced by the systemic racism of the land remained in the hearts of many Canadians.

4

Japanese Canadians 1877–1946
The Hoax of Pearl Harbour

It is fortunate that the use of the bomb should have been
upon the Japanese rather than the white races of Europe.
—Prime Minister Mackenzie King, August 6, 1945

Sirens pierced the morning's calm. Most dismissed the excitement
as another drill. But this was no drill. Smoke and fire filled the sky.
Anti-aircraft blasts and the crashing thunder of roaring engines
tangled with officers' barking orders and the chilling screams of the
wounded. In a flash it was over. Eighteen ships and two hundred
aircraft were destroyed. Three thousand seven hundred lay dead or
wounded. The surprise Japanese attack on the naval base at Pearl
Harbour on December 7, 1941 brought the United States into the
Second World War. It also tore into the lives of thousands of
Canadians.

Tsungo Mineoka was one of them. At the time of the Pearl
Harbour attack, forty-four-year-old Mineoka had lived in Steveston,
British Columbia, for six years. He owned his home and made a
good living as a fisherman. He attended the local Christian church
and was secretary of the Japanese Fishermen's Union. He and his
wife were relaxing after dinner on the evening of December 7 when
a loud knock on the front door announced the arrival of two RCMP
officers. They told Mineoka that he had five minutes to pack, for he
was being taken into custody for a few days.

Mineoka was whisked to the Immigration Hall in Vancouver,
where he was interned with thirty-seven others of Japanese descent. Visits from family or friends were not allowed. After two

months, and without notification to his family, he was suddenly moved to a prisoner-of-war camp in northern Ontario, where he languished for the next three years. He worked in chain gangs under armed guard during the day and slept behind barbed wire in Spartan barracks each night. Meanwhile, Mrs. Mineoka had been taken to the cattle barns at Vancouver's Hastings Park. After several horrible weeks of penned captivity, she was banished to an old mining ghost town in the Fraser Valley. She was quartered with other refugees in a small hut, far from her home, her family and news of her husband's fate. They did not see their home again. Their property, house and contents were sold without their permission by a government agency for only $150. Government expenses were deducted before payment was made in small monthly instalments. They received nothing for their boat.

The Mineoka family's story is sadly not unique. From 1942 until 1946, every person of Japanese descent in Canada was harassed, evacuated from his or her home, imprisoned or deported. Property was impounded, left to rot, made available to looters, sold for a fraction of its real value or stolen outright. Twenty-three thousand people were so affected. Only 5,924 were Japanese nationals, many of whom had been waiting for years for Canadian citizenship, while 3,159 were naturalized Canadian citizens. The majority, some 14,119, were Nisei. That is, they were second-generation Canadian citizens born in Canada, educated in Canadian schools, with English as their first language.

Those who acted against the Japanese-Canadian people claimed many motives. The most common was that Japanese military aggression had rendered it likely that an attack on the North American west coast was possible and perhaps imminent. Nativist logic dictated that the loyalty of Japanese Canadians was suspect; consequently, they had to be removed from the coast as a matter of national security. While the indignities and hardships suffered by the Japanese Canadians was unfortunate, the argument goes, a democracy must suspend itself in times of war to survive. Others have argued that the increased Japanese military activity in the Pacific, and especially the capture of Canadians at Hong Kong, had fanned the flames of anti-Oriental racism that had long burned in British Columbia. Japanese Canadians had to be evacuated from the coast to save them from the racist violence that was about to be visited upon them. Still others have contended that Prime Minister

King was reacting to having tied Canada's economic and defence policies and plans to those of the United States, which afforded Americans the right to directly influence Canadian decisions. American generals wanted all Japanese Canadian people interned.

The arguments have been bantered about for decades, but all are based on one accepted notion: the government of Canada acted in a racist fashion by treating all Japanese-Canadian people as one body. The racism inherent in such action is seen in the fact that there were also German and Italian Canadians interned during the Second World War but each was investigated, charged and imprisoned as an individual. There was no mass round-up of German or Italian Canadians. The arguments ignore the fact that because anti-Japanese officially sanctioned discrimination was already well engrained before the war, it was easy to step up the ladder to exclusion and expulsion. Pearl Harbour and Hong Kong were simply excuses used by a systemically racist society to do what it had been trying to do to Japanese Canadians for years.

•

Teenagers have always been rebellious. They have always sought adventure while ignoring danger. Manzo Nagano was no different. Nagano was a nineteen-year-old Japanese sailor whose ship docked at New Westminster in 1877. Breaking his captain's rules, he went ashore, and breaking even more rules, he stayed there. Young Nagano became the first Japanese settler in Canada. He travelled to the United States and worked as a labourer in a number of towns before returning to Victoria in 1892, when he employed his wit and charm to establish a salmon-exporting business. The business grew so successful that he moved to a large, stately home with his beautiful bride and growing family. Nagano was able to enjoy the company of very few other Japanese people.

At that time Japan was emerging from three hundred years of strict military, political and cultural isolation. Beginning in the 1500s, Japan had been ruled by Tokugawa Shogunate and his heirs. Mostly in an attempt to maintain their totalitarian power, the shoguns had created a culture in which the Japanese people were taught to fear foreigners as barbarians whose inferiority in all matters led them to lust after all that Japan possessed. The strains of maintaining an impossibly tight rein on society tore the land asunder in 1867. The shogun was overthrown in a well-organized and widely popular bloodless coup.

The new emperor was a quiet and polite fifteen-year-old named Meiji. Meiji and his many advisers decreed an end to Japan's isolation. The emperor's Charter Oath of 1868 encouraged Japanese people to travel and seek out new ideas, cultures and trade possibilities. Many accepted the challenge. Many others simply sought to escape the poor living conditions that had left millions in crushing poverty and on the edge of starvation. There were 190 farmer revolts in the decade following Meiji's ascension. New laws were passed and new ways of taxation developed, but the average peasant's standard of living did not significantly improve.

Those seeking to leave found few places to go. Beginning with Australia, most nations of the British Empire had passed white-only immigration laws. The United States, while having no mandated policy, had regulations that rendered it very difficult for non-white people to enter the country. America had its hands full at the time, having just finished butchering itself in civil war and renewing its genocidal slaughter of the Native nations on its western frontier. Hawaii and Peru offered the only places of refuge for significant numbers of Japanese emigrants. The conditions they were forced to endure were abominable, but still better than those they had left.

Japanese officials realized that Canada and the United States held an undeniable attraction for many of Japan's people. The country saw its negotiation of emigration agreements with the two governments as opportunities to build its stature and reputation for dependability in the world community while also impressing other nations with the quality of its people. It created companies to handle emigration to North America. Consulates were established, and those already in existence were granted additional monies and personnel. The consulates fed newspapers stories that praised Japanese emigrants as economically beneficial to the host countries and bragged of their superiority to all others. Japanese officials were instructed to ensure that only a good class and quality of emigrant moved to North America. Fees for emigrating and the control of passports and visas were used to effect this end. Poor or illiterate people were weeded out at the source.

From 1897 to 1901, 15,280 Japanese people entered Canada, all going to or through British Columbia. They arrived with an average of $39.59, which was second only to Scottish immigrants and higher than the average wealth of English immigrants at the time. Nearly all were single men who found work either as fishermen or in fish-processing plants. By 1901, only 4,738 Japanese people remained in Canada. The others were either sojourners who had saved money and returned home or transients who had used Canada as a stepping-stone to the United States.

Nearly all Japanese immigrants who settled in Canada came from Wakayama, Shiga, Kagoshima and Hiroshima. Significant cultural and linguistic differences split the groups. Traditional tensions and rivalries accompanied them to Canada. The Okinawans, for example, formed the nucleus of Japanese immigrants working on railway construction. They discouraged Japanese immigrants from anywhere other than Okinawa from joining them. This disunity later haunted and hurt all Japanese Canadians.

Travelling to Canada was often horrendous. The one- to three-month journey had immigrants living like caged animals below decks. They survived on poor and often rancid food. There were no provisions for washing clothes or bathing. British Columbia's newspapers, having gained experience in dealing with Chinese immigrants, had become adept at blaming the victims of unfortunate circumstances for their situation. They were quick to use the Japanese immigrants' physical mistreatment and pitiful conditions on the immigrant ships as weapons against them to initiate ugly Japanese stereotypes. On April 20, 1900, for instance, a *Vancouver Colonist* reporter visited the steamer *Milos* and wrote,

> A visit to the [Japanese] quarters…was sufficient to prejudice anyone against the Japs as a clean people, their filth filling the alleys and their noise so odious filling the air. No one needed to be told where the *Milos* was lying—she could be immediately located by the varied and nauseating smells.[1]

The civic leaders and citizens of British Columbia did not need to be instructed by racist newspapers about the undesirability of Oriental people in their midst. The petitions, racist legislation, town hall meetings, segregation laws and business and union practices that were in place to deal with the Chinese "threat" automatically applied to the Japanese. Few made the distinction between Japanese and Chinese people. The "yellow peril" splashed all with the same brush. While facing a common set of challenges from similar quarters, few Chinese or Japanese Canadians, however, perceived themselves as allies. The animosity had long and deep cultural and historic roots. Neither the 1894-1895 Sino-Japanese war nor the transplanted Japanese tradition of seeing Chinese people as inferiors helped smooth relations. The Canadian government could not afford to consider Japanese and Chinese people as one. China had no power on the world stage and Japan had plenty. As Japan's economic and military strength grew, it earned more. As an acknowledgement of its growing clout, Britain signed the Treaty of Commerce and Navigation with Japan in 1894. Part of the treaty allowed Japanese people to enter and reside in any of Britain's colonies or former colonies. Prime Ministers Thompson and Bowell had fought against the provision but their protests were ineffectual. Canada still enjoyed little control over its external affairs.

Laurier took up the fight after winning office in 1896. He felt pressure from many sides. British Columbian federal and provincial politicians joined business, religious and labour leaders in writing letters, gathering petitions and lobbying Laurier directly. They demanded that Oriental immigration be banned completely, or at least that Japanese immigrants be forced to pay the same head tax levied on Chinese immigrants. Meanwhile, the British colonial secretary wrote terse letters reminding Laurier of his obligation to adhere to the British-Japanese treaty. The Japanese government grew concerned that its people were being publicly maligned and mistreated in Canada. It too applied pressure. Japanese consul Shimizu wrote to Laurier in 1898 about the idea of a head tax. He wrote,

> If the bill has any great number of supporters...the Japanese nation cannot be helped considering it as the attitude of Canada towards their country [and] it may hinder the development of the trade and commerce between both countries which bids fair to grow year after year.[2]

It was Laurier's wont to seek the "sunny way" of compromise in potentially untenable situations. Laurier negotiated an informal "gentleman's agreement" with the Japanese government. He agreed to stand against British Columbia's racist fulminations, and the Japanese government agreed to limit emigration to Canada to four hundred people a year. Both sides upheld their ends of the bargain. While acting against Chinese Canadians, Laurier ensured that all *ultra vires* legislation aimed directly at Japanese Canadians was disallowed.

Meanwhile, segregation laws aimed at the Japanese and Chinese minorities continued to proliferate. Japanese-Canadian children were kept out of public schools. Their parents were denied seats in restaurants, theatres and trains and could not purchase business licences in many towns or own land in many counties or join white-only unions throughout the province. Japanese Canadians enjoyed no political efficacy, as they were legally denied the right to vote because of their race.

The Japanese defeat of Russia in the 1902-1905 war led to increased Japanese influence in the world. A new British-Japanese treaty signed in 1906 reaffirmed the free movement of people and trade between Japan and the British dominions. Laurier's "gentleman's agreement" was forced to the archives as the new treaty brought 5,571 Japanese immigrants to British Columbia. Racism in British Columbia reached a boiling point.

The 1907 election brought a proudly racist Conservative government to power in Victoria. Meanwhile, the Anti-Asiatic League was formed and the Vancouver race riot occurred. In reaction to the increasing political pressure and violence, Laurier dispatched Canadian minister of labour Rodolphe Lemieux to Japan to negotiate a new gentleman's agreement. Japan again agreed to voluntarily limit emigration. Under the Lemieux agreement only four hundred Japanese people a year would come to Canada. A subsequent addendum rendered it illegal for people to skirt the restriction by entering Canada via Hawaii. The agreement's effect was seen in the reduction of Japanese immigrants from 7,601 in 1907 to 495 in 1908. Ironically, at the same time as these restrictions were being implemented, government-funded immigration agents were scouring the British Isles and northern Europe, bribing and cajoling prospective white emigrants to consider settling in Canada. Canada needed immigrants but only those of the right colour.

With racist governments firmly in control in the B.C. legislature and in nearly all municipalities, with London and Ottawa supporting racist immigration laws, with Oriental people disenfranchised and segregated, the racist fervour abated. In 1914, the attention of most Canadians turned to the European killing fields. Japanese

Canadians volunteered to fight with the Canadian armed forces. They worked at their jobs, raised their families and thought the worst was over. They were wrong.

•

William Lyon Mackenzie King become the prime minister in 1921. Many people have tried to unravel the mysteries of King's mind. He was born into a Victorian, Protestant, upper-middle-class world and retained those strict values throughout his life. He sincerely believed he was doing God's work. He was also an unabashed political opportunist. The secret of his political longevity seemed to be an uncanny ability to sense where and when Canadians wanted to move, and to never stray too far in front of public opinion. His actions regarding Japanese Canadians must be seen as his interpretation of what the people of British Columbia and Canada wanted and his attempts to give it to them. King's confidant and biographer, the extremely influential civil servant Jack Pickersgill, noted that "King in his heart did not approve of the [Japanese] policies.... He recognized that opinion in British Columbia counted as far as votes were concerned [and] could not be ignored."[3] These considerations aside, as was seen in his actions regarding Jewish questions, King often found himself allied with the forces of racism and intolerance.

In his first year as prime minister, King wrote to the government of Japan demanding that it respect the old Lemieux agreement. It acknowledged King's concern, but noted that in 1920 only 120 Japanese nationals, well under the agreed-upon four-hundred ceiling, had immigrated to Canada. King insisted that the sharp increase in the number of Japanese people in B.C. was evidence that Japan had broken the agreement. He ignored the fact that the birth rate among Japanese-Canadian women was nearly seventeen percent higher than the provincial average. Beginning in 1909, the natural increase of Japanese Canadians far outstripped the increase due to immigration.

Facts did not seem to matter. Governor General Grey had made this observation in a 1909 letter to Laurier in which he argued that, despite an absence of evidence, many people in British Columbia had become convinced that "their province is to be, as a result of a deep plot and design to be taken possession of by a quiet, persistent and systematic Japanese invasion."[4] King seemed to believe the paranoiac nonsense. In 1925, the Japanese ambassador to Britain visited Canada. King told the surprised Ambassador Matsui that the rising number of Japanese women arriving and children being born in Canada supported the belief that Japan was indeed trying to colonize British Columbia. He demanded further cuts to Japanese emigration. Negotiations began, culminating in a new agreement in 1928. It restricted Japanese immigration to 150 farmers, servants, clergy, or wives and children of men already here. Throughout the depression-ravaged 1930s, an average of fewer than one hundred Japanese people per year entered Canada. Most joined long-established families.

While moving to exclude Japanese immigrants, business, labour and government leaders colluded to increase the rigidity of anti-Japanese economic segregation laws and regulations. This activity can be seen using the example of the B.C. fishing industry.

As far back as 1893, many municipal Trade and Labour Councils had pressured the B.C. government to stop granting fishing licences to fishermen of Japanese descent, even if they were Canadian citizens. The segregationist idea was supported by many other labour organizations including the important Fraser River Salmon Canners Association and the B.C. Fishermen's Union. In 1900, a strike involving the price of sockeye turned ugly. A rumour was circulated that Japanese-Canadian fishermen would accept twenty cents per fish while the strikers were demanding twenty-five. Union leaders blasted the Japanese-Canadian fishermen, ignoring the fact that the rumours were false, that their Japanese counterparts actually supported the strike and that many had even marched with white strikers. Japanese-Canadian fishermen organized a rally to show their support of the twenty-five-cent demand. Police waded into the crowd with clubs. Rock-throwing white citizens drove the Japanese-Canadian fishermen to the river and away. The next season saw armed white fishermen sabotaging Japanese-Canadian boats and cutting their nets. The tension waned as the summer of 1901 became the richest ever, but the hatred created in the strike was not forgotten.

The overt violence subsided, but white fishing groups maintained lobbying efforts to purge the industry of Japanese Canadians. In 1919, the federal Department of Marine and Fisheries surrendered to British Columbia's government and fishing unions.

It announced support for reducing, then eliminating, the Japanese presence in the fishing industry regardless of whether the fishermen were Japanese nationals or naturalized Canadian citizens. A report on the matter issued in 1922 stated bluntly that "The question...is not whether Oriental licences should be reduced in number but what percentage of reduction should be decided upon in order to bring about the displacement of Orientals by white fishermen in the shortest possible time without disrupting the industry."[5] By the end of 1925, one thousand Japanese fishermen, many of them Canadian citizens, had their licences revoked. The clearly racist federal law had effectively cut the number of Japanese-Canadian fishermen in half. Adding to the difficulties of those who managed to retain licences, many municipalities passed by-laws stating that fishing boats owned by Japanese Canadians could no longer use gas-powered motors.

B.C. member of Parliament Allan W. Neill was known for his anti-Oriental racism. He once rose in the House of Commons to assert, "To cross an individual of a white race with an individual of a yellow race is to produce in nine cases out of ten, a mongrel wastrel with the worst qualities of both races."[6] Prime Minister King appointed Neill to chair the federal government's Select Standing Committee on Marine and Fisheries. Not surprisingly, its 1926 report endorsed the racist goals of 1922. It recommended that "The licences issued to other than white men and Indians be reduced by ten percent of the number issued in 1926, and the same reduction in each future year, so that these licences will be entirely confined to whites and Indians."[7]

Japanese-Canadian fishing organizations attempted to fight the regulations, municipal by-laws, and provincial and federal legislation. They tried to protect their boats, nets and homes from vandalism and their families from harassment. It was a futile battle. Finally, expensive and time-consuming legal action was taken. The Supreme Court of Canada eventually declared that the federal economic segregation laws restricting Japanese-Canadian fishing licences were illegal, for the government could not withhold or remove business licences from Canadian citizens who had committed no crime. The federal government appealed the ruling to the Judicial Committee of the Privy Council in London, which also declared the laws illegal. The King government then engaged in a quick political shuffle. It rewrote the legislation without naming

Japanese Canadians but giving itself the power to withdraw business licences from whomever it pleased. The cynical manoeuvre allowed the unconstitutional program of removing Japanese Canadians from the fishing industry to continue according to Neill's schedule.

From 1922 to 1930, 1,253 more Japanese-Canadian fishermen lost their licences. The majority were Canadian citizens. By the summer of 1941, only twelve percent of the fishing licences in British Columbia were held by Canadians of Japanese descent. Federal officials promised that number would eventually be zero. The attack on Pearl Harbour was still four months away.

Meanwhile, King had to deal with an increasingly militaristic and dangerous Japan. In the 1920s and early 1930s, overpopulation, food shortages and rising resource prices had plagued the small island nation. The economic problems increased the power of imperialists who promoted rapid territorial expansion as a panacea to all the country's difficulties. Taking advantage of China's interminable political struggles, the Japanese military swept into Manchuria in September 1931. Governments that had welcomed Japan to the world community began to fear its new power and designs. In 1932, Japan was forced out of the League of Nations. The American government threatened economic sanctions. Most importantly, the Americans threatened to end steel exports. The Japanese government felt itself increasingly isolated, and turned to the only nations that offered their hands. The Comintern Pact of 1936 united Japan with Nazi Germany and Mussolini's Italy. The rape of Manchuria continued.

Japan's growing military power, and the ruthlessness with which it was employed, naturally concerned Canadian and American military planners. The idea of a direct Japanese military threat to Canada was introduced to the public by Archdeacon F.G. Scott in 1937. Speaking in Quebec City, Scott stated that Japanese naval officers were entering Canada illegally and posing as British Columbia fishermen. The RCMP conducted an immediate and thorough investigation of the charges and declared them without foundation. The only shred of truth uncovered was that some elderly Japanese-Canadian fishermen had decades earlier served as conscripts in the Japanese navy.

Prime Minister King remained unsatisfied. Rather than allowing the rumour to die, he inflamed it by demanding another investigation. Hugh Keenleyside, a B.C. native and federal external affairs bureaucrat, was placed in charge. He also reported the concerns to be baseless. His report also stated what most reasonable people had long suspected: "The great majority of those politicians, editorial writers and others who had been most voluble in spreading the impression that Orientals were entering Canada illegally in large numbers were making those assertions without facts—or even second-hand knowledge of the facts."[8]

While Japanese Canadians posed no internal threat, Japanese imperialist expansion remained quite real. The Canadian military acted responsibly in preparing for a possible attack. It had been telling the government for decades that it was under-gunned and understaffed on the west coast. With world tensions mounting, King increased the military budget in 1937 and directed a portion of the funds to that region. Fixed defence positions were built in 1939 in Vancouver, Prince Rupert and Esquimalt. Air bases were built and others were spruced up. Ships found their way to secure harbours. Despite these actions, Canada remained dreadfully unprepared for war.

King, nonetheless, expressed confidence in Canada's war readiness, for he had an American ace up his pinstriped sleeve. Prime Minister King and President Franklin D. Roosevelt had a relationship that is rare in international politics. They enjoyed a genuine friendship. The two dined together, spent relaxing evenings together and were so close that King once even sat at the President's bedside and read him to sleep. That their friendship led to a familial closeness in Canadian-American relations was evidenced in the Hyde Park and the Ogdenburg agreements. The deals inextricably bound the two governments' wartime economies, military structures and defence planning. The two friends entered the Hyde Park agreement with such casualness that neither consulted their cabinets during negotiations and they sealed the treaty with Roosevelt scribbling on a corner of the document, "Done by Mackenzie and F.D.R. on a grand Sunday in April."[9]

The Permanent Joint Board of Defence was created to implement new, interdependent defence policies. One of the first issues discussed was the danger posed by Japan. Canadian and American officers agreed that a full-scale Japanese invasion would not happen. If anything, they concurred, diversionary air attacks were much more likely. Despite this agreement, United States Army

Chief of Staff General Malin Craig stated at an early meeting that he feared the reaction of Japanese Canadians in the remote event that a Japanese attack actually occurred. Canadian military officials reported that they had already investigated the loyalty question and concluded, in studies dating as far back as 1921, that Japanese Canadians would remain loyal to Canada. The more recent RCMP and Keenleyside studies were used to afford even greater credence to the argument. The Americans remained unconvinced. Craig stated in a November 1938 meeting that the Japanese in Canada "most likely" had radio communications set up, reaching from Japan to B.C. He offered no evidence to back his fears but recommended that all Canadians of Japanese origin be interned immediately upon the beginning of any hostilities involving Canada or the United States with Japan.[10] Canadian military leaders continued to disagree. American military officials tenaciously continued to pressure the Canadian government to prepare plans to intern all Japanese Canadians.

The prime minister created the Interdepartment Committee on Emergency Legislation in 1938 to prepare for the war that everyone knew was imminent. It recommended the imposition of the War Measures Act immediately following a declaration of war. The act was declared for the second time in Canada's history as Hitler's blitzkrieg razed Poland in September 1939. The act rendered legal a long list of flagrant violations of civil and human rights. It suspended habeas corpus and allowed censorship, the seizure of assets and property, and much more. It authorized the RCMP to arrest not only anyone who acted in ways that posed a threat to Canada but, more disturbingly, anyone who the RCMP suspected might act in such a fashion.

Canada was still not at war with Japan. Those long harbouring racist hatreds and those subscribing to American fears, however, began demanding that the Canadian government use its enabling legislation against Japanese Canadians. In October 1940, for example, the Vancouver city council passed a motion declaring Japanese Canadians untrustworthy and demanded that all Japanese-language schools and newspapers be closed. British Columbia attorney general Gordon Wismer stated that he believed "Japs" could never be trusted. He convened meetings of police and municipal officials to decide not whether, but how, Japanese Canadians were a threat to Canada.

Meanwhile, despite the harassment and insults, most Japanese Canadians continued to consider Canada their only home. Many Nisei tried to enlist in the Canadian armed services. After all, they were Canadian citizens who reacted with the same patriotic commitment to king and country as the thousands of other Canadians who volunteered to fight. They were turned away. The reason for refusing to allow Nisei to enlist was expressed by Attorney General Wismer, who said, "If these men are called upon to perform the duties of citizens and bear arms for Canada, it will be impossible to resist the argument that they are entitled to the franchise."[11] The prime minister backed the B.C. government's action and advice.

Many Nisei were frustrated by their inability to enlist. Many of their parents had fought for Canada in the First World War. It was they who had sheathed Vancouver's Powell Street in union jacks and red, white and blue bunting to celebrate the royal visit in June 1939. They were forced to accept the official message that only white Canadians could be patriotic Canadians.

Unable to fight, many sought other ways to help their country. The Japanese Canadian Citizens League pledged its support for the war effort. The most widely read Nisei newspaper, the *New Canadian*, pledged total support for the war. A Nisei-organized fundraising campaign raised $55,000 for Canada's first war loan drive in 1940. By the summer of 1941, $340,200 had been raised. Japanese-Canadian fishermen, despite nearly all being pushed out of business by racist regulations, donated 5,508 cans of salmon to Britain during the blitz. By the war's end, one hundred Nisei managed to join the Canadian army and fight in a segregated unit in Europe. Many others joined the American military and served with distinction. None of these patriotic efforts seemed to matter to minds clouded by racist hatred.

In the face of increasing agitation from British Columbia's political leaders and pressure from the United States, King created yet another committee to investigate options regarding Japanese Canadians. Keenleyside became its chair. Members included Lt. Col. A.W. Sparling from the Department of National Defence, RCMP Assistant Commissioner F. J. Mead, and historian and Japan expert Sir George Sanson. It reported in December 1940, noting a belief among many British Columbians that a Japanese spy network, or fifth column, existed in B.C. and that Japanese Canadians would side with Japan in a war. It concluded that the belief was based on rumour and hearsay. One bit of "proof" of the presence of a Japanese fifth column presented to the committee was news that a Japanese-Canadian farmer had cleaned scrub brush from his fence rows and burned it in large piles. They could be signal beacons. More evidence was that another Japanese-Canadian farmer had planted tomatoes in rows that pointed directly toward an air field. They could be direction markers for incoming Japanese bombers.

The real culprit in the tension, the report stated, was the racism under which Japanese Canadians had been suffering for years. It concluded that Japanese people in Canada had "an admirable record as law-abiding and decently behaved citizens.... [But suspicions were] deliberately inflamed by certain individuals for reasons which can only be ascribed to a desire for personal political advantage."[12] The prime minister accepted the committee's findings. He stated, "The great majority of the people of the Oriental racial origin who are now in Canada are thoroughly loyal to their adopted, or in the case of the large percentage who were born in Canada, their native land."[13] The report should have finally settled the matter. It didn't.

Despite the findings, and despite the insistence of military leaders that a Japanese invasion was highly unlikely, the committee advised King that while Japanese Canadians could be trusted, the white racists could not. It suggested that to calm racist fears, all those of Japanese descent over the age of sixteen should be registered with the RCMP. King and his cabinet agreed and the appropriate Order in Council was passed. From March until August 1941, 14,700 registered, and details of 8,300 children were noted. There was little resistance. Many Nisei saw their registration as yet another way to show their loyalty to their country by calmly obeying its laws. The attack on Pearl Harbour remained four months away.

Meanwhile, Japanese military and political strategists recognized an opportunity to expand their empire further while the world's attention was turned to the madness in Europe. Indochina, Indonesia and the islands of the southwest Pacific were taken. Japanese submarines appeared on the Australian and New Zealand coasts. The United States-imposed sanctions threatened to quickly sap the Japanese economy and military of essential resources. On December 7, 1941, the same day that 360 Japanese planes attacked

Pearl Harbour, equally successful attacks were launched on military bases at Guam, Wake Islands and the Philippines. The attacks were designed to destroy enemy fleets while illustrating that Japan would rule the Pacific. President Roosevelt had no option but to enter the war.

Canada felt the sting of Japanese aggression. In the fall of 1941, as a result of an ill-conceived and foolhardy decision that flew in the face of all military and civilian advice, orders had been issued to defend the British colony of Hong Kong at all costs. Two thousand Canadian soldiers were dispatched along with British, Indian, and a small contingent of Chinese troops. On the day after Pearl Harbour, Japan attacked Hong Kong with a brilliantly coordinated land, air and sea assault. After fierce and brave fighting, and with their commander dead, the Canadian troops surrendered on Christmas Day.

Stories of Japanese atrocities at Hong Kong filled Canadian newspapers. One told of Japanese soldiers tearing into a Red Cross hospital and bayoneting the wounded in their beds. Others told of prisoners tortured, mutilated and killed. Many of the stories were true. Many inexcusable acts of torturous cruelty occurred. Many of the stories reported at the time, however, were either greatly exaggerated or completely fabricated. Truth is war's first casualty. Canadians read the stories and reflected on the defeat and imprisonment of Canadian troops and on the battle's forty percent casualty rate. They pondered too that Japan had already attacked the United States and had the ability to attack Canada. They recalled that for years Canadian newspapers and political leaders had spoken of a Japanese conspiracy to colonize British Columbia and that for years their civic, religious, business and labour leaders had worked to rid the province of the "yellow peril." Coupled with the stress of having already fought nearly three years of total war against the madman in Germany, these ruminations sparked a firestorm of nativist, xenophobic, racist hatred directed against Japan and Japanese-Canadian people among even normally reasonable citizens.

Under these circumstances it would have taken strong political and social leaders willing to stand for the principles of fairness and tolerance to persuade Canadians to direct their anger and desire for revenge against Japan and not the Japanese Canadians in their midst. Canada's leaders, however, had already showed their colours.

The treatment of the Chinese and Japanese on the coast, the Ukrainians on the plains and the Jews in central Canada made the scurry up the ladder easy to predict. King ignored facts, his advisers and his own beliefs. He saw where the parade was going, grabbed his flag and ran.

•

Thirty-eight Japanese nationals living in British Columbia were arrested and interned only hours after the Pearl Harbour attack. The next morning, Japanese-Canadians found their bank accounts frozen and their life and property insurance policies cancelled, with cash values confiscated. Japanese Canadian children found pad-locks on their schools, as fifty-nine Japanese-language schools were closed overnight. Japanese-language newspapers were shut down. Hundreds of Japanese-Canadian workers found their jobs gone. A great number of Japanese-Canadian-owned businesses were burned, vandalized and looted. Business and personal contracts between whites and Japanese-Canadian entrepreneurs were declared null and void. Twelve hundred fishing boats were impounded. Order in Council PC 9591 ordered all Japanese nationals to register with the RCMP as enemy aliens.

To the panicked people of Canada's west coast, these actions were not enough. Nanaimo's Liberal member of Parliament Alan Chambers demanded that Japanese people be barred from all economic activity, especially the preparation of food. He further demanded that all Japanese Canadians of military age be interned for the duration of the war. Allan Neill, Independent member of Parliament for Comox Alberni, went a step further and led a contingent of British Columbia MPs in a demand that all those of Japanese descent be evacuated from the west coast. Others screamed for mass deportations.

Newspapers were nearly unanimous in their cries for evacua-tion, internment and deportation. City and town councils passed resolutions supporting the ideas. Service clubs met to pass similar resolutions. The Victoria Kiwanis Club stated that all those of Japanese descent, including second- and third-generation Cana-dian citizens, could not be trusted and must be evacuated from the coast or deported. It stated that it was impossible to distinguish "between the loyal and disloyal, especially when one is dealing with a people who have given ample demonstration of their treachery and deceit."[14] No examples were cited. Alan Neill had put it more succinctly the previous February in a statement in the House of Commons that became popular and repeated as a cant: "once a Jap always a Jap."[15] Some were dismayed by what they were seeing. Even the usually racist *Vancouver Daily Province* pleaded for reason. Its December 8, 1941 editorial stated that the problem,"is with Japan, not with the Japanese national here or people of Japanese blood. To these, in a very difficult situation they are compelled to face, is due every consideration."[16] The appeal was perhaps heartfelt but it was clearly years late.

Pearl Harbour and Hong Kong quickened everyone's pulse. The enabling legislation already in place made the arrests and seizures of money and property quick, easy and legal. Racist violence appeared imminent. Troops were dispatched along Vancouver's Powell Street to protect the Japanese community. The usually moderate Caribou member of Parliament J.G. Turgeon wrote to the prime minister on January 6, 1942 advising him that "If the government does not take drastic action, the situation will get out of hand. Either delay, or a lack of thorough action, may cause violence."[17]

It was not in King's nature to act quickly. He created an advisory committee with Ian Mackenzie as chair. Mackenzie was the president of the Great War Veterans Association, a former British Columbia MLA, current ember of Parliament for Vancouver Centre, and minister of pensions and national health. The hard-drinking Mackenzie was also a virulent racist. Other committee members included high-ranking officials in external affairs and all branches of the Canadian armed services.

Reason battled with emotion. Logic struggled with blind hatred. Canadian military officials maintained their stand that there was no danger of Japanese invasion and no domestic Japanese fifth column. It was noted that Winston Churchill and Franklin Roosevelt had recently dismissed the possibility of a Japanese invasion of North America. Chief of the General Staff Lt. General Stuart reported on recent investigations and stated that "From the Army point of view, I cannot see that they constitute the slightest menace to national security."[18] Vice Admiral of the Navy H.E. Rei stated that there was no need for concern, due to the confiscation of all the Japanese-Canadian fishing boats. RCMP Assistant Commissioner

Mead reported that all even-slightly-suspicious Japanese nationals had already been rounded up and interned. He expected no subversion or sabotage from those who remained, as they were largely Canadian citizens and most were Nisei. The point was also made that all those of Japanese descent in Canada should be treated well, for any further mistreatment, and certainly the internment of large numbers of Japanese Canadians, could lead to retaliatory action by the Japanese government, which still held Canadian prisoners of war.

Mackenzie then waded into the discussion. He and others, such as Labour Minister George Pearson, disputed the findings of the military and police officials. It was insisted that Japanese Canadians would side with Japan, that they harboured spies and that they should be removed from the coast for the good of the country. Many at the meetings expressed shock at the racist hatred that guided the thoughts of members of Canada's federal cabinet. Escott Reid was a junior external affairs minister who witnessed the meetings. He later wrote, "I felt in that committee room the physical presence of evil. They were speaking of the Japanese in the way that the Nazis would have spoken about Jewish Germans."[19]

At the end of the deliberations, the majority view was that no mass evacuation or further internments were necessary, nor should they be contemplated. Mackenzie then took the findings to cabinet. He ignored the majority findings and recommendations and argued strongly in favour of the minority position. He pointed to the portion of the report that stated that because of the difficulty in "satisfying the residents of British Columbia that there is no need to fear subversive activities on the part of Japanese national able bodied males, Japanese nationals must be removed from the coast, provided with suitable employment, and, where circumstances permitted, be joined with their families."[20] Federal bureaucrat Ernest Trueman was present during the discussions. He explained later that few believed Japanese Canadians posed any danger whatsoever. He said, "The reason for the mass evacuation was not because of the Japanese but because of the whites. The problem was one of mass hysteria and prejudice."[21]

The prime minister accepted Mackenzie's interpretation of the committee's recommendations. The necessary Orders in Council were quickly issued. Japanese nationals and Canadian citizens of Japanese descent were to be rounded up and torn from their homes and families. Those who resisted the injustice would be interned as prisoners of war.

The British Columbia Security Commission (BCSC) was established to coordinate the undertaking. It was granted the power to make regulations, enter into contracts, hold property, employ staff, and fine and jail those who disobeyed its rulings. It was promised the full cooperation of all federal departments. The BCSC was chaired by Vancouver businessman Austin Taylor. He was assisted by RCMP Assistant Commissioner F.J. Mead, B.C. Police Assistant Commissioner John Shirras and a mostly silent committee of twenty-one advisers. The BCSC reported to Justice Minister and future prime minister Louis St. Laurent.

The BCSC created a department called the Custodian of Enemy Alien Property. Its first job was to confiscate all radios, cameras and cars. Receipts were provided. The BCSC imposed a dawn-to-dusk curfew on all those of Japanese descent regardless of work hours. All mail to or from Japanese Canadians was opened and indelicately censored with scissors. The BCSC reopened the *New Canadian* as a vehicle to communicate with the Nisei community.

The round-up and evacuation began in earnest in March 1942. Four thousand Japanese Canadians were given only two or three hours' notice of their evacuation. Their houses were boarded up and their possessions either left inside or taken by the Custodian of Enemy Alien Property. Businesses were similarly treated. Families were allowed 150 pounds of personal property per adult and seventy-five per child. One couple wanted to bring along a piano that had been in their family for three generations. Officials would not allow its transport and ordered it to be auctioned. The priceless family heirloom sold for fifteen dollars. Rather than accept that indignity, the family pushed their piano into the harbour.

A common sight was that of white neighbours descending on Japanese neighbourhoods after the exodus. Houses and businesses were stripped to the bare walls. The director of the Fraser River Fishermen's Union in Steveston later spoke of feeling revulsion upon going into a Buddhist temple to find ashes strewn about the floor. The families had been promised that their church and the cremated remains of their loved ones inside would be protected. It was one of far too many lies. Police did nothing.

The refugees were taken to Vancouver's Hastings Park Exhibition Grounds. They were housed in rat- and flea-infested livestock barns. The buildings reeked of manure, and although the refugees scrubbed every day, the smell never left. There was no privacy. Bunks were placed three feet apart, and they held old, lumpy straw ticks and First World War surplus army blankets. Blankets were hung to form partitions, but the sounds of crying babies, coughing and conversation created a constant din. Toilets consisted of a sheet-metal trough with no walls. There were ten showers for fifteen hundred people. Food was served at a cost of less than ten cents per person per day. Ptomaine poisoning and diarrhoea were common. Armed guards kept order. One woman who spent time in Hastings Park said later that "My first night in there was the only time in my life where I thought 'Jesus, this is a good time to commit suicide.'"[22]

A committee was formed to liaise between the prisoners and the BCSC, but, unfortunately, the BCSC appointees were chosen to serve the commission's interests rather than those of the prisoners. Long-time police informer and loan shark Etsuji Morii, for instance, was appointed to the three-person committee. Further, appointees were first-generation Japanese Canadians, known as Issei. They did not represent the prisoners, who were almost all Nisei. The BCSC's insensitivity and failure to understand its prisoners made an intolerable situation even worse. Hastings Park was a temporary transition centre. Most people spent two to four weeks in the barns. Single and married men aged eighteen to forty-five were separated from their families and lined up to register for employment in the Interior. Armed guards, often snapping riding crops and shouting racist insults, kept the long lines straight. Men were assigned to road-building crews, logging camps or timber-clearing jobs. They were afforded a moment to wish their families goodbye, then taken away. The businesses in which they were placed thrived. Slave labour always increases profits.

Most went to road crews. By June 1942, there were 1,233 Japanese Canadians doing roadwork. Hundreds of communities applied to the BCSC to have roadwork done and new roads constructed. Roads were built from Yellowhead to Blue River, from Hope to Princeton, and from Revelstoke to Sicamous. The work was hard, tents were old and leaky, supervisors were often cruel, tools were inadequate, and the mosquitoes were ravenous. The men were paid but after deductions for room, board and other expenses, most cleared only about five dollars a month. Worst of all was that the men not only missed their families but were also not told of their whereabouts. There were several protests in which men demanded not improved conditions or pay but news of their loved ones. Protest leaders were routinely arrested and sent to internment camps.

The internment camps were for those the BCSC deemed troublemakers or direct threats to Canada's security. They were located far from the west coast in northern Ontario at Angler, Petawawa and Schreiber. The Department of National Defence had established them as prisoner-of-war camps and ran them as such. Angler was the largest. By the end of 1942, it imprisoned 758 Japanese Canadians. It was surrounded by two sixteen-foot fences topped with barbed wire. Constant roll calls were often scenes of brutality and terror, as guards sometimes fired live ammunition over the heads of prisoners who did not line up straight enough or within the prescribed ten minutes. Back-breaking work through the mosquito- and black fly-infested bush cleared a new railway line, using anachronistic tools and techniques. The Red Cross was allowed to supply P.O.W. relief packages. Prisoners wore rough-hewn red-and-white-striped uniforms, on the back of which was sewn a large red circle. Officials claimed the circle represented the Japanese flag but prisoners said it was a target for the guards.

In Vancouver, 103 Nisei had refused to be taken to work camps until they were assured of the safety of their parents, wives and children. They were arrested and interned at Schreiber. Their brave protest led Nisei organizations to encourage people to cooperate with the BCSC to avoid being sent to the camps. Japanese Canadian Citizens League general secretary Kuino Shimizu wrote in the *New Canadian*, "We do not feel that it is in the best interest of the family to have oneself interned. I therefore make an appeal to you to comply with the government order to evacuate as soon as possible for the national safety of Canada."[23] Regardless of the admonitions of the JCCL and others, some continued to choose internment. One prisoner at Angler wrote to his wife explaining that he chose imprisonment to "protest the hairy beast racist discrimination."[24]

While most of the men were being placed in work gangs or prison camps, women and children became refugees. They were moved to towns in the Interior. Most were consigned to ghost towns abandoned by mining companies. Slocan was the largest. By October 1942, it housed 4,776 Japanese Canadians. Tashme had 2,584 and New Denver 1,825. Roseberry, Greenwood, Kaslo and Sandon each had over one thousand. Barbed wire was unnecessary, for the towns were so isolated that escape was impossible. Still, each detention centre was guarded by an armed RCMP detachment, and permits were needed to leave or enter the town. Registration cards had to be carried by everyone over the age of sixteen.

Refugees arrived more quickly than builders could construct accommodations. In Slocan, twelve hundred people greeted the winter in thin tents. There was no electricity or running water. Some made do in abandoned, condemned hotels or other buildings. The H-shaped government-built huts were ready by February. Two families, almost always meeting for the first time at the front door, shared each fourteen- by twenty-four-foot structure. A common stove in the middle of the H was used for cooking and heat. The huts were built too quickly and without care, and often with green lumber that quickly warped. Insulation was installed late in the second winter. Communal outhouses served all.

Some families were sufficiently wealthy to establish separate, self-sustaining communities. The BCSC assisted in those efforts. The settlement at Taylor Lake was among the most successful. One hundred and eighty Nisei formed the community, which supported itself by cutting pulpwood. Other successful self-supporting communities were at East Lillooet, Minto, Bridge River and McGillivray Falls. About four thousand people lived in these communities. The Nisei in the detention centres and internment camps called the communities the *kanemochi mura*, or "villages of the rich." The self-supporting communities that failed did so most often due to the hostility of the predominantly white communities around them. Such was the case at Grand Forks. Racist taunts, and a refusal to buy products from or sell to Nisei settlers, doomed them to hardship and ultimate failure.

A close, extended family was an element of Japanese culture that had been retained faithfully in Canada. This fact meant that while the physical and economic hardships could be endured, the splitting of families was insufferable. As Kane Tanaka said later, "Our families were not allowed to be together. This struck into the heart of all Japanese."[25] Protests flared and refugees continued to insist that families be reunited. In May 1942, 139 young men refused to leave Vancouver's Immigration Building until their complaint was heard. They overpowered the guards and caused twelve hundred dollars damage before being subdued and arrested, then interned without a hearing. The action brought attention to their cause. By mid-July, the BCSC announced that able-bodied men whom the government had slated for roadwork could join their families in the detention centres. Slowly, more and more families were reunited.

In some cases, refugees were placed near or within established towns. This practice became more common after the decision to try to keep families together was made. Some communities welcomed the sudden influx of refugees. Kaslow, for example, had a population of only 468 in March 1942 when six hundred new men, women and children arrived. By the end of the year there were eleven hundred newcomers. Among the refugees was a dentist, two doctors and *New Canadian* editor Thomas Shoyama. The local economy boomed, and services long lost to Kaslow were revived. The white and Japanese communities were completely integrated, to the benefit of both.

Other towns were different. In Kelowna, for instance, the Okanagan Fruit Growers Association wanted refugees to work as pickers in local orchards. The town council tried to block their arrival, and the Board of Trade sought assurance from the BCSC that the refugees would be gone at the war's conclusion. A *Kelowna Courier* editorial stated, "They are just as much a danger as their fathers or uncles who were born in Japan and to pretend that they are harmless and allow them to go and come as they will, is folly."[26] Large signs proclaiming "No To Coastal Japs" were posted downtown and on many farm fenceposts in the valley. A dusk-to-dawn curfew on all refugees was strictly enforced. They were not allowed to join community organizations or to form their own. They were allowed to come to town to shop and conduct business only on Mondays.

The refugees tried their best to carry on regardless of the type of community near or within which they found themselves. A primary concern was education. The British Columbia legislature asked that the British North America Act be amended to relieve it of the responsibility of providing education for the children of its Japanese-Canadian citizens.

The request was denied but the federal government allowed the BCSC, rather than the provincial education ministry, to control the education of the refugees. The B.C. government thereby wiggled out of its constitutional responsibility without an amendment. Fifty Nisei girls, most of them senior secondary-school students, were brought to Hastings Park, quickly trained, then dispatched as teachers. The BCSC insisted that all classes be taught in English, which was a relief to the young teachers as very few of them knew Japanese. After having missed a year of school, about twenty-three hundred children sat in classrooms far from their old friends and homes, with relatives in prison camps, studying their civics books and learning about Canadian democracy and civil rights.

Sixty Nisei university students had been enrolled at the University of British Columbia in 1941. They were kicked out. Most tried to enrol in another university to continue their studies. Some universities made excuses, such as Ontario's Queen's which stated that they had all applied too late, or Quebec's McGill, which claimed that defence research made their presence impossible. Others, such as the University of Toronto, simply rejected every applicant with a Japanese name. American political activist Pearl Buck observed in *Time* magazine that Canadian citizens of Japanese descent were being barred from universities in Canada "on the frank contention that serfs of an inferior race deserve no education."[27]

By the end of 1942, a good deal of the panic about a Japanese invasion of the west coast had subsided. Even the sightings of Japanese submarines off the coast and their launching of a couple of torpedoes at uninhabited shorelines had been written off as grandstanding by a Japanese navy intent upon making a point about American coastal defences. The American fleet had recovered quickly from Pearl Harbour. The battle of Midway had begun the slow, island-hopping drive that doomed Japan. If it were true that Japanese Canadians had been robbed, evacuated, enslaved and interned because of the threat of an invasion, they would have been released in the spring of 1943. Since the external threat had not been the real reason for the actions taken against them, their ordeal continued.

Throughout 1942, the Canadian government had done much as the American government had done. Japanese Americans had also been removed from their coastal homes and many had been interned. As in Canada, racist hysteria rather than a genuine military or national security need had motivated the actions taken. This is seen in the fact that while Pearl Harbour remained the centre of the

American Pacific war effort, Japanese Americans living in Hawaii were not interned. Even the Japanese Americans who worked at the Pearl Harbour base and other Hawaiian government and military establishments were allowed to continue their work and retain their security clearances.

In January 1943, the Canadian government moved beyond the Americans, taking a step that Roosevelt had dismissed as wrong and unnecessary in the United States. Even many Canadians who had supported the mass evacuations believed the step was unfair, unjustified, unnecessary, and illegal. There were many others, however, who believed that despite the conditions in which the refugees were held, and the indignities they had been forced to endure, too much tax money was being spent coddling enemy aliens. Further, many editors and civic leaders began to express the fear that with the threat of Japanese invasion gone the federal government might free the refugees, who would logically return to their homes on the west coast. Still others argued that many of the businesses, and especially the fishing boats that were sitting idle, could be used by white people to turn a profit. These considerations were apparently more persuasive than thoughts of justice or morality. The odious step came with Order in Council 469, issued in January 1943. It authorized the sale of enemy alien property.

The local committees established to organize auctions faced a number of problems. Much of the property had been broken or had rotted in poorly maintained storage areas. Cars and boats had been left to the elements, and much was smashed or stolen. The committees gathered what they could and began moving it. From 1943 to 1946, 741 commercial and residential properties were sold. Boats, cars, furniture, clothing, books, musical instruments and everything else that had been confiscated and was still saleable went to the auction block. The owners had no say in the matter. Most found out about the auctions long after they had taken place.

Things sold for a fraction of their true value. Confiscated farms, for example, were purchased by the government, then given to white veterans. Many quickly sold them for their real value. One Salt Water Spring farm was purchased by the government for $235 and resold by a veteran for $2,000. Frances Saito received $50 for her house and $8.50 for its contents. A car belonging to Mr. Kudo was appraised at $400 and sold for $11.

Expenses for the sale of property and the storage of goods were deducted, then payments made in instalments. The instalments allowed for the creation of an interest-earning pool of capital to finance future resettlements. Each family was charged $22.50 for each month of their internment, which represented nearly half the average monthly wage at the time. The robber was submitting a bill to the robbed. Those who felt cheated could appeal to the Japanese Property Claims Commission, but the process was so costly and intricate that only a fraction of those involved even bothered. Twenty-five percent of those whose property had been stolen could make no appeal because it had been taken before the Custodian of Enemy Alien Property was created in March 1942. The non-appeal ruling applied to every confiscated fishing boat.

While Japanese Canadians were being robbed and cheated they were also moved. St. Laurent believed that rather than being allowed to rebuild their lives, the refugees could better serve Canada by adding to the number of Japanese-Canadian slave labourers. In February 1943, the Department of Labour was given the power to move Japanese Canadians anywhere in the country that a labour shortage existed. George Collins, put in charge of the new program, created placement offices in Nelson, Winnipeg, Lethbridge, Toronto and Montreal. His job was not easy. Collins found violent resistance to the notion of moving Japanese-Canadian families to areas even where severe labour shortages existed. The municipal councils of all the cities in which the placement offices were located passed resolutions, stating that they would not allow Japanese-Canadian people in their communities. Other cities and towns followed with similar resolutions including Calgary, Edmonton, Oshawa, St. Catharines and many more. The city council of Georgetown, Ontario, was blunt but typical in openly declaring its racism: "If one or two Japanese are...employed, it will not be long until a colony of them will be established here."[28] In Beamsville, Ontario, a farmer agreed to accept Japanese-Canadian farm hands. He awoke one morning to find a huge wooden cross burning in his laneway. Signs stating "No Japs Allowed" sprang up in cities and towns across the country.

Some of the plans to relocate refugees were cruel. For instance, Claire Booth of the Vancouver office of the Ministry of Labour could not understand why Japanese-Canadian parents did not like the idea of allowing their teenage daughters to drop out of school, leave their home and families, and accept work as maids in Ontario. Her insensitive idea was eventually scrapped.

British Columbia's provincial and municipal governments did all they could to ensure that Japanese Canadians would not return and that those still in the province would leave. A provincial law stated that if the head of a Japanese-Canadian family was laid off, the government automatically won the power to move the family out of town or out of the province. Employers reacted by laying off scores of Japanese-Canadian workers. Police escorted them away. Other laws stated that Japanese-Canadian children could not attend public schools but that parents could not organize separate schools. Japanese Canadians could not apply for business or fishing licences and could not buy or lease farmland.

By the spring of 1945, Labour Department officials had persuaded enough eastern municipalities to accept Japanese Canadians that movement could begin. The *New Canadian* published articles encouraging the moves. Many refugees were met with violence. In Ingersoll, Ontario, a mob of two hundred white people swarmed the house of a Nisei family that had lived in the community for two generations, and savagely beat the terrified, defenceless people. Police reacted by advising all people of Japanese descent to stay off the streets at night. In many cities and towns there were rigidly enforced restrictions placed on where Japanese Canadians could live. Many shops, theatres and restaurants added Japanese to the list of races that were either not allowed or segregated.

There were a few exceptions. Ironically, although Montreal was notoriously anti-Semitic, its people were generally magnanimous in their treatment of Japanese-Canadian refugees. The charitable notions and actions were led by the Catholic church. Many eastern newspapers also began to urge tolerance. The mistakes that had been made and the magnitude of the injustice that had been perpetrated on innocent people had begun to dawn on a number of Canadians. A refugee from Tashme detention centre named Margaret Hayward explained, "We had people who came into the camp in stretchers and left on stretchers. Now, what in the world were they going to do against Canada?"[29]

Not all people and certainly not all politicians, however, were yet willing to see what had really happened and what was still going on. The government of Alberta agreed to accept Japanese-Canadian refugees to work on sugar beet plantations. The deal specified, however, that the refugees could not move to cities or towns, could not buy land or start businesses, and had to be removed six months after the war ended. Many refugees welcomed the move to Alberta, for not only could they leave the overcrowded conditions of their detention camps but also they had been promised that their families could be kept together. They were soon disillusioned. One family spoke later of being housed in a quickly cleaned out chicken coop, and others spoke of small unheated shacks. The work was very hard and children were expected to help. Wages were so low and deductions for food, water, and lodging so high that the federal government began topping up the slave wages by ten dollars a month per adult and five a month per child. The money was most often used to pay the fees charged to attend local public schools, where local laws allowed racial integration. Japanese Canadians were the only citizens so charged. Many communities put the school fees out of reach of refugee families, resulting in hundreds of tired children being instructed at nights by parents exhausted from fourteen-hour days under the scorching prairie sun. By 1945, sixty-five percent of all sugar beet workers were Japanese Canadians. Their hard work and slave wages built the industry.

•

The problem of what to do with the refugees after the war had begun to concern St. Laurent by the middle of 1944. He personally wanted every one of them deported.[30] He nonetheless developed three options for cabinet. The federal government could free the refugees unconditionally and allow them to return to the coast or wherever they pleased, it could control where they resettled, or it could deport them. When St. Laurent reviewed the options in cabinet, Ian Mackenzie promised to resign and take every British Columbia caucus member with him if the Japanese Canadians were allowed to return to the coast. A poll released in the summer indicated that sixty-four percent of white British Columbians wanted the refugees deported.

On August 4, 1944, King announced his government's plans. He noted that not a single Japanese-Canadian person had been suspected of or charged with an act of sabotage or had engaged in any disloyal activities. He, consequently, found it difficult to support forced deportations. He announced the formation of a commission to arrange the deportation to Japan of any refugee who wished to go and the forced deportation of any deemed by the commission to be disloyal.

Reaction to the plan was mixed. The United, Roman Catholic, Baptist and Anglican churches, in a rare display of unity, issued a joint declaration denouncing the forced deportations as wicked and smacking of Nazism. British Columbia's newspapers, on the other hand, criticized the plan as too lenient. The *Victoria Colonist*, for instance, repeated its long-held assertion that a Jap was a Jap whether born in Canada or Japan. It questioned the ability of the commission to "determine the loyalty to this land of one born of enemy stock."[31]

The determination of loyalty became a sticky issue. Minister of Labour Mitchell placed full-page advertisements in the *New Canadian* and posters in all detention centres and prison camps in March 1945. Two options were outlined. The first offered free passage to Japan. Despite the fact that the majority of those at whom the option was directed had never even visited Japan, much less lived there, the option was called repatriation. Those choosing repatriation were promised that they could take all assets with them. Those not choosing repatriation, and who were later deemed to be disloyal, would be deported and allowed to take nothing. A second option offered free transportation and movement of personal effects to any location in Canada east of the Rocky Mountains. Neither option allowed a return to homes on the west coast.

RCMP officers were dispatched to conduct interviews and record decisions made. The officers were to fully explain each option, allow adequate time for reflection and family consultation, record the head of the family's decision and secure a signature. It seldom happened that way. An inadequate number of officers were assigned to the task. There were language difficulties with some of the older people. Most officers interviewed an average of four hundred people a day. That speed left little time for discussion or reflection. Those who signed for repatriation were promised pay raises and other perks. Those who refused to sign often found their jobs jeopardized and suffered other forms of harassment.

Most refugees found the decision very difficult and expressed a desire to control where they were going to move, where they would be working, their housing, their children's education and other details. Although their homes and property were gone, most wanted to return to the coast, where many had lived for two or, in a few cases, three generations. All wanted to ensure that their families would remain together, but the stress-inducing process split families asunder. Nisei naturally almost all wanted to stay. Issei parents were often of two minds. Many signed for repatriation not because they wanted to go but because they had been pressured in a hurried interview or were seeking to keep fracturing families together. By the first of August 1945, 10,397 or forty-three percent of all Japanese Canadians had signed for repatriation.

In April, Adolf Hitler had put a revolver in his mouth and blown out what remained of his brains. The European war ended days later. On August 6, 1945, a single atomic bomb obliterated the Japanese city of Hiroshima. The predominantly Christian city of Nagasaki was destroyed by a second bomb two days later. The government of Japan surrendered. Canadian prisoners of war from the battle at Hong Kong returned home. With war's end, those still clinging to the lie that the treatment of the Japanese Canadians was due to Pearl Harbour or the threat of invasion were left naked.

The program of repatriation and relocation, nonetheless, continued. The absence of logic was not lost on those Nisei who had been tricked or bribed into signing up to be banished to a devastated country they had never seen. From V-J Day until the end of 1945, the Department of Labour received 4,720 requests from Nisei asking to be removed from the repatriation lists. The government refused. Church leaders, several eastern newspapers and the Cooperative Commonwealth Federation led the protest against the government's intention to proceed with the mass deportations. The prime minister stated that if a person declared himself willing to go to Japan then that person must be disloyal and, therefore, should be deported.

In the face of mounting questions about the legality of the forced mass deportation of law-abiding and predominately Canadian citizens, King issued a new Order in Council. It allowed the cabinet to continue the War Measures Act despite the fact that the war was over. Clause G of Bill 15 allowed cabinet the power to deport and revoke the citizenship of anyone it pleased. Order in Council P.C. 7338 stated that people would be deported if they were over sixteen years of age and had made a request for repatriation before they were interned or before the surrender of Japan, or if they were the wife or child of a person being deported. Labour Minister Mitchell was placed in charge of implementing the new rules. The American military ruler of vanquished Japan, megalomaniacal General Douglas MacArthur, wired that he was prepared to accept any Japanese Canadians whom Canada wished to send.

Many new, painful, family-destroying hearings were held. Many opted to quit and be deported rather than continue to fight a government they had long ceased to trust. Finally, on January 16, 1946, five months after the threat from Japan had been unquestionably removed, a ship crammed with eight hundred Japanese Canadians left Vancouver for Japan. It was the first of five. The *Vancouver Daily Province* reported on June 1, 1946,

> Six hundred and seventy solemn-faced Japanese...sailed from Vancouver Friday night bound for the land of the rising sun.... There were few smiling faces among the boatload. Solemnness was written on their faces; only indifference they showed.[32]

A newly formed Cooperative Committee of Japanese Canadians led the fight against further deportations. Public meetings were held in Ottawa, Winnipeg and elsewhere. A letter-writing campaign was organized. Several newspapers took up the cause. The December 22 *Toronto Star* editorial, for example, stated, "One of the crimes charged against the Nazis, is the deportations of Civilians on racial and religious grounds. This is precisely what Canada is doing in respect to her Japanese citizens."[33] The Canadian Council of Churches sent delegations to King asking him to stop the deportations. At a meeting at Jarvis Collegiate in Toronto, Rabbi Feinberg spoke to a large crowd that included senators, municipal politicians and business leaders. He demanded an end to the deportations, arguing,

> I am here on behalf of six million Jews who were slaughtered...for no reason other than being Jews...the ghost of Hitler still walks in Canada. The thing for which Hitler stood has been inscribed on the Order in Council which punishes little children for crimes they couldn't commit.[34]

Not all opposed the deportations. The *Halifax Herald*, the *Toronto Telegram*, the *Vancouver Sun*, the *Victoria Colonist* and many more newspapers supported them. Many business and labour leaders also expressed their support, as did many elected officials. British Columbia attorney general Maitland offered that "Japs" were "still a menace to Canada and good riddance to them all."[35] Meanwhile, the military had begun to recruit Nisei to work as interpreters to assist with Canada's new role in postwar Japan. Before any of the new interpreters could begin, however, it was discovered by embarrassed officials that they needed crash courses in the Japanese language and culture, which, it turned, out they knew little about.

A court challenge was initiated in the names of prospective deportees Yutaka Shimoyama and Yae Nasu demanding that Louis St. Laurent issue a writ of habeas corpus for every deportee. The case went to the Privy Council in London, which decreed that the government of Canada had indeed been acting illegally. It did not matter. King had already seen a new parade and had already ended the mass deportations. By that time, 3,964 people had been deported. Of those, 1,355 were Japanese nationals, many of whom had tried to become Canadian citizens long before the war but had been entrapped in the web of government bureaucracy that had frustrated their attempts. Over half of those deported, some 2,509 people, were Canadian citizens.

Before the Second World War, British Columbia had been home to ninety-five percent of Canada's Japanese-Canadian people. By December 1946, only thirty-three percent lived in the province. Many considered that percentage still too high. In a March 1948 House of Commons debate, nearly three years after the American war against Japan had ended, Ross Thatcher of the C.C.F. argued that restrictions that still existed on the movement of Japanese Canadians should be lifted. MPs on both sides of the floor rose to shout down the suggestion. B.C. premier Byron Johnson dismissed Thatcher's idea as unthinkable. He predicted that every politician who supported the lifting of restrictive laws would lose his seat in the next election. Thatcher's proposed amendments were defeated. Even though all pretence of national security was gone, and no one even tried to argue that the actions against the Japanese Canadians had any motive other than racism, the federal and B.C. governments still wanted no Japanese Canadians west of the Rockies. The number of Japanese Canadians in British Columbia dropped from 23,224 in 1941 to 15,733 in 1944, to and 7,169 by 1951. The ending of the mass deportations allowed the state to step slightly down the racist ladder, but exclusionary immigration policies and segregation laws and practices that remained in place made that step a small one.

Those who were deported, robbed, imprisoned, evacuated and enslaved had all been guilty of the same offence. Their crime was their race. As with Chinese, Ukrainian and Jewish Canadians, that crime had been deemed sufficiently heinous to justify abuse and mistreatment in a country whose veins coursed with racism.

5

Black Canadians 1791–1970
Slavery, Segregation and Evacuation

I can have a million dollars, I can have ten university degrees—but what happens when I try to join a golf club, the yacht squadron, and many churches? Isn't this society's way of saying, "You may escape from servitude, you may wipe out ignorance, but you can never belong to the family of man."
—Dr. William Pearly Oliver, 1967

Slavery is as old as humanity itself. The pyramids were built by slaves. The ancient Greeks, who gave birth to our western civilization, owned slaves. Thomas Jefferson, who captured the spirit of the Enlightenment with the revolutionary assertion that all men are created equal, owned slaves. A wide variety of powerless groups of people have at one time or another found themselves enslaved by those who, for a time, possessed power.

In the sixteenth century, the empires of Europe seemed to have all the guns and all the money, and the nations of Africa had none. The idea of enslaving Africans is credited to a Catholic priest who accompanied Columbus on his second voyage to the New World. The priest was sickened by Columbus' ongoing slaughter of Haitians who had been enslaved to search for gold. Over 100,000 had died. He believed that Africans would be better able to do the job. The first African slaves arrived in the West Indies on Portuguese ships in 1518. Fifteen million African slaves eventually followed them to the New World. The Portuguese word for black is *negro*.

The European notions of inhumanity and slavery found their

way to what became Canada. The first Canadian slaves were Native people. Jacques Cartier kidnapped the Iroquois chief Donnaconna and several of his people and toured them through France like a circus act. Most died of European diseases and none returned to their homes.

The first African slave in Canada was Mattieu da Costa. He arrived with explorer Pierre Du Gua De Monts, who, with Champlain in his employ, founded Port Royal in 1605. The young da Costa spoke several languages and, as interpreter, was instrumental in the success of the expedition. The first African slave to settle in Canada was a six-year-old from Madagascar. He arrived in 1628 as cabin boy on a pirate ship captained by the ruthless English rogue David Kirke. Kirke captured Quebec City in a violent raid, then sold it back to France four years later with the boy part of the bargain. He was purchased by a priest who renamed him Olivier Le Jeune.

Quebec governor Jean Talon pressured King Louis XIV to allow slavery in New France. Despite the fact that it had been abolished in France it was allowed to continue in the colony. Slaves were purchased from Africa, the West Indies and the United States and were owned by nearly all of the business and political elite as well as the leaders of the colony's Jesuit, Franciscan and Dominican Orders. Slavery continued in Quebec after the 1759 Conquest placed the British in control. The articles of capitulation, signed after the fall of Montreal in 1760, guaranteed the continuation of slavery in the colonies. In 1763, newly appointed British governor James Murray sent a message to New York asking for more slave fieldworkers and domestic servants.

Slavery was also common in the Maritimes. Slaves were used to build the new colony of Halifax in 1749. The growing city became a centre for the maritime slave trade, with public auctions used by maritime slave merchants to turn tidy profits. The only known public opposition to slavery came from Halifax's small Quaker population. It was ignored.

The American Revolution brought thousands of Loyalists northward. The British government offered them and war veterans land, assistance, and permission to bring their slaves. The government also offered freedom and land to any slave who fought for the Crown. The twin offers meant that thirty-five hundred of the Loyalists fleeing to Nova Scotia, representing ten percent of the total migration, were Black slaves or freedmen. Slaves also moved with their owners to what became Quebec, New Brunswick and Ontario. The powerful Mohawk leader Thayendanegea (Joseph Brant) had fought bravely for the British and brought thirty African slaves whom he had captured as booty to his land grant along the Grand River. Slaves built his handsome home near present-day Burlington. Slave labour also contributed to the building of loyalist communities at Prescott, Niagara, Belleville and elsewhere.

Freed slaves fared little better than those still in bondage. Five hundred freed slaves were granted land in Nova Scotia. Most were in the Annapolis Valley, with a few near Shelbourne, Guysborough and Halifax. Whites were afforded land grants of fifteen to 150 acres and given their choice of location. Freed Blacks were given an average of less than twenty acres and were assigned land that was nearly all rocky, swampy or far from fresh water. If a white family wished to have a Black family's land they could take it without compensating its owner. Many stores refused to sell supplies to Black families or buy farm produce from them.

Conditions and future prospects were such that in 1792, twelve hundred freed Blacks took advantage of an offer by the Sierra Leone Company of London and left the colony for an unknown future in west Africa. Four years later Nova Scotia governor John Wentworth reluctantly accepted six hundred Jamaican refugees, called Maroons, who had been leading a rebellion against British domination of their homeland. Soon after arriving, nearly all became so discouraged by their treatment that they too decided to risk the perilous Atlantic voyage and the uncertainty of Sierra Leone rather than stay in Nova Scotia. By 1800, only 450 Blacks remained in the colony.

African-American slaves as far south as Texas knew of Canada. Many called it the Lion's Paw and dreamed of escaping to live under the benevolent protection of the British Crown. The lure of escape grew when Upper Canada's Attorney General John Beverley Robinson declared, during the War of 1812, that any slave arriving in Canada would be automatically freed and his or her pursuers would be stopped at the border. An all-Black regiment was formed, and Black soldiers joined a number of other British regiments. About fifty Black soldiers defended Canada at the decisive battle at Queenston Heights. Around two thousand escaped slaves found their way to Canada during and immediately after the war.

The early 1800s saw slavery flourish in the American South where the cotton industry had become dependent upon slave labour. The Canadian economy, however, was much different. Slavery was not an economic necessity. The British government had banned the slave trade in 1791, leading each of the British North American colonies to begin enacting legislation to restrict, then ban, slavery. The British Imperial Act of 1833 officially abolished slavery in the British Empire. The act had little effect on Canada, since by that time its slaves had nearly all been freed. As the freed slaves of Nova Scotia had discovered, however, slavery's death did not mark the birth of true freedom.

As bad as things were for Blacks in Canada, they were worse in the United States, especially in the South. As more slaves sought to escape to Canada, more northern abolitionists came forward, willing to risk imprisonment to help them. By the 1830s, Pennsylvania Quakers had honed a system whereby an intricate network of abolitionists used their farms and homes as checkpoints for fleeing slaves. The secret network used railroad terms such as "conductors," " trains" and "stations" to confuse authorities, and so was dubbed the Underground Railroad. The stations were about fifteen miles apart. The people at each station knew only about those at the next, thereby ensuring that the discovery of one would only temporarily cut the line. Harriet Tubman was instrumental in the Underground Railroad's success, risking capture and death by repeatedly returning to solidify the network and directly escorting over three hundred people to freedom. She was called Black Moses. By 1860, the Underground Railroad had helped around sixty thousand escaped African-American slaves to Canada.

The Underground Railroad's main terminals were Collingwood, Windsor, Amherstburg, St. Catharines, Toronto, Montreal and Saint John. Each city's story is much the same. Negative Black stereotypes and racist suspicion led to the quick creation of discriminatory laws and practices, which isolated, segregated and humiliated Blacks. The same litany of restrictions that plagued the lives of nearly all non-white, non-Christian Canadians faced the newly arriving Black refugees. Schools were segregated according to race, and Blacks could not attend private schools. Restaurants, theatres, hotels, railroads and other establishments either segregated Blacks or banned them outright. It was illegal for Blacks to run for public office or sit on juries. In many counties it was illegal for Blacks to purchase land or business licences or to sign contracts.

Black people were forced to look to themselves for help, guidance and a sense of community. The church became the centre of cultural and political activity. The first Black Baptist Church had been created in Nova Scotia by Richard Preston in 1815, and many others had followed. Church leaders struggled along with their communities to ascertain a route around the racist roadblocks to true freedom and dignity.

Three people represented the clearest options. Josiah Henson was an escaped slave who lived near Buxton, Ontario. It is said that he was the model for Harriet Beecher Stowe's Uncle Tom, although he was quite unlike the book's spineless sycophant. A Methodist minister, community leader and fearless spokesman for Black interests in his adopted homeland, Henson believed that white Canada would never accept Blacks. Consequently, he argued, Black people must completely segregate themselves and form self-sufficient communities. His British American Institute, which purchased over two hundred acres of land, allowing five hundred Black people to live independently, was his proof that his ideas were sound. Mary Ann Shadd disagreed. Shadd was a former schoolteacher and a social activist who promoted women's rights and racial tolerance. Shadd edited a newspaper called the *Provincial Freeman* in Windsor. She was North America's first woman newspaper editor. Shadd argued that Blacks should struggle for equality and total integration with the white community. Only then, she argued, would Black children be assured of a fruitful future. Henry Bib disagreed with both. Bib edited a newspaper called *Voice of the Fugitive*. His strongly worded editorials argued that there was no hope for Black people in Canada, for white Canadians would never abandon their racist beliefs, would never allow Black communities to thrive and would never accept Black people as equals. Therefore, he concluded, the only road to salvation lay in moving to Africa.

The competing options of segregation, integration and exile split Black communities. The options remained hotly debated when Confederation created a new country and offered new opportunities. The Black communities in Canada never produced one person or one group that represented all Blacks or decisively advocated one of the three options. As the young country grew, however, it became increasingly clear that most Canadian Blacks saw integration with the dominant white society as the most viable option. The white society that was barricading the gates of justice before Chinese, Ukrainian, Jewish and Japanese Canadians, however, was not about to throw them open to Blacks.

•

The systemic racism that Black Canadians were up against was illustrated clearly by the reaction of governments, the media and other community leaders to the movement of Blacks from Oklahoma to Western Canada in 1910.

The Oklahoma territory was part of Thomas Jefferson's 1803 Louisiana Purchase. It was deemed Indian territory in 1820 but it did not stay Indian land for long. As white government officials and settlers encroached on the land, African slaves were often given to the Creek Indians as payment. The Creek allowed Blacks to own land, and a great many became very successful farmers. Interracial marriage was not encouraged by Blacks, whites or Indians, but it happened. Hormones beat pigmentation every time. When the territory was thrown open to white settlement in 1889, there were approximately sixty-eight hundred so called Creek Negroes. Many were successful doctors, teachers, lawyers and business people. Many Black landowners had become quite well off when oil was discovered in the territory. The granting of statehood in 1907 restricted federal power in Oklahoma. Segregationist Democrats took office. Laws that robbed Blacks of land and businesses were created and Jim Crow laws stole their civil rights. Ku Klux Klan lynchings became commonplace.

Meanwhile, the Laurier government's campaign to fill the Canadian West was in full swing. Oklahoma newspapers wrote of free land and adventure in the far North. American business and government leaders ensured that Blacks heard the news and encouraged them to go. Many families undertook the two-thousand-mile journey on their own or in small groups. In 1910 a Black community leader named Henry Sneed organized a large group of Black families that brought over four hundred people to Alberta.

The first to arrive faced hardships typical of frontier settlement. The largest settlement was Pine Creek, about twenty miles east of Athabasca. The settlers renamed it Amber Valley. The densely wooded area was cleared throughout the hot, mosquito-infested summer in time for makeshift log cabins to greet the arctic blast of the prairie winter. Approximately one thousand Black settlers soon found their way from Oklahoma to Alberta. Nearly all were educated, experienced farmers or business people, and most were financially self-sufficient. Amber Valley became Canada's largest Black community and soon boasted a church, school and community hall.

If racism had had no home in Canada, the settlers would have been welcomed as perfect examples of the kind of people the young country needed. The racist attitudes that had met Ukrainian settlers and others on the prairies, however, were already well entrenched. Despite the service of Black soldiers, the promises of the British and colonial governments, and anti-slavery legislation, Black people were not welcomed in Canada. Stereotypes had already pegged Black people as stupid, lazy, dishonest and uncivilized. A widely read and often-reprinted *London Times* November 13, 1865 editorial, for example, had argued, "It seems impossible to eradicate the original savageness, of the African blood.... whenever he attains to a certain degree of independence there is the fear that he will resume the barbarous life and the fierce habits of his African ancestors."[1]

The Canadian media adopted the same ideas and tone to greet the Oklahoma settlers. *Saturday Night* magazine ignored the successes in Oklahoma and the Amber Valley and argued in an April 11, 1911 article that Black people could succeed only under strict white control. The reason, it stated, was that Black men are by nature "indolent, prodigal and shiftless. In other words, he is by nature unfit for carving out for himself a home in the wilderness."[2] A 1911 *Maclean's* magazine article noted that white mothers in Nova Scotia frightened children into obedience by threatening to abandon them in Black neighbourhoods. The article stated that Black communities were "the abode of little more than innocent shiftlessness, but such places are adopted to the breeding of vice and crime."[3]

A number of prominent newspapers were quick to take up similar editorial stands. The *Globe and Mail*'s April 27, 1911 editorial issued an ominous warning: "If negroes and white people cannot live in accord in the South, they cannot live in accord in the North.... If we freely admit Black people from that country (U.S.A.) we shall soon have the race troubles that are the blot on the civilisations of our neighbours."[4] The *Lethbridge Daily News* spoke often of the "Black Peril" and its April 8, 1911 editorial was entitled "Keep the Black Demon Out of Canada."[5] The *Calgary Herald* was like many other newspapers at the time in consistently using the words "nigger," "coon" and "pickaninnies" when referring to Black people.

As the stereotypes were endlessly repeated they became easier for many to believe, and rendered actions taken against Blacks easier to justify. The business communities in many towns advocated stepping up the ladder from segregation to exclusion and organized efforts to stop Black immigration and settlement in the West. In 1910 and 1911, the Boards of Trade of nearly every prairie town, as well as the cities of Winnipeg, Calgary and Edmonton, passed resolutions demanding that Black immigration be stopped and that those already in Canada be either strictly segregated or, even better still, deported. Most claimed to be speaking on behalf of their entire community and not just the business elite. The Athabasca Board of Trade wrote to Ottawa stating, "When it was learned around town that those negroes were coming out there was a great indignation, and many threatened violence, threatening to meet them on the trail out of town, and drive them back."[6] The Edmonton Board of Trade circulated a petition to ban Blacks from the city and collected thirty-four hundred signatures. A number of municipal governments reacted to the growing racist fervour by either enacting or toughening segregation and curfew by-laws. The Edmonton city council went a step further and in April 1911 passed a resolution completely banning Black people from the city.

While there were some exceptions, most notably the *Winnipeg Free Press*, most newspapers endorsed racist actions. The *Edmonton Capital*, for instance, wrote in its April 13, 1910 editorial,

> The Board of Trade has done well to call attention to the amount of negro immigration which is taking place into this district. It has already attained such proportions as to discourage white settlers from going into certain sections. The immigration department has no excuse for encouraging it at all.[7]

Racist editors, municipal governments and business leaders, in fact, had little reason for concern because the federal government was reshaping its already exclusionist immigration policies to stop Black immigration. Black people were not the northern European "stalwart peasants in sheepskin coats" that Clifford Sifton had in mind. The Department of the Interior had stated in a report to cabinet in 1899 that "it is not desired that any negro immigrants should arrive in Western Canada."[8] Deputy Assistant Secretary of Immigration Lynwood Pereira had instructed a Kansas City immigration official that "it is not desired that any negro immigrants should arrive in Western Canada, under the auspices of our Department or that such immigration should be promoted by our agents."[9] In 1902, a Black man from Shawnee, Oklahoma, was denied permission to enter Canada by the following note from the secretary of the Immigration Branch, L.M. Fortier: "The Canadian government is not particularly desirous of encouraging the immigration of negroes."[10]

Frank Oliver was Sifton's successor. He shared Sifton's views on non-white immigration. Upon hearing of the movement of Black settlers from Oklahoma to Manitoba, Oliver stated in the House of Commons that "At no time has the immigration of [negroes] been encouraged by the government."[11] He ordered that newspaper advertisements inviting settlers to Canada's West be kept out of the Black areas of Oklahoma. Oliver even hired a Black Methodist minister named G.W. Miller to travel to Oklahoma to encourage Black families to stay where they were.

With his views and the views of his government already clear, but with the racist storm gathering strength in the West, Oliver cynically appointed an inspector to determine whether Oklahoma Blacks would be suitable immigrants. The inspector, ironically named White, spent only five days in Oklahoma. His report was based on the premise that spurred Canada's anti-Chinese, anti-Japanese racism but would appal modern geneticists. It stated,

> The Indian has brought into the mixed race the cunning that the Indian is credited with, and has raised the lower and more harmless instincts of the negro, but only to a more brutal level, and with the combination becomes a more undesirable person.[12]

White then ignored the fact that not a single Black person had ever been convicted of a violent crime in the history of the Oklahoma territory and that Black families had been successfully farming for two generations in concluding that " There is so much Indian in the coloured man of Oklahoma, carrying with it the evil traits of a life of rapine and murder, that it will not easily assimilate with agrarian life."[13]

With the White report in hand, and with media support and the resolutions and petitions of western municipalities and Boards of

Trade in his pocket, Oliver approached cabinet. Laurier had already made it clear with his handling of the Chinese question in British Columbia that he would support racist policies if it were politically expedient to do so. On May 31, 1911 the Laurier cabinet passed Order in Council 115. It banned all Black immigration to Canada.

As had happened with the Japanese-Canadian question, politics entered the picture. At that time, Laurier was negotiating his doomed free trade agreement with the United States. American officials made it clear that they did not mind at all if Blacks wanted to leave the United States but minded a great deal that the Canadians were planning to stop them. Consequently, before the immigration ban could be put into effect, Laurier quashed it. It was weakly explained that the order was invalid since the minister of immigration had not been present when it was passed.

Where laws fail, however, bureaucracy succeeds. Using the same tactic that was later used against prospective Jewish immigrants, Immigration Ministry medical inspectors were used to turn away Black applicants. Blacks found their medical examinations ridiculously more stringent than those of their white counterparts and were turned back for the flimsiest medical reasons. If only one member of a Black family was found to have the slightest medical malady, the entire family and often all those travelling with them were refused entry. Doctors were offered a bonus for every Black immigrant they turned away.

Oliver had stories planted in Oklahoma newspapers that made it clear that Blacks were not welcome in Canada and that all would be stopped at the border. When asked in the House of Commons about the stories and rumours of unfair medical examinations, Oliver rose to clearly state his government's support of the racist practices:

> The immigration policy of Canada today is restrictive, exclusive, and selective.... there are many cases where the admission or exclusion of an immigrant depends on a strict or lax interpretation of the law, so that if the immigrant is of what we would call the desirable class they [sic] are administered laxly and if he is of the presumably less desired class they [sic] were administered more restrictedly.[14]

Railroad companies cooperated completely in the unofficial ban on Black immigration. Although the CPR had agents throughout northern Europe and the United States persuading white people to join the Canadian adventure, it had no agents in Asia, Africa, the West Indies or American Black communities. Further, while often reducing or waiving fares for white families travelling to settle in the West, it either charged full fare to Black families or refused to carry them at all. In March 1911, a train entering Canada at the Manitoba border was stopped by CPR officials, and 165 Black people were removed and the train sent on its way. The kidnapped people were placed on the next train south. Immigration inspector White expressed the gratitude of the Canadian government to the president of the CPR for its racist policies and practices in a January 4, 1911 letter in which he stated, "I think the action you have taken is a wise one and I believe it will help to keep out the class of people that to my mind are undesirable."[15]

Federal Opposition members were nearly unanimous in their support of the restriction of Black immigration. The Conservative MP for Lanark North, William Thoburn, stood on April 3, 1911 to demand even stricter regulations to stop Black immigration "to preserve for the sons of Canada the lands they propose to give to the niggers."[16] Many others expressed similar views. The Conservative MP for Lisgar, William H. Sharpe, argued for a total ban on Black immigration to "preserve Canada for the white race."[17]

The federal government established an exclusionist wall but, despite the wishes and efforts of many, did not move to expel Black Canadians. Meanwhile, throughout the country, segregation remained enthusiastically and ruthlessly enforced. Laws and common practice made it clear to Black Canadians that the dominant white, British-French society no more wanted Black Canadians as full and equal citizens than it wanted Chinese, Japanese, Jews, Ukrainians or others.

•

The First World War offered Canadian Blacks an opportunity to demonstrate their patriotism. Hundreds of young Black men showed up alongside young white men to enlist. They were turned away. Local recruiters were given the power to accept the men they wished, but military and government officials made it clear that only whites were acceptable. Fifty Black men arrived to enlist in Sydney and were told by the recruitment officer, "This is not for you fellows, this is a white man's war."[18] Despite attempts to enlist in Manitoba, Alberta, Ontario, New Brunswick and Nova Scotia, not a single Black person was accepted into the Canadian military in the fall of 1914.

Despite assurances by the greatest military minds of the day, the boys were not home by Christmas and the decisive cavalry charges that were to have won glorious victories had surrendered to the stalemate of the trenches. The desperate need for fresh blood led military leaders to consider accepting non-white enlistment, and some Japanese and Chinese volunteers quickly entered the service. Toronto's General Logie became the first to break the Black colour barrier when, in January 1915, he accepted forty Black recruits into a regiment he was having difficulty building. Black men in the Maritimes were told to go to Toronto if they wanted to fight, and some did. Most generals, however, remained adamant in their opposition to Blacks in the service. General Gwatkin wrote,

> The civilised negro is vain and imitative; in Canada he is not being impelled to enlist by a high sense of duty; in the trenches he is not likely to make a good fighter; and the average white man will not associate with him on terms of equality.[19]

Prime Minister Borden took a personal interest in the matter. He elected to allow Blacks into the armed services but acknowledged the concerns of the military officials and white soldiers by bringing segregation to the military. He appointed Daniel Sutherland to lead Canada's first all-Black regiment but with orders that all officers were to be white. The regiment was quickly filled by Black recruits eager to serve. The Black soldiers who had volunteered in Toronto were transferred to the regiment, and all subsequent Black recruits served as reinforcements.

The hastily trained regiment soon learned that the Number 2 Construction Battalion (Coloured) would see no action. Number 2 was sent overseas through the U-boat-infested waters of the north Atlantic without escort. It built bridges, dug trenches and cleared roads and, in so doing, helped secure the victory of 1918. One thousand Black soldiers served in the Canadian forces in the First World War.

After the war, soldiers of the Number 2 were among those stuck in antiquated English barracks at Kinmel Park Camp awaiting repatriation. They lived in segregated barracks and ate at segregated tables. One evening, a Black sergeant arrested a white soldier for drunkenness and had two Black soldiers escort him to jail. When news of the arrest spread, a race riot ensued. The arrested man was released. Later, the Number 2 was attacked on the parade ground by white soldiers who had brought the racism they had learned in Canada with them to Europe and found it untouched by battle experience.

The veterans of the Number 2 descended the gangplank in Halifax in 1919 to find Canadian apartheid unchanged. Like their fellow veterans, they wanted nothing more than to return to their jobs, homes and families but, also like their fellow veterans, found few jobs available during the postwar recession. Black veterans joined all other Black Canadians in discovering that even after the recession ended and the prosperous 1920s began, systemic racism locked them out of good jobs and into menial or servile work or dead-end occupations. W.D. Scott, the superintendent of immigration, observed in 1918 that "Coloured labour is not generally speaking in demand in Canada and it is not only regarded as the lowest grade, but it is the last to be taken on and the first to be discharged in most cases."[20]

Too young for the war, Roy Williams grew up on his family's prosperous farm and attended an unsegregated school. He knew of the racism that stood before him and all Black Canadians, but long after his retirement he recalled being shocked by the vehemence of the hatred he and his family encountered. He spoke of his brother Carl, who lost his job as a plasterer in Saskatoon because white workers refused to work with a Black man. He recalled,

> I did not notice the discrimination until I left the farm looking for work. I was never told, "We won't hire you because you are Black" but it was always, "We don't need any help today." The young white boys I went to school with would go to North Battleford and get work of their choice."[21]

The economic segregation laws and practices stacked against Black Canadians can be seen clearly in the example of sleeping-car porters. Before air travel, sleeping cars were the common means of travelling across the country. They were havens of the rich, nearly rich or pretend rich who travelled in relative luxury. Their every whim was tended to by sleeping-car porters, who made beds, cleaned sheets, dusted, moved baggage, shined shoes, pressed clothes, served meals and provided other services. It was the policy of all Canadian railroad companies that only Black men serve as porters. The policy was based on the belief that as Blacks they could be paid less than white workers, that the social distance between them and the white customers would be maintained, and that the condition of servitude of the Black race would be perpetuated.[22]

Many Black men found that being a porter was often the only job available to them. Some found the job quite acceptable, for it afforded them opportunities to see the country, wear a clean uniform and work steadily. Most were paid about seventy-five dollars a week, but once food, lodging and work expenses such as the uniform, shoe polish and cleaning supplies were deducted, they netted very little. Many porters were terribly over-qualified. Emerson Mahon had a B.Sc. in zoology from the University of Manitoba, Clay Lewis a degree in business administration, and Stanley Clyke a B.Sc. from Acadia University. These and many other similarly educated men were forced to accept jobs as porters because no other jobs, and certainly none in their professions, were available to them as Black men.

Canadian National Railroad and Canadian Pacific Railroad executives made a deal with the Canadian Brotherhood of Railway Employees (CBRE) in 1926. The deal established two job classifications. Group two was porters. Group one was everyone else. Different pay rates and benefit packages were established for the two groups. An employee's seniority and thus job security could only begin if he was in group one. Everyone in group two was forced to sign an agreement stating that he could be summarily fired and left anywhere along the line without notice or stated cause. Another stipulation was that no one could change groups. The porters were understandably upset with the racially tiered work system but powerless to change it. Those who argued were fired.

A. Phillip Randolf had been instrumental in creating the Alberta Association for the Advancement of Coloured People. In 1942, he was instrumental in the creation of the Brotherhood of

Sleeping Car Porters (BSCP). Railroad executives tried to skirt the BSCP. Their most ambitious union-busting action began with the claim that there were suddenly no qualified porters or men who could be trained in all of Canada, necessitating the importation of Black porters from the United States. Many of those who had publicly supported the new union were sacked and replaced by Americans. The federal government put an end to the importation scheme. The district superintendent of immigration made it clear, however, that rather than recognizing a need to protect Canadian workers who happened to be Black, the government's action was based on its continuing insistence that Black people must be kept from immigrating to Canada. The minister explained in August 1943 that

> For obvious reasons I do not think we would want to add to our coloured population and I do not believe that the arrangement with the Canadian Pacific Railway for the admission of these coloured porters contemplated the entry of their families. We have been discouraging their admission as visitors or otherwise, by every means possible here on this assumption.[23]

The BSCP signed its first contract in 1945, winning better pay and working conditions. The two-tiered contract system remained. In 1953, the federal government passed the Canada Fair Employment Practices Act, which aimed to ban racial discrimination in the workplace. It was consistent with the growing egalitarianism of the day and reflected the government's intent to re-examine racist policies and regulations it had long supported. The government was opposed in this and other attempts to decodify racism, however, by many in positions of power, including business groups and labour leaders. Railroad executives insisted that their two-tiered system was based not on race but job description and, consequently, fell outside the act. They ignored the fact that there were still no Blacks in group one, or whites in group two. The two-tiered system was allowed to continue notwithstanding the new well-intentioned but clearly toothless law. By 1957, the system had been in place for so long, and the Black workers' fear of losing their jobs was so great, that in a free vote the majority of workers in both groups elected to retain the system.

The tiered system was brought to the attention of the Canadian Labour Congress in 1961. An investigation was conducted by Sid Blum of the CLC's Human Rights Committee. Blum recognized the racist system for what it was and reported that "These restrictions appear to have been influenced by the discriminatory employment policies of the company in the years up to the passage of the Canada Fair Employment Practices Act."[24] He suggested that the system be abolished.

Finally, after months of new negotiations, the two groups amalgamated in January 1964. Black employees were able to break through the glass ceiling, and many were eventually promoted to an array of positions of responsibility. The victory was sweet, but it had taken over three-quarters of a century. The victory was tainted by the realization that railways were only one of many Canadian companies and unions in which promotion or employment itself remained dependent on race.

•

The Canadian military began the Second World War planning to maintain the segregated service it had employed in the First. As Hitler raced across Europe and the war's outcome grew disturbingly uncertain, the government attempted to quickly press as many people into uniform as possible. The desperate situation forced the desegregation of the Canadian armed services. The decision allowed Black servicemen and women to again demonstrate through their courage in action how wrong anti-Black stereotypes had always been. Many Black service-people, however, found themselves subjected to the same discrimination to which they had grown accustomed. Stanley Grizzle was a Black veteran who served in Europe. He recalled,

> While overseas, considerable pressure was exerted on me by my officers to become a batman—that is to shine their uniform buttons and shoes. I refused to perform these menial tasks reserved for Blacks. This resulted in my being taken off rotating duties, which all soldiers enjoyed, and being placed on permanent latrine duty.[25]

The discriminatory treatment endured by Grizzle was typical. In many regiments, Black soldiers were allowed to associate, bunk and eat only with other Black soldiers. Throughout the war, the Red Cross carefully maintained separate supplies of Black blood and white blood.

The Black veterans of the Second World War returned to a much different Canada than the one they had left. The Holocaust had shown all thinking people how horrific it was when ideas such as ethnic allegiance, social Darwinism and biological determinism where truly put into practice. The international questioning of the ideas upon which racism was based afforded a window of opportunity to those who had been fighting systemic racism in Canada.

The first battle by Black Canadians involved racial discrimination laws. An important soldier in that battle was Viola Desmond. Desmond was a beautician and entrepreneur who had formed the School of Beauty Culture for Girls in Halifax. One evening in 1947, Desmond attended a movie at the Roseland Theatre in New Glascow. The theatre was segregated, with Blacks allowed only in the balcony. Blacks were charged thirty-two cents, with two cents tax, for their balcony seats, and white customers were charged forty-two cents with three cents tax. Desmond bought an upstairs ticket but then stated that she wished to see the movie from a closer, cleaner downstairs seat. She offered to buy a downstairs ticket but the theatre manager refused and ordered her upstairs. Desmond walked past the manager and began to watch the movie from a downstairs seat. The police were called. The manager and a police officer violently yanked Desmond away, injuring her leg and hip. She was charged with sitting in the white section of the theatre and with defrauding the government of one cent. A judge sentenced her to thirty days in jail or a twenty-five dollar fine. Desmond paid the fine.

Dr. William Pearly Oliver was a Baptist minister, educator and social activist. In 1945, Oliver was instrumental in forming the Nova Scotia Association for the Advancement of Coloured People (NSAACP). The organization was based on the same principles, used the same tactics and sought the same goals as the American NAACP, which had been helping African Americans fight segregation in the courts since 1905. The NSAACP took Desmond's case through the Nova Scotia court system and to the Supreme Court. Black church groups, white liberals, liberal labour groups and others wrote letters to newspapers and to members of Parliament in support of the NSAACP case. Canada's Black communities were unified as never before.

Victory was not certain. There was a long history of Canadian courts upholding segregation laws. In 1919, a Black man sued a Quebec City theatre that had refused him an orchestra seat and the Quebec court held for the theatre. In 1924, a Black man sued a restaurant in London for refusing to serve his family and the Ontario court held for the restaurant. Most significantly, in 1939 a Montreal tavern was sued for refusing to serve Black people. The case was appealed to the Supreme Court of Canada and lost. The Dominion Law Reports of 1939 recognized the importance of the Montreal case, reporting that it constitutionally enshrined systemic racism through supporting racial segregation. They stated, "This would appear to be the first authoritative decision on a highly contentious question and is the law's confirmation of the socially enforced inferiority of the coloured races."[26]

With the winds of liberal egalitarianism gathering force after the Second World War, a few brave attempts to challenge the tradition and legal basis of segregation became more common. For example, Harry Gairey's ten-year-old son had returned one afternoon from the Icelandia Arena explaining that the manager had refused to admit him to public skating because he was Black. After receiving nothing but insults from the arena manager, Gairey took his case to the Toronto city council. He argued that as Canadian citizens he and his family should enjoy all the rights of citizenship. A group of University of Toronto students took up the Gairey cause and picketed the Icelandia Arena. Finally, in January 1947, the council passed an ordinance banning the segregation of recreation and amusement establishments licensed by the city police. The ordinance was not enforced. Segregation remained as much a fact of life in Toronto as elsewhere—even at the Icelandia Arena.

The Viola Desmond case was designed to challenge the legal basis of segregation in Canada once and for all. The Supreme Court cleared Desmond. In so doing it reversed its stand taken in the Montreal case and deemed all segregation laws unconstitutional. Dr. Oliver later stated,

> Neither before nor since has there been such an aggressive effort to obtain rights. The people arose as one and with one voice.... It is my conviction that much of the positive action that has since taken place stemmed from this [incident].[27]

The Supreme Court decision afforded Black Canadians the legal foundation to challenge all segregation laws. Inspired by Martin Luther King, by brave, charismatic local leaders, by the cracks in the walls of segregation in Canada and by a growing sense of moral outrage, many displayed acts of incredible personal courage. They walked into segregated restaurants and demanded to be served, and into segregated theatres and demanded to be seated. Many were harassed, insulted and spat upon. Many were beaten up.

Their actions, coupled with simultaneous but uncoordinated initiatives by Chinese, Japanese, Jewish and other individuals and groups, inspired white liberals. As notions of ethnic tolerance and universal human rights became increasingly popular, or at least more widely debated, more laws that tore at the heart of Canada's racist state were passed. Municipal governments across the country began purging their books of segregationist by-laws. Provincial governments reacted as well. Ontario's Racial Discrimination Act of 1944 was the first provincial legislation to ban discrimination according to race. Saskatchewan enacted similar legislation in its 1947 Bill of Rights. Ontario's 1951 Fair Employment Practices Act was followed by similar legislation in Manitoba, New Brunswick, British Columbia and Saskatchewan in 1956 and Quebec in 1964. Legislation outlawing racial discrimination in accommodations was passed by Ontario in 1954 and Nova Scotia, New Brunswick, Saskatchewan and Manitoba in 1959. British Columbia's 1961 legislation was an important step but it applied only to publicly owned accommodations, and Quebec's 1963 law applied only to hotels and campgrounds. On the federal level, John Diefenbaker's government enacted Canada's first Bill of Rights in 1960. For the first time, the rights of Canadian citizens, including the right to be free from discrimination according to race, were written in a federal statute.

The burst of legislation appeared to mark the end of legally sanctioned racial segregation in Canada. Minister of Immigration Ellen Fairclough announced at a press conference in 1960 that "Canada has no racial problem. Nor has Canada a racial policy. And that's the way its going to stay."[28] Fairy tales are fun but even children do not really believe them.

Segregation and discrimination remained facts of life in many Canadian communities despite all the well-intentioned legislation and the actions of people courageous enough to challenge illegal but entrenched racist practices. Segregation remained common in health clubs, sports clubs and service clubs across Canada throughout the 1950s and into the 1960s. Many real estate agents and landlords worked according to unspoken rules to ensure that non-white, non-Christian families remained out of white, Christian neighbourhoods and thus out of white schools. Author and social activist Adrienne Shadd observed, "Southwestern Ontario may as well have been below the Mason-Dixon line in those days."[29]

Many churches also remained segregated, reserving back pews for Black parishioners. Many banned the burial of Black people in church-owned cemeteries. Segregation was especially prevalent in churches in the Maritimes. Dr. William Pearly Oliver had led the fight against the hypocrisy of Nova Scotia's segregated churches. He had observed in 1949 that "The largest segregated institution that remains is the church.... How can these differences exist in a society whose religious ideals affirm the fatherhood of God and the brotherhood of man?"[30] His tireless efforts were often thwarted by white church leaders who made no effort to mask racist beliefs. Reverend James Stahl of the Full Gospel Church in Nova Scotia proclaimed in 1966, "The bible teaches God made us separate in race.... I can't see why they should be united."[31] The situation had altered little by 1970, when Reverend Lucius Walker observed Nova Scotia's segregated churches and stated, "I refer to it as Halifax, Mississippi...in that it has the same characteristics of depression, repression, and opposition."[32]

Meanwhile, Canada's immigration policies also ignored the flowering of racial tolerance and anti-discrimination legislation. Their racist nature was discovered by prospective Black immigrants and by many Black Canadians, one of whom was Anthony Hughes. Hughes was born in Jamaica but had lived in Canada for ten years, had graduated from a Canadian university and had worked for six years as a successful accountant. In 1951, he decided to become a Canadian citizen and, carefully following the rules, applied for landed immigrant status as the first step in the naturalization process. His application was rejected. Hughes was told by the immigration department that Jamaican people could not withstand harsh Canadian winters, and, consequently, for his own good he would be deported. He was shocked. Immigration officials were unmoved by Hughes' argument that he had been surviving the ravages of downtown Toronto winters for a decade. He contacted his member of Parliament, who took his case to the minister of immigration and threatened to raise it in the House of Commons. Suddenly, landed immigrant status was granted, and in due course Hughes became a Canadian citizen.

Climate had long been an excuse used by immigration officials intent upon maintaining a white Canada. In 1912, Borden's superintendent of immigration, William Scott, had stated, "It is to be hoped that climatic conditions will prove unsatisfactory to those new Black settlers, and that the fertile lands of the West will be left to be cultivated by the white race only."[33] In 1952, the minister of citizenship and immigration was asked in the House of Commons to explain the blatantly racist ruse of using climate to restrict non-white immigration. He said,

> In the light of experience it would be unrealistic to say that immigrants who have spent the greater part of their life in tropical or semi-tropical countries become readily adapted to the Canadian mode of life which, to no small extent is determined by climatic conditions. It is a matter of record that natives of such countries are more apt to break down in health than immigrants from countries where the climate is more akin to that of Canada.[34]

The minister was asked to produce the record to which he referred. He had no record. The use of climate as a clumsy means of continuing to stop Black immigration became embarrassing. In 1953 it was dropped from the immigration act.

The elimination of climate as a racist ploy, however, did not end the racism inherent in Canada's immigration practices. Policies of the 1950s and 1960s based immigration criteria upon four racial classifications, prioritized according to desirability. Class one included immigrants from Britain, Australia, New Zealand, France and the United States, class two comprised Germans and Dutch, class three Italians and class four all others. There were quotas attached to the grab bag of fourth-class immigrants, and their entry was entertained only when there were no applicants left from the other three, all-white classes.

Diefenbaker's minister of citizenship and immigration, Richard Bell, acknowledged no problem with being a minister of the government that had created the Canadian Bill of Rights while overseeing the clearly racist immigration policy. He stated in the House, "If we adopted an immigration practice that was truly non-discriminatory, it wouldn't last longer than a year and that government that set it up would be defeated."[35] Meanwhile, Canada maintained immigration offices in all of the countries of the first three classifications but none in Africa or the West Indies.

Britain changed its immigration laws with the Commonwealth Immigration Act of 1962. The act restricted Black immigration to Great Britain. It is believed by many that the countries of the Commonwealth were then pressured to accommodate Britain by allowing more Black immigrants through their gates.[36] The Canadian classification system that had blocked non-white immigration ended shortly after the Commonwealth Immigration Act was passed. The number of non-white immigrants allowed into Canada rose. In 1967, race was expunged from Canada's Immigration Act with the creation of a point system that ostensibly judged the suitability of prospective immigrants not according to race but to their ability to be self-sufficient contributors to Canadian society.

The law was new but the time-honoured trick of using bureaucratic barricades was old, and it was dusted off to be used again. All races were allowed entry on an equal basis, but nearly all non-white immigrants were asked to post bonds proving they had adequate money to support themselves. In 1967, the year the government stated that race no longer mattered, five thousand immigrants passed through the Toronto International Airport. Every one of the two thousand non-white immigrants was asked to post a bond. Not a single white immigrant was so asked.[37]

As the number of non-white immigrants continued to rise, the government began to feel pressure to return to a racially based, restrictive immigration policy. A 1975 green paper on immigration noted a concern among some Canadians that too many non-white immigrants were coming to Canada and supposedly threatening the fabric of Canadian culture. A senior immigration official explained that members of the government and the bureaucracy shared this concern. He said, "What this means is that we are worried like hell about the influx of coloured people and want to clamp down."[38]

As Black Canadians continued to fall victim to lingering racist policies and practices, many began to support organizations dedicated to fighting systemic racism. The organizations were founded on courage and determination but were tempered with bitter cynicism. Dr. Oliver noted the suspicious nature of many Black Canadians in his 1967 report of the African United Baptist Association. He wrote, "The philosophy of this Committee is such that it is not deluded by hand-outs that degrade, paternalism which is another form of discrimination, nor by false victories that fail to make any real change."[39] Political activist Buddy Daye expressed a similar point in 1969, noting, "When I think of Black people working together, one of the greatest problems is the liberal whites who go into the Black communities and divide them."[40] Similarly, University of Windsor professor Howard McCurdy, who would later serve as a distinguished member of Parliament, said in 1969, "It is time for liberal whites to stop trying to choose leaders for Blacks."[41]

The hypocrisy of many white politicians and some white liberal community leaders claiming that racism was dead while it remained entrenched in many levels of society continued to stir bitterness among Black-Canadian leaders. The hypocrisy was laid bare in Africville.

•

Africville was created in 1842 by a land grant awarded to Black families who had emigrated from the United States. The original grant consisted of sixteen single-acre lots on the shore of the Bedford Basin, which at the time was separated from the city of Halifax by thick woods and a nearly impassable road. There were eight original families. The settlement expanded as Black families, seeking to escape Halifax's racism and the poor land grants of the surrounding area, purchased land and constructed homes. The community thrived as Halifax boomed, with the fishing and shipbuilding industries providing employment for men and with many women working as domestic servants. Many men travelled as sleeping-car porters.

The community was originally called Campbell Road. Africville was a pejorative nickname that stuck. The Seaview African United Baptist Church became the community's cultural centre. Richmond Elementary School was built in 1883 but closed in 1953, after which children were bussed to Halifax. A post office was opened in 1936. Two convenience stores provided basic necessities. Africville's minor softball and hockey teams competed in Halifax leagues.

179

Throughout the 1940s and 1950s, Africville was visited by many famous and important people. Retired boxing champion Joe Louis visited when officiating at Halifax wrestling matches. Duke Ellington was a frequent visitor, having married Mildred Dixon, whose father lived in Africville. Ellington performed in Halifax but, like Louis, was not allowed to stay in any of the city's segregated hotels.

Halifax grew to the point that it touched and then, by the early 1950s, encircled Africville. The city council had by that time made it abundantly clear that it did not like the idea of a Black community by doing all it could to encourage the residents to quit and leave. Despite the fact that Africville residents paid Halifax city taxes, the road to and through Africville was unpaved, poorly maintained, and seldom ploughed in winter. Hydro ended at Africville's border. There were no streetlights. There were no sewers. Africville residents were forced to draw water from a central well that the 1852 Halifax city council had dug as a "temporary" measure. Halifax police seldom patrolled Africville, and responded to calls slowly or not at all. The fire department claimed that without sewers there was little they could do to fight fires. Insurance companies refused to sell home insurance policies to Africville residents because of the lack of adequate fire protection. Banks often refused mortgages or home improvement loans for the same reason. A 1947 fire destroyed seven homes. The fire department had not responded.

Africville residents petitioned successive councils for an improvement in services, but to no avail. With respect to water and sewage, for example, most outhouses disappeared from Halifax in 1909 but requests to extend sewers into Africville were ignored. In 1935, a petition was presented to city council and a promise to investigate the possibility of water service obtained. Nothing happened. In 1944 the issue was discussed again but again nothing happened. In 1947, the Halifax Public Health and Welfare Department recommended that sewers be extended into Africville, and city council allocated $20,000 to complete the job. Nothing happened.

The city's neglect of and abhorrence for the people of Africville was further illustrated in its locating nearly every distasteful addition to the city next to the community. Permission was granted for a slaughterhouse, an oil refinery and a tar factory to locate on

Africville's borders and fill the air with their effluence. Later, a stone-crushing plant located nearby, with the crashing of the machines and the roar of the trucks deafening neighbours. The city council decided that a hill overlooking Africville was the perfect location for its Infectious Diseases Hospital. The Bedford Basin Railroad punched a line through Africville with land taken but only partially paid for. Two more lines later slashed the community even further. In 1955, city council located a new dump only 350 feet from homes in Africville's west end. Two years later an incinerator was constructed only fifty yards from homes in the south end.

By the 1950s, the years of neglect were taking their toll. Africville had developed into three distinct parts. So-called "mainliners" lived in Africville's original area. They were middle-class people who owned clean, well-kept homes on the land of their grandparents and great-grandparents. The area known as Around the Bend became home to transients, some of them white, who rented small, run-down houses. Big Town teemed with crime, bootlegging, prostitution and illegal drinking houses. Most white people who visited Africville arrived after the Halifax bars closed at 11:00 p.m. and found what they were seeking in Big Town. In 1960, a young law student named Brian Mulroney visited Big Town and left with a souvenir that took a hospital stay to cure.[42]

Few outside observers were sufficiently astute to recognize or willing to admit publicly that Africville, like most communities, had its good and bad characters and good and bad areas. Most considered the community as one and based their perceptions on the raucous Big Town. An Africville mainliner recalled, "I remember when someone got killed in Big Town. The police came down and herded everyone up like a bunch of cattle. This is how Africville got a bad name."[43]

That racism was at the heart of the misunderstanding and mistreatment of the people of Africville was accepted by all. A white Halifax business owner explained that the Halifax city council "didn't regard, I suppose, the people as people, certainly not as citizens; and apathy, prejudice, fear, discrimination existed."[44] An Africville mainliner recalled,

> If they had been white people down there, the City would have been in there assisting them to build new homes, putting in water and sewers and building the place up....

> There were places around Halifax worse than Africville was, and the City didn't do to them what they did to Africville.[45]

What the council did was consistent with the treatment the people of Africville had received for decades. Beginning in 1962, the city of Halifax scooped them from their homes and razed the entire community. The relocation decision had been coming for some time. It had been discussed in city council meetings as early as 1945. The drive to remove the citizens of Africville began in earnest, however, with the publication of the Stephenson Report in 1956.

Gordon Stephenson was a University of Toronto professor hired by the city to study the Africville situation. He was one of the early proponents of the notion of community relocation as a means of urban renewal. The bulldozing style of urban renewal had been growing in popularity in Canada and the United States. From the early 1950s, increasing numbers of communities were emptied then flattened. Stephenson recommended that such a program of urban renewal would be good for both the city and the people of Africville.

The City of Halifax Development Department was placed in charge of the relocation. Its 1962 report noted that the majority of the people of Africville wanted not relocation but the services they deserved and had been paying for. The report nonetheless concluded that relocation should proceed so that the people could live in better neighbourhoods and so that industry could move into the area. It recommended that those without legal title to their land should receive five hundred dollars for their homes and those with legal title could receive market value. All those without adequate funds to purchase a new home in Halifax, it recommended, should be placed in subsidized housing. While they were asked about their willingness to relocate, at no time were the people of Africville told that relocation was imminent. Nor were they consulted about the terms of relocation.

Many Africville residents were shocked by the Development Department's report, and several groups were quickly formed to respond. The Africville Ratepayers Association was comprised of seven residents, five of whom were elders from the Seaview Church. The Halifax Human Rights Advisory Council was comprised of Black people from Halifax and Africville along with some concerned white people, and was led by Peter Edwards and Frank

Macpherson, whose wife's family had lived in Africville since the 1840s. The Canadian Labour Congress dispatched Alan Borovoy from Toronto.

The groups staged public meetings at the Seaview Church. The initial meetings were well attended, with over a hundred people generally present. It quickly became evident that the people of Africville were split. Some wanted to continue the long fight for a better deal, some wanted to fight for more services, and others wanted to fight the outsiders, who they suspected did not really represent their interests. Many in the community's three distinct districts wanted to fight each other. The only consensus was that the majority of Africville residents wanted to stay. They wanted to save their community. While well-intentioned, the groups failed to coordinate their efforts, and none won the support of the majority of Africville residents.

Peter Edwards made an impassioned plea before Halifax city council on October 24, 1962. He spoke of the community's history and explained how most residents wanted to stay and, with the city's help, wanted to make the community better. He castigated the council for the heartless manner in which it was proceeding and for acting without consultation. He noted the racist nature of the council's actions and insisted that "If they were a majority group, you would have heard their impressions first."[46] The council thanked Edwards for his presentation and agreed to consult with the people of Africville before further actions were taken. The council met the very next day, however, and with unanimous consent outlined the timetable, strategy and remuneration schedules for the relocation. Africville's people read about it in the newspaper.

In the fervour created by the blunt announcement of the relocation plans, the council was pressured into hiring a consultant to again examine the situation. Dr. Albert Rose was a professor of social work at the University of Toronto. As Rose had written *Regent Park: A Study in Slum Clearance*, the council knew he would support their plans for Africville. None were surprised when he did just that.

The people of Africville, meanwhile, had become completely demoralized. It had become clear after the Edward presentation that city council would speak with them only through individuals and groups that enjoyed little or no community support and would even then ignore their real concerns. Their only option was to secure the best deal for their homes. Families attended interviews with social workers from the city council's Africville subcommittee. They assessed each family's assets and needs and awarded a sum of money. Their decisions were final.

The residents received an average of five hundred dollars for their homes. It was later discovered that only thirty percent of the residents had been told of the city's offer of social assistance. Only fifteen percent of that group accepted the assistance. Many who had been self-sufficient homeowners were forced by the low prices their homes had fetched into government-assisted housing. Those placed in one particular government-subsidized housing project soon found themselves on the move again, as the project had been scheduled for demolition before their arrival. While most stayed in Halifax, some left friends and family and resettled in Toronto, Montreal and Chicago.

By 1968 the people were gone. Heavy machinery had flattened the homes and erased the streets. Africville's last resident was Aaron "Pa" Carvery. Part of his land had been expropriated without consultation or payment in 1941, and more taken in a similar manner in 1957. When the social workers came again he had refused to bargain. By the fall of 1969, his house stood alone amid the rubble and dunes that had once been Africville. The city was anxious to complete construction of the MacKay Bridge between Dartmouth and Halifax and needed Carvery gone to do so. A city worker with a suitcase crammed with $14,000 in cash failed to move him. Local and national newspapers picked up on Carvery's story and took up his cause.

The entire Africville episode had, in fact, become acutely embarrassing for the city. The *Halifax Mail-Star* quoted the Halifax welfare director as stating,

> The City has fallen down on its responsibility to Africville. Providing proper water and sewage facilities for these people, when needed, would have enabled them to give as good an account of themselves as any other families in the area and would have made relocation unnecessary.[47]

In January 1970, Pa Carvery left. Africville was gone. The city had claimed to need the land for industrial development but instead created a park. The Seaview Memorial Park was named after the church. A monument erected in 1985 dedicated the park to the people of Africville. The names of the original families are engraved. Reunions are often held, with grandchildren shown their family roots. A former resident recalled sadly, "Out home, we didn't have a lot of money but we had each other. After the relocation, we didn't have a lot of money—but we didn't have each other."[48]

Africville remains alive. It lives as a symbol of the more than three hundred years of systemic racism with which Black Canadians lived and against which they fought and continue to fight. It stands as an example of how an increasingly liberal, tolerant country, while dismantling racist segregation and immigration laws, can still allow racism to blind it to the legitimate needs and aspirations of others.

6

Native Canadians 1867–1991
Attempted Cultural Genocide

> Our land is more valuable than your money. It will last
> forever. It will not perish as long as the sun shines and the
> water flows, and through all the years it will give life to men
> and beasts. We cannot sell the lives of men and animals, and
> therefore we cannot sell the land. It was put here by the
> Great Spirit and we cannot sell it because it does not really
> belong to us.... As a present to you we will give you
> anything we have that you can take with you, but the land
> we cannot give.
> —Crowfoot

Nineteen-ninety was the year of the Indian. Near the town of Oka,
Quebec, a group of Mohawk protesters met the violence thrust
upon them with violence of their own to protect ancestral burial
grounds. Blockades supporting the Mohawk struggle sprang up on
highways and bridges across Canada. In the Manitoba legislature,
MLA Elijah Harper sat quietly holding an eagle feather and said no.
His no effectively killed the decentralizing constitutional amendments known as the Meech Lake Accord, which had been designed
by the prime minister and ten premiers with no consultation with
Native leaders or acknowledgement of Native concerns. Finally,
the Supreme Court ruled that despite the insistence of the federal
and provincial governments, a man named Sparrow of the
Musqueam band had the right to fish when he pleased. The decision
meant that for over a century the federal government had been
wrong in its assertion that treaties signed with Native nations were

meaningless. After 1990, things would not be the same again.

The most amazing part of the events of 1990 was that there were any Native people left to ponder the year's significance. All racial minorities have had to struggle against the systemic racism that has been an integral part of Canada's political culture. The Chinese, Ukrainian, Jewish, Japanese and Black examples have illustrated, however, that Canada's social, political and economic leaders have moved both up and down the racist ladder. The Native example is different. Native people did not come from elsewhere and thus could not be stopped through immigration laws or sent back. Colonial and then Canadian leaders placed their states firmly on the ladder's top rung from their first encounter with Native people. They did not budge. Canada's Native people have survived an intentional, sustained, well-financed and cleverly executed program of cultural genocide perpetrated by the government of Canada.

The government's tactics were not as brazen as those of the British, who had offered smallpox-infected blankets to Native peoples, sparking plagues that nearly annihilated them. The government was not as macho or bold as the Americans, who turned their Civil War-hardened army on Native villages under the command of General Sheridan, who once exclaimed that "the only good Indian is a dead Indian."

The Canadian government's program of cultural genocide took a more Canadian form. It was to be death through bureaucracy. Treaties were signed then ignored. A web of racist laws and regulations intended to assimilate Native peoples into the dominant culture were created and ruthlessly implemented. Native nations were to be killed by stealing their past through eradicating their culture, by stealing their future through kidnapping their children, and by stealing their present through attacking their pride. It nearly worked.

Government officials have never made a secret of their beliefs or intentions. Duncan Campbell Scott was the deputy minister of Indian affairs from 1913 to 1932. Early in his career he said, "The happiest future for the Indian race is absorption into the general population, and this is the object of the policy of our government."[1] In 1920, he again explained the purpose of the federal government's Indian policy, stating, "Our object is to continue until there is not a single Indian in Canada that has not been absorbed into the body politic."[2] In 1970, Prime Minister Pierre Trudeau sought to rip up treaties and expropriate reserve land. In explaining his ideas he stated, "It is inconceivable that one section of a society should have a treaty with another section of a society. The Indians should become Canadians as have all other Canadians."[3] Little had changed. Cultural genocide remained the goal, bureaucracy the means, and systemic racism the glue that held it all together.

•

The relationship between Native nations and the federal government is based upon treaties and a federal statute called the Indian Act. One must consider the two separately while understanding that both have been used to forward the government's destructive goals. Let us begin with the treaties.

The 1763 Proclamation Act bound the British government to make treaties with Native nations to, among other things, win access to Native land. The government signed eight "Peace and Friendship" treaties based on the act's assertion and, in so doing, officially recognized the sovereignty of Native nations, for only states may enter into treaties.

By the mid-1800s, Native nations were no longer needed economically or militarily. They were simply in the way. Consequently, they were to be robbed of their rights and their land so as to shuffle them aside to make way for territorial expansion. They were to quietly and willingly surrender to white society all that made them unique and all upon which their cultures were based. The newly formed Canadian government would see to it. Indian Commissioner J.A.N. Provencher explained these beliefs and goals in a December 31, 1873 speech in which he stated, "Treaties may be made with them simply with a view to the extinction of their rights, by agreeing to pay them a sum, and afterwards abandon them to themselves."[4]

As lost to the Canadians as it had been to the British was the unique Native concept of nationhood. The Canadian nation-state bases its legitimacy on its recognition by other nation-states. Native nations base legitimacy on recognition by the Creator. The western concept of nation is political while the Native concept is spiritual.

Lost also on the Canadian treaty negotiators was the Native idea that all things exist in nature for a reason and that people must accommodate themselves to those things. One does not seek to change a river's rapids but to work with or around them. That white people and their ways existed did not invite attacking but accommodating them. The treaties, and all that they entailed, were seen by many Native leaders as part of that accommodation. They allowed the new white intrusions to become part of their lives. The treaties were not seen by Native people, as they were by many whites, as admission of defeat or surrender of one culture to another. Social Darwinism was a stranger to Native minds.

It was across this chasm of cultural differences that the treaties were negotiated. It is little wonder that they gave birth to two centuries of misunderstanding and mistrust. Neither should it be surprising that Native leaders did not anticipate or recognize the Canadian government's real intentions. A brief look at how the Canadian government negotiated treaties with the Plains Cree illustrates the nature of the Native-Canadian negotiations and the role they played in the federal government's program of cultural genocide.

The Cree people were quite adaptive to change. With the arrival of French fur traders, and later the British fur-trading companies, they recognized opportunities, altered their way of life and became an integral part of the western fur-trading industry. With the fur trade's decline, the Cree changed again. The semi-nomadic lifestyle of the buffalo culture developed. By the late 1800s, the white people's destruction of the buffalo led to the evolution of an agrarian lifestyle. It was at that time that the Canadian government entered into treaties with the Cree and other plains nations. It is clear that, far from being the backward barbarian or noble savage blindly clinging to a dying past envisioned by officials of the day and historians who followed, the Cree were willing and eager to embrace change and accept new realities. The new reality meant co-existence with the new white regime.

The leaders of the largest Cree groups were Piapot, Big Bear, Little Pine and Poundmaker. Poundmaker took treaty early. The others acted alone and sometimes in concert to influence negotiations in an attempt to win guarantees of Cree autonomy and, in exchange for the land and the complete abandonment of the buffalo culture, guarantees of adequate farm tools and training. The three moved their people south to the easily defended Cyprus Hills area to demonstrate their resolve and disdain for Canadian orders to stay where they were. Treaty commissioner Edgar Dewdney feared the growth of an Indian Confederacy but agreed to reserves at Cyprus Hills while promising increased farm assistance.

Dewdney believed it necessary to illustrate that he remained the boss. In a letter to Prime Minister Macdonald, who acted as his own minister of Indian affairs, Dewdney wrote, "The only effective course with the great proportion [of Indian bands] to adopt is one of sheer compulsion."[5] He broke every promise made. He refused to allow Big Bear and Little Pine to have adjacent reserves. He cut rations to their followers and increased rations to all others. Farm implements were of insufficient number and quality to allow real farming to begin.

As the Cree struggled to adjust to an agrarian lifestyle in new surroundings and with inadequate tools, food grew short. Guns that had been promised to allow the hunting of food and protection of domesticated animals were withheld. Starvation became commonplace as Dewdney cut rations further. Police officers broke up council meetings. New regulations prohibited leaving one's reserve without the written permission of the Indian agent. Thirst Dances, which were the centre of the Cree's cultural, political and spiritual lives, were banned. Macdonald received regular reports on the treatment of the Cree and, obviously pleased with Dewdney's activities, added the position of lieutenant-governor to his responsibilities.

Ignoring government restrictions, Cree leaders met at Duck Lake to plan a response to the broken promises. A united council of all the Cree and Blackfoot was discussed. The meeting was attended by Métis leader Louis Riel. Riel was listened to, then dismissed with the decision that the Cree would not join him in his planned confrontation with the federal government. Dewdney assumed, however, that the Cree had allied with the Métis, and called for reinforcements.

In March 1885, only months later, the Riel Rebellion began with a clash with police near the site of the Duck Lake meeting. Things then got messy. Without the sanction of their leader, a number of Cree families left Poundmaker's reserve and travelled to Battleford to trade for food. Fearing an Indian uprising, white citizens abandoned the town. The Cree families arrived, took what they needed, and left for home. They travelled part of the way with several white families from neighbouring farms who were on their way to the police post for protection against reported bands of rampaging

Indians. All was calm but police reports screamed that Battleford was under siege.

Meanwhile, several young men from Big Bear's reserve decided to use the confusion to seek revenge on a particularly ruthless Indian agent at nearby Frog Lake. Nine white people were killed in a short but violent exchange. Big Bear arrived on the scene and stopped the melee. He freed terrified white citizens who had been tied up, helped the police restore order, and then moved his people back to his reserve. Newspapers dubbed the incident the Frog Lake Massacre.

Insisting that the events at Frog Lake and Battleford were part of the Riel Rebellion, Dewdney finally had the excuse he needed to declare war on the Cree. Police were told to arrest any Cree found off their reserves. When police reported that they were unable to find any, Dewdney ordered the occupation of the reserves. Poundmaker and Big Bear were arrested and charged with treason-felony.

The trials were travesties of justice. No witnesses could be found to prove that either man had planned or participated in either the Frog Lake or Battleford incidents. Police reports indicating that both leaders had actually helped quell the incidents were ignored. The all-white jury convicted both Big Bear and Poundmaker and sentenced both to three-year prison terms. Both died within a year of release.

The Cree people's spirit was broken. Military force, the removal of leaders and the withholding of food from starving children were used to mute Cree protests about the blatantly unfair trials and the continuing disregard for treaty promises. The injustices suffered by the Cree people typified the attitudes and manner in which the Canadian government dealt with Native nations and leaders and way it negotiated and enforced treaties.

The second component of the federal government's relationship with Native nations is the Indian Act. Even before treaties were signed, the Canadian government had begun constructing a phalanx of legislation to control and eventually eliminate Native nations. At the time of Confederation, a mess of overlapping laws was on the books. In 1876, all laws pertaining to Native peoples were swept into one new law called the Indian Act. The Indian Act is among the most inherently racist pieces of legislation passed at any time by any government. The fact that cultural genocide was at its heart was made clear by Sir John A. Macdonald, who explained to the House of Commons that "The great din of our legislation has been to do away with the tribal system and assimilate the Indian people in all respects with the inhabitants of the dominion, as speedily as they are fit for the change."[6]

The act stripped Native people of their humanity by defining who was and who was not an Indian. An Indian became a person who lived on a reserve and was a registered member of a registered band. All others, regardless of heritage, were no longer Indians. Until Bill C-31 amended the act in 1985, any Indian woman who married a non-Indian man was declared a non-Indian. All Indians were stripped of their names and assigned numbers.

The legal definition of Indian split the Native peoples of Canada by placing thousands outside the law. The entire Métis nation legally ceased to exist. The Inuit people, then referred to by the derisive term "Eskimo," meaning "meat eater," also fell into judicial limbo. The legal definition allowed the government to violate the constitution, for the British North America Act clearly stated that the federal government was responsible for all aboriginal people. It allowed Newfoundland, which had witnessed the total annihilation of the Beothuk nation, to enter Confederation in 1949 claiming that not a single Indian lived within its jurisdiction.

The government continued its divide-and-conquer strategy by trying to split those within its already narrow definition of Indian. One method was the creation of location tickets. The scheme allowed those who surrendered their Indian status to win a ticket for a plot of reserve land. After a probation period of three years, they would be awarded legal title to the land. Indian commissioner Reed explained the purpose of the location ticket idea, stating, "The policy of destroying the tribal or communist system is assailed in every possible way and every effort is made to implant a spirit of individual responsibility instead."[7] There was tremendous opposition to location tickets. Indians recognized the ploy as an attempt to bribe them with their own land. Only a handful took the government's offer, and those few quickly found life on reserves rather unpleasant. The plan failed, but it alerted all to the manner in which the government could use its new legal definition of Indian as a weapon.

Beyond attacking their humanity, the Indian Act attacked the political and cultural heritage of Native nations. They had been organized for generations according to a matriarchal system that tied political decision-making with spiritual awareness. The Indian Act destroyed the highly organized and effective system by dictating that Indian bands would be governed by elected, male band councils. There would be an elected chief and one councillor for every one hundred people. The very limited powers of the band councils were listed. Their toothless nature was made clear by the fact that no decisions could be made and no money spent without the express approval of the Indian agent. Band councils were to have mouths and hands but not ears, brains or hearts.

Delaying tactics were devised to prevent the imposition of the despised band council system. An 1880 amendment allowed Indian agents to create a band council whether the band wanted one or not and, if they refused, to simply appoint a chief and council. The agent could dismiss any chief he did not like and appoint his own at any time. Many band councils were elected or appointed, then largely ignored by elders who tried to maintain their legitimate power in their communities.

Perhaps more devastating than the imposition of the foreign and impotent system of government was the banning of traditional cultural ceremonies. The ceremonies were Native societies' core, connecting a community's economic, political, spiritual and social strands. Sweat lodges, pipes, sweet-grass ceremonies and other traditions became illegal. On the plains, Thirst Dances and Sun Dances were banned.

The importance of the ceremonies and the significance of their banning can be seen through the example of the Potlatch of the west-coast Tsimshain nations. A Potlatch involved calling guests to witness and affirm the host's newly gained status through marriage or inheritance or to ratify a new treaty or trade arrangement. Potlatches usually lasted three days and involved dozens of people from neighbouring communities. Ritual dances called *Tamanawas* were performed by people who were carefully chosen and meticulously trained. Elaborate costumes, masks and ingenious props were used. During the dramatic cannibal dance, for instance, performers appeared to actually eat human flesh. A Potlatch's climax was the distribution of gifts. The gifts were of such a number and quality that their bestowal often impoverished the host. In one Kwakiutl ceremony, for example, ten thousand blankets were given away. The giving was welcomed, for, according to the

Tsimshain culture, wealth was measured not by how much one accumulated but by how much one gave away.

Christian missionaries had been trying unsuccessfully for nearly two centuries to persuade Native peoples to abandon their spiritual beliefs. They had derided shamans as witch doctors and bribed and pressured generations of young Native people to ignore their teachings and question their power. Missionaries saw the Potlatch as yet another heathen ritual to be eradicated on the road to the Christianization of the pagans. Catholic missionary William Duncan explained, "The Potlatch is by far the most formidable of all obstacles in the way of the Indians becoming Christian, or even civilised."[8]

A number of business leaders petitioned the federal government to ban the ceremonial rituals. Mine owners and CPR officials were most adamant in their demands. The rituals, it was explained, sometimes kept Indians from their jobs and disrupted work schedules. The federal government saw the ceremonies as excuses for Indians to travel from one reserve to another and, in so doing, possibly create a united front to oppose federal laws and regulations. The ceremonies were also recognized as means through which cultural uniqueness and pride could be maintained. Further, they allowed Indians to sidestep the newly created band council systems.

In 1884, the federal government amended the Indian Act to abolish the Potlatch and all other cultural ceremonies. Anyone found participating in one of the banned ceremonies, or even encouraging others to participate, would be imprisoned for two to six months. Masks, pipes and other articles used in the ceremonies were confiscated. Many found their way to government offices and the homes of bureaucrats. Many can be seen today in museums, and many more gather dust in museum basements.

The banning of the ceremonies drove yet another dagger into Native communities. The generational cleavage between those who recognized the value of the old ways and the young who were taught by white people that those ways were evil was devastating. The ceremonies went underground as some tenaciously clung to culture as a weapon to fight the destructive intentions of the federal government.

Beyond these broad attacks, the Indian Act insidiously removed all vestiges of self-reliance, independence and dignity from

Indian people. It became illegal for Indians to buy, make or possess liquor. As late as the 1950s, it was illegal for Indians to enter establishments that sold liquor. This meant that after serving with distinction in two world wars and in Korea, Indian veterans could not set foot in a Canadian Legion.

The government controlled the personal finances of all Indians through a number of Indian Act clauses. Except under special circumstances, Indian people could not own land on reserves. Without land ownership they had little collateral. Without collateral, obtaining mortgages and most other bank credit was difficult or impossible. The sale of livestock or crops was illegal except as organized by the Indian agent. The Indian agent's approval had to be sought before cutting wood on reserve land. His approval was also needed to seek off-reserve employment.

The Indian Act afforded the government the legal right to appoint justices to administer Canadian laws on reserves. All Native laws and traditional systems of justice were banned. A 1927 amendment banned the raising of money for Native political action groups or the spending of band money to support such groups. The amendments rendered it illegal for bands or individual Indians to pursue legal claims against the government or Indian agents. The Indian Act even declared that the government had the right to control and, if deemed appropriate by the Indian agent, rewrite wills. The government attacked Indians even in their graves.

The Indian Act was created and evolved without consultation with the people against whom it was directed. Indians became wards of the state. With Victorian, colonialist, Burkean social Darwinist views, Canadian government officials saw Native people as children and treated them as such. Sir Hector Langevin, after whom the Langevin Block on Parliament Hill that now houses the prime minister's office is named, stated the idea clearly in an 1876 House of Commons debate. He said "Indians were not in the same position as white men. As a rule they had no education, and they were like children to a very great extent. They, therefore, required a great deal more protection that [sic] white men."[9]

The government's treaties and laws had stolen their past and attacked their present. The Indian Act also awarded the government the means to steal their future. It stole the children.

•

The United Nations General Assembly Resolution 96, passed in 1946, catagorized genocide as physical, biological and cultural. Within the definition of cultural genocide were listed the many means used to carry it out. Among them was the forcible transfer of children from the group under attack to the society's dominant group. Years before the UN definition was written, that is exactly what the Canadian government did. It began the transfer under the guise of education, then initiated a campaign of outright kidnapping. In 1868, the federal government awarded itself the responsibility to educate Indian children. If the government's sole intention was education, then schools would have been established on reserves and adequate funds to run them would have been allotted. The government, however, had much more on its mind than education.

An 1892 amendment to the Indian Act empowered the Department of Indian Affairs to establish and operate Indian boarding schools that Indian children between the ages of six and sixteen were obliged to attend. Christian church leaders were consulted, and they approved the legislation. Indian band councils were not consulted. They were informed only after the legislation was passed. Indian bands were allowed to continue to operate their own schools provided that they met new government regulations regarding teachers and curriculum. Few could or wished to meet the stringent, foreign regulations. Funding was cut every year. Soon, very few bands were able to continue to educate their own children in their own schools. Indian parents were pressured to surrender their children to priests and Indian agents and the distant residential schools.

The residential schools were designed to kill Native nations by turning their children white. The 1889 Department of Indian Affairs annual report made the goal clear, stating,

> The boarding school disassociates the Indian child from the deleterious home influences to which he would otherwise be subjected. It reclaims him from the uncivilised state in which he has been brought up. It brings him into contact from day to day with all that tends to effect a change in endeavour to excel in that will be most useful to him.[10]

Residential school facilities were hastily erected. They were all far from reserves. Day-to-day administration was left to the churches.

At their peak, Anglican, Baptist and Presbyterian churches ran thirty-six residential schools, and the Oblate and Sisters of the Child Jesus Orders of the Catholic church ran forty-six. Missionaries established curricula and procedures, and church leaders hired the teachers. Teachers were often priests who had no education training. They were first and foremost missionaries, who saw it as their job not to educate children but to convert them. Other teachers were often of the poorest quality. More often than not they were rejects from white schools, dismissed for incompetence or acts of indecency. Some teachers could speak a Native language, but nearly all spoke not a word of any Native language, and some even found their command of English inferior to that of their students.

With the schools ready, they went for the children. The fall round-ups, as they became known, were horrendous, tragic affairs. In many cases, the RCMP arrived in force. They encircled the reserve to stop runaways, then moved from door to door taking school-age children over the protests of parents and the children themselves. The children were locked in nearby police stations or cattle pens until the round-up was complete, then taken by train to the schools. Parents could protest but could really do nothing, for legislation rendered it illegal to refuse to surrender one's child. Any who hid children, or fought the police too vehemently, could be fined or imprisoned. In Alberta in 1893, several mothers rode to the train and held children's hands through the windows to try to stop the departure. RCMP officers climbed up the sides of the cars and ruthlessly whipped and kicked the hands apart.

As the years went by, round-ups became less violent but just as sad. Author Basil Johnston recalls an Indian agent coming for him and his older sister. His sister had poison ivy and could not leave. The agent said gruffly that he had come for two kids and must leave with two kids, so Johnston's four-year-old sister was taken. His mother protested, but to no avail.

Brothers and sisters were split, as schools were segregated by gender. Upon arrival, boys lost their traditional braids as heads were shaved. Clothes were taken and burned, and rough-hewn, prison-like uniforms distributed. Beds in large dormitories were assigned. There was no privacy.

Routines were quickly established. A normal day at a typical residential school saw the children up at 6:00 a.m. for morning prayers. Classes generally took place in the morning. Afternoons were spent working at various tasks to render the schools profitable or at least self-sufficient. Organized sports after supper were followed by silent study, more prayers, then bed. The routine was broken only by holidays, when children were allowed to sleep until 6:30 a.m., to work all day with no classes, and to take an extra hour for recreation.

The schools were clearly not about education. Children were often placed in grades according to their height, as school administrators were told to disbelieve any claims of children or parents regarding previous scholastic achievements. The curriculum was similar at all residential schools. Children learned rudimentary arithmetic, reading and writing for the very few hours they actually attended classes each day. Some boys were taught trades and all were taught to be farmers. Girls were taught to sew and cook. Most important for the missionaries who designed the curriculum was the daily religion lesson.

Until the 1940s, all residential schools ended at grade eight. Requests from students and parents for secondary-school education were denied. A northern Ontario residential school administrator expressed the desire of many of his students to expand the program to include grade nine but was told by his inspector, "If we let the Indian people go at Grade 9, then they'll want Grade 10, and then they'll want to go to university. That's not what we want."[11] Many schools continued to deny secondary-school education to Native children well into the 1960s. Government policy stated that if Indian students insisted upon attending university they had to first renounce their heritage by dropping their Indian status.

The chief administrator of the Anglican residential schools in the 1890s was Reverend Wilson. That he understood the reason for the schools was seen in his reporting to the government that the Indian students should "become one in language, one in pursuits, tastes, ambitions, and hopes.... we want them to become apprenticed out to white people and to become, in fact, Canadians."[12]

A racist song that children were forced to sing every day at a number of Anglican-run residential schools also made the real objective of the schools quite clear. To the tune of "God Bless the Prince of Wales" the children sang:

In days of old our fathers, bold
In arts of war must chase
To bend a bow, or scalp a foe
Gave strength the highest place

Then let us praise the peaceful ways
Of that Queen Mother's rule,
Whose kindly laws must give us cause
To love our Indian school

'Tis ours to learn the thoughts that burn
In Christian hearts, to train
Both head and hands in heathen lands
From work true strength to gain.[13]

The heart of every culture is language. The best way to kill anything is to strike its heart. All residential school lessons were taught in English. It was forbidden for any student to speak his or her language even in private conversations. Letters home had to be in English even if parents did not speak the language. Those breaking the English-only rule suffered incredibly torturous punishments. There were regular and brutal beatings. David Blacksmith recalls his grandfather speaking tearfully of being beaten with a four-foot-long whip with marbles at its end, for speaking his Native tongue. At the girls' residential school near Chilliwack the punishment for speaking one's own language involved having one's mouth held open and one's tongue pierced with a knitting needle.

Abuse was the norm. Humiliation was often used to modify behaviour. At a Manitoba residential school, children were forced to stand naked in the classroom before their classmates after being caught the night before engaging in a pillow fight. Incidents of sexual abuse went unreported at the time, but in the late 1980s victims began coming forward. Crushingly painful trials revealed that few children had been safe from violent and unrelenting sexual abuse and humiliation. A dorm supervisor at the St. George's Residential School in British Columbia, for example, was convicted of six counts of indecent assault and eleven counts of buggery, but in handing down his sentence the judge spoke of seven hundred other incidents of sexual assault for which the accused had been suspected but not charged. In a 1991 British Columbia inquiry, it was revealed that more than half of the Native people interviewed had suffered sexual abuse while residential school students.

There were cases of runaways at every school, every year. Punishments for running away varied from beatings, to being tethered to a flagpole for twenty-four hours, to solitary confinement. Charlie Wenjack was an Ojibway child who tired of the beatings and ran away from the residential school near Kenora. He planned to walk the four hundred miles home to his family. Police found him thirty-six hours later, frozen to death on the same CNR tracks that had brought him to school.

The children were taught to hate their Native culture. Many young residential school students were caught rubbing their skin raw, trying to remove the colour. Many girls burned themselves attempting to dye their hair blond. Children found returning home for summer vacations chillingly difficult, for their parents represented everything they had been taught to consider reprehensible. Graduating students faced even greater problems. They became cultural refugees. They were divorced from their own people, while segregationist laws and practices barred them from entering white society. Political activist Harold Cardinal has written, "The child went to school an Indian. The young man emerged a nothing."[14]

As decade after decade witnessed no changes in the residential school system, Native societies were faced with generation after generation of lost souls. They were left with few ideas regarding effective parenting, for they were allowed little experience with the values and everyday give-and-take that are essential to a loving, nurturing family environment. William Thomas stated in 1982, "I personally attended Indian residential schools for eleven years and on leaving it took me another eleven years to mentally undo the devastation perpetrated therein by religious and other fanatics...."[15] Dysfunctional families, alcoholism, drug abuse, family violence and more were the legacy of the schools. In the 1980s, Canadian psychologists began to call the cycle of denial, self-hatred and anger the Residential School Syndrome.

Even government and church officials could see something was wrong. From 1946 to 1948 a special Joint Committee of the Senate and the House of Commons examined the issue of Native education. It was forced to admit that its residential schools were failing to drive the Indian-ness out of the Indians while saddling them with destructive psychological and social problems. It suggested changes. Residential schools began to close in 1951. The Indian Act was amended to allow provincial governments to share the responsibility for Indian education. An Educational Division of Indian Affairs was established, and procedures were put in place to bus Native students to the closest public schools. Assimilation through segregation and indoctrination was abandoned in favour of assimilation through integration and indoctrination.

The Joint Committee interviewed a number of church and government officials in coming to its conclusions about residential schools and its recommendation to begin the integration of Indian children into white communities. It did not, however, interview Native leaders. Further, band councils and Native parents were not consulted about the decision to bus children far from home every day to integrate them with white children. It was the 1950s but the mentality remained that of the 1880s.

The plans for integration met a great deal of resistance from many white parents. Their resistance is understandable when one considers how Natives who had left reserves had been treated. Many unions would not allow Indian membership. Many businesses would not hire Indian employees. Many landlords would not rent to Indian tenants. Many real estate agents quietly steered Indian customers from certain neighbourhoods. Many stores, restaurants, theatres and hotels refused to serve Indian patrons. The racist discrimination they faced was part of the systemic racism that blocked the integration of Chinese, Japanese, Jewish and Black Canadians at every turn.

As with other ethnic groups, the anti-Native racism had been fed by generations of a steady diet of negative stereotypes that remained firmly entrenched in Canadian society in and beyond the 1950s. A November 1959 *Saturday Night* magazine article is typical. It said,

> Because the Indian has a built in sense of irresponsibility many employers who demand good, steady, sober personnel are averse to Indian labour…. The Indian never worries. What tomorrow will bring is of no concern today. He won't put in a sustained effort at anything. He can do it, really, but just hasn't the inclination.[16]

The stereotypes were supported in schools. A popular Canadian secondary-school textbook published in 1951 instructed school children about Indians coming to North America across the Bering Strait explaining,

This experience developed in them a stolidity and endurance that gave them exceptional physical vigour and courage, but it deadened their minds; it killed their imagination and initiative…. the Indian was wholly unfit to cope with the more civilised, more intelligent White man.[17]

Most other textbooks ignored Native peoples altogether, dealt with them in anthropological terms as ancient people who once existed but had since disappeared, or perpetuated cruel stereotypes. Meanwhile children joined their parents in watching cowboys and soldiers saving town after town from evil, marauding, yet rather dumb Indians on television and in movies.

Under the new system of integration, the Native child was forced to enter this racist society during the day, endure a non- or anti-Native curriculum, then return home each evening to a culture he was being taught was inferior and worthy of being relegated to the dustbin of history.

By 1964, only eighteen percent of Native children were left attending residential schools. Nearly all were from areas where busing to white public schools was unfeasible due to the remoteness of reserves. The residential schools were going but their victims remained. If the government was really interested in helping to heal the wounds it had inflicted, it had the necessary resources and would have enjoyed the assistance of Native organizations. Destruction, and not rebuilding, however, remained the official policy.

This fact came to the fore in the discussions surrounding the United Nations resolution on genocide. General Assembly Resolution 96 defined genocide and proclaimed it an international crime but left it to UN signatories to pass enabling legislation to address it. Canada signed the resolution but then narrowed genocide's definition when it came to the House of Commons in 1952 by remaining silent on the resolution's third article, which dealt specifically with cultural genocide. It was thus with a clean conscience and narrow, whitewashed legislation that a new weapon was developed to continue the genocidal attack. Children were again the target. The kidnapping was about to begin.

•

There was a great increase in all forms of social welfare in the wave of liberal ideas that followed the Second World War. The postwar economic boom gave governments the money, and the horrific experience of the war gave them the incentive to change. Chinese Canadians were enfranchised, Japanese Canadians were released from detention camps, restrictions on Jewish immigration were revisited, and Black segregationist legislation was questioned. Native people should also have benefited from the burgeoning reforms but they did not.

The notion that Indian children needed to be rescued from the catastrophic social problems caused by generations of residential school abuse had been recognized by the Special Joint Committee of the Senate and House of Commons. Representatives from the Canadian Association of Social Workers had appeared before the committee and suggested ideas to help children scarred by the schools. They believed, and the committee concurred, that the best way to address the problems the government had created was to remove Native children from their homes and place them with white families. The idea was accepted. It was to be state sanctioned kidnapping planned and initiated by government bureaucrats while their compatriots were still wrestling with watering down Resolution 96.

The kidnapping began in 1955, when provincial government inspectors and social workers arrived on reserves. Children were taken from homes where there was even the slightest evidence of alcoholism, where amenities normally found in suburban houses were absent, or where children were being tended to by grandparents during even a temporary absence of parents. The children were placed in foster homes. The homes chosen were often out-of-province, and in many cases even out of the country, to dissuade the children from running away. Social agencies claimed to try to keep brothers and sisters together, but siblings were nearly always separated.

The program began slowly, but by the 1960s nearly every Native community had lost children. Although it took place in every province, the statistics for one tell the tale. In 1955, there were 3,433 children in protective care in British Columbia. Less than one percent were Native children. By 1964, B.C. had 4,228 children in protective care, but thirty-four percent were Native.[18] Many Native children needed to be saved from dangerous or unhealthy situations, but these figures indicate that there was more going on than social work. B.C. social workers refer to the era as the "Sixties Scoop." They admit to taking Native children from their homes on flimsy pretexts that would never have been accepted as justification for similar action with white children.[19] Most of the non-Native children taken into protective care across Canada returned within a year to their parents. Conversely, few Native children ever saw their parents again.

The cultural differences between whites and Natives had again been ignored. Native child-rearing traditions allow children much more freedom than western, European traditions. Social workers viewed Native parenting as too permissive by white middle-class standards and, consequently, deemed it bad parenting. The possession of material things is far more important in the dominant Canadian than in the Native culture. Social workers mistook an emphasis on interpersonal relationships and a closeness to nature as a lack of ambition. Poverty knows no race, but social workers automatically perceived impoverished Native parents as bad parents, assuming that love and compassion should be measured by a parent's ability to provide western material goods.

If the social agencies had not been blind to the cultural differences they would have recognized that many Native communities were addressing the problems of bad parents. Native customs suggest that the entire family, and indirectly the entire community, is responsible for raising children. Nearly every community told of situations where grandparents or aunts or uncles had taken children into their homes and then worked with the parents to address whatever problem had rendered them unable to care for their children, with the goal of reuniting the family. The Sixties Scoop did not recognize the legitimacy of the practice.

Native parents protested vehemently but in vain about the abductions. Band councils had not been consulted about the plan and were not informed when social workers arrived. Band councils and other Native leaders tried to stop the abductions but were ignored. Parents who attempted to hide their children or stop the social workers were fined or imprisoned. At least when children were taken to residential schools the parents knew where they were and that they would return. The Sixties Scoop stole children forever.

Beginning with the residential schools in the 1890s, and

continuing with the child abductions, the Canadian government had been attacking Native people through their children for nearly a century in pursuit of cultural genocide. In the middle of the child abduction programs the Canadian government attempted a legal flanking action to more quickly attain that goal.

•

Canada fell in love in the summer of 1968. The object of her affection was an aloof, intellectual, millionaire bachelor with the temerity to wear sandals to the House of Commons, drive a sports car and claim while running for prime minister that he really did not want the job. The job was his on a platter.

Pierre Trudeau subscribed to the liberal political philosophy that argued that everyone's freedom in a society is guaranteed if the rights of individuals supersede the rights of groups. Consequently, everyone's freedom is endangered if special rights are awarded to groups such as Québécois, women or Native peoples. It was this philosophy that led to his fight for the Canadian Charter of Rights and Freedoms and his opposition to Quebec nationalism and, later, the Meech Lake and Charlottetown constitutional proposals. Shortly after taking office, Trudeau introduced a set of ideas that attempted to put theory into practice with respect to Native peoples. The ideas were contained in a thirteen-page document called *The Statement of the Government of Canada on Indian Policy*, but it was quickly dubbed the White Paper. Trudeau's minister of Indian affairs and northern development who was in charge of the White Paper, was populist Quebec M.P. Jean Chrétien.

The White Paper's creation began in the fall of 1968 when a pamphlet called *Choosing a Path* arrived in every Indian household in Canada. The pamphlet contained thirty-four questions about the future of government-Indian relations. Chrétien dispatched Minister without Portfolio Robert Andres to various reserves to discuss Native responses to the questions.

Native people had been growing increasingly politicized in the politically charged 1960s. Part of the reason for this development was a 1951 Indian Act amendment that after seventy years finally awarded Indians the right to leave reserves without seeking permission from Indian agents. Another 1951 amendment removed the 1927 prohibition on the creation and funding of Indian political organizations. These changes allowed the development of Native political action groups representing the needs and desires not just of Indians but of all Native people. The Native Indian Council was formed in 1954. By 1968 it had split into the Canadian Métis Society and the National Indian Brotherhood (NIB). The NIB, led by David Courchene, was the most influential Native voice of the 1960s and early 1970s.

Of great importance to the politicization of Native communities was the fact that in 1960 Native people had for the first time been given the right to vote in a federal election. Indians won that right in Newfoundland and the Northwest Territories in 1949, in Ontario in 1954, in the Yukon, Manitoba and Saskatchewan in 1960, in New Brunswick, Nova Scotia and P.E.I. in 1963, in Alberta and B.C. in 1965 and finally in Quebec in 1969. The awarding of this fundamental democratic right had taken nearly a century. Native people were the last group in Canada denied the right to vote because of their race. The new power of enfranchisement, and the new ability and desire to organize politically, meant that Chrétien was dealing with a much different clientele than his predecessors.

Robert Andres departed from many Native communities surprised by the political astuteness of Native leaders. They claimed that the government's thirty-four questions ignored the most salient issues facing Native people. Andres was repeatedly told that treaty issues, a clear definition of aboriginal rights, Native control of education, and an end to the kidnapping of Native children were not included in the questions but needed to be addressed before any of the less relevant matters raised in the pamphlet should be examined. As the reserve meetings proved a bust, Chrétien organized a week of meetings with Native leaders in Ottawa in May 1969. Native leaders again insisted that the thirty-four questions dealt only with government and not with Native concerns. The meeting ended with nothing agreed upon except the need to develop a mechanism for more fruitful consultation.

Chrétien invited several prominent Chiefs and the leaders of Native political action groups to return to Ottawa on June 25, 1969. They met briefly with the minister at a wine and cheese reception, then were led to the public gallery to observe the House of Commons in action. They were shocked to see Chrétien rise in the House and introduce the White Paper. They were even more shocked to hear him claim that the document was the result of extensive consultations with Native bands. David Courchene was among those in the gallery. He later said, "We didn't know anything about the 1969 White Paper until we were called to Ottawa by the minister.... And he said he had consulted with us. That is bullshit."[20]

The White Paper made five points. It admitted that the Indian Act was the "legislative and constitutional basis of discrimination"[21] and proposed to scrap it. It proposed to complete the process, begun in 1951, of transferring responsibility for Indian affairs from the federal to the provincial governments. It stated the principle that those in the most need must receive the most help and that new programs would be developed to help Indians "catch up" to white Canadians. It stated that treaty obligations had to be kept but that their anachronistic and limited nature must be recognized. Finally, it proposed that title to reserve lands should be given to band councils to be distributed among Indians living on the land. The proposals seemed reasonable. Native leaders, however, could read between the lines.

The day after the White Paper's announcement, thousands of form letters spewed from the Department of Indian Affairs and Northern Development to editors, provincial governments and Native leaders. They outlined the five points and paternalistically argued that once Native people had time to digest and understand the White Paper they would support it. Chrétien then undertook an extensive speaking tour. At every reserve he was booed and heckled. Band councils warned that they could not guarantee his safety. In Winnipeg, a copy of the White Paper was burned and left flaming on the floor while every Native person walked out, leaving Chrétien and his assistants alone behind the head table.

Meanwhile, the White Paper united Native people and invigorated Native political action groups. Leaders requested six months to prepare a response to the White Paper. Chrétien promised three. He also promised that while awaiting the Native response, his department would not begin implementing the proposals, which were, he assured them, still just proposals.

While Native leaders began honest consultations with their people, the federal Indian Policy Group that had designed the White Paper changed its name to the Implementation Group. It began planning the changes that would be necessary to implement the White Paper proposals. In a letter dated February 20, 1970, Chrétien assured the premier of Alberta that the Implementation

Group would work with provinces to provide services to reserves but that funding would be phased out as provinces eventually assumed full responsibility for all Indian affairs. In the same month, a letter from Chrétien to Manitoba premier Ed Schreyer discussed the money that had been allotted to his province to implement White Paper plans. The letter tried to calm Schreyer's concerns by predicting that within twenty years there would be no Indians left on any of Manitoba's reserves.[22]

Prime Minister Trudeau expressed support for the White Paper and disdain for Native opposition. In a television interview he stated, "No society can be built on historical might have beens.... We'll keep them in the ghetto as long as they want."[23] It was clear that Indian people would have input only into how the proposals would be implemented, but not their substance.

There were three formal responses to the White Paper. A Native contingent petitioned the Queen. It argued that treaties were signed with the Crown, that reserve land was held in trust by the Crown, and that the government's White Paper was threatening this arrangement. It was not made public whether Her Majesty was amused. In October 1971, the National Indian Brotherhood published *Waubung–Our Tomorrow* and presented it to the prime minister. A year earlier, in July 1970, the Indian Association of Alberta had presented the federal government with *Citizens Plus*. It become known as the "Red Paper". Because it was first, and because the NIB document echoed many of its ideas, *Citizens Plus* was and has remained the most important Native response to the White Paper.

Citizens Plus was designed mostly by the Indian Association of Alberta's twenty-four-year-old president, Harold Cardinal. The document was a scathing indictment of the White Paper, the process used in its design, and the not-so-cleverly-hidden agenda it betrayed. *Citizens Plus* agreed that the Indian Act was paternalistic and inherently racist, but argued that it remained necessary until aboriginal rights, treaty claims and land questions were settled. As long as the Indian Act remained, Native people would be the federal government's responsibility, and that reality would allow Native groups to prod thorns into the government's side to win changes that respected traditions, recognized past injustices and benefited Native communities. Further, the document argued, Indian affairs should never be transferred to the provinces because there were no treaties with provincial governments. Such a transfer would split Native groups as they began dealing with twelve governments rather than one. Ignored as well in the proposed transfer of responsibility were Native nations whose borders crossed provincial, territorial and national lines. The document argued that if the federal government was truly willing to help Indians "catch up" to white citizens, it could establish on-reserve economic development projects without the White Paper. However, in promising to transfer money to provinces to initiate programs, it was promising only to create another level of bureaucracy and lose a good deal of the money earmarked for Native economic development in the process. It argued that the spirit as well as the letter of treaties had to be recognized. The government must not pay lip service, as suggested by the White Paper, but recognize the moral and legal obligations inherent in the treaties. It must rectify the historic injustices created by generations of neglect of treaty terms and narrow interpretations of their intent. Finally, *Citizens Plus* argued that reserve land did not belong to the federal government but was, as the petition to the Queen said, owned by Native people and merely held in trust for them by the Crown. This applied even to reserve lands carved out of federally owned land and not covered directly by treaty. The government had no legal right to split the land among its present occupants, for, "The true owners of the land are not yet born."[24]

In short, *Citizens Plus* assailed every White Paper proposal by showing each to be designed only to help the federal government by allowing it to surrender its responsibilities to and for Native people. The petition to the Queen, *Waubung–Our Tomorrow* and *Citizens Plus* all exposed the White Paper as yet another attempt to destroy Native people. In a book entitled *The Unjust Society* Harold Cardinal wrote, "It is a strange government and a strange mentality that would have the gall to ask the Indian to help implement its plan to perpetuate cultural genocide on the Indians of Canada."[25]

Many band councils and Native groups had been consulted and had played a role in designing *Citizens Plus*, so all were quick to endorse it. Provincial governments had showed themselves squeamish about the White Paper even before the Native reaction was widely known. Saskatchewan premier Ross Thatcher, for example, became a firm opponent of the White Paper and said, "We do not want the problem thrown on our hands."[26]

Left with no support, the government quietly withdrew the

White Paper. It is interesting to note that Chrétien apparently completely misunderstood Native opposition to the White Paper even after the controversy was over. In his 1985 autobiography he wrote, "After that, no one could use the old rhetorical exaggerations about the reserves or the special laws because the Indians themselves had chosen to keep them."[27] Perhaps his misunderstanding of what really happened is not surprising when one reads that to Chrétien "The department [Indian Affairs and Northern Development] was a fascinating one, and because of its range and authority, I used to refer to myself jokingly as the last emperor in North America."[28] The White Paper's death meant that there would be more emperors after all. Equally certain was the fact that Native groups would be quick to draw attention to any new clothes.

The White Paper fight had galvanized Native political action groups and Native people in general. At the insistence of the NIB, Chrétien had offered bands one dollar per capita to develop groups to discuss the White Paper. As the groups grew in strength and resolve they raised more money and earned more support. After the White Paper's death, however, the government appeared willing to continue funding only certain Native groups, which sparked a counterproductive competition among them. Many lost popular support. Despite these problems, the fire started by the White Paper fight was not extinguished. Many newly charged political action groups focussed their attention upon saving the children.

•

Parents and band councils had been protesting the existence of residential schools and the racist curriculum in integrated schools for years. In 1967, for instance, a group called the Native Alliance For Red Power had organized a protest event to publicize the crisis in Native education. A conference of administrators and superintendents of reserve and residential schools in Vancouver was picketed. Among the signs were "Priests Make Converts Not Graduates," "Residential Schools Are Prisons," and "Stop Cultural Genocide." A leaflet handed to conference participants, the media and passers-by said in part,

> The breakdown of family and community life has been the
> result of Indian Residential Schools and the educational

policy was not determined by our people.... Residential schools are perfect training grounds for the integration of Indian people into the penitentiaries and skid-rows of our land....[29]

Also in 1967, Howard Hawthorne had compiled the comprehensive *A Survey of the Contemporary Indians of Canada: Economic, Political, Educational Needs and Policies* for the Department Indian Affairs. His report was praised by editors, academics and politicians for its scholarly approach and meticulous research. Hawthorne supported everything that Native people had been saying about the education of their children. His report was very critical of the government's Native education policy, stating that it was based on an "isolationist and paternalistic ideology."[30] Among the report's recommendations was that all funding for church-run residential schools be immediately ended. It recommended that for the good of Native children, of Native nations and of Canada as a whole, Native parents and communities should be given the means and power to control housing, health care and economic development. While praising the Hawthorne report, federal officials shelved its recommendations. The report, and other changes to legislation that were attacking systemic racism at the time, nonetheless, indicated that times were changing.

Upon this shifting ground, and with fresh memories of the White Paper struggle, the National Indian Brotherhood took up the fight for the children. In 1971, it undertook a study of aboriginal education in the United States. NIB members saw Native people controlling their children's education, and it strengthened their resolve to win that control in Canada.

In November 1972, the NIB worked in concert with other Native groups from across the country to develop a document called *Indian Control of Indian Education*. It argued that only if Native parents influenced the hiring of teachers and the setting of curricula could Native children learn to appreciate their history and culture. Only this appreciation, it was argued, would address the social problems plaguing Native communities that were the legacy of white control of Native education. It proposed the creation of Band Education Authorities to oversee the education of Native children. It proposed affording Native parents the right to keep their children in integrated schools but the changing of provincial legislation to ensure

Native representation on appropriate school boards. Federal funding for Native students worthy of attending post-secondary institutions should continue. Finally, it proposed the creation of Native adult-education programs.

In February 1973, Jean Chrétien officially accepted the document and expressed full agreement with its accusations, arguments and recommendations. Chrétien said,

> I have given the National Indian Brotherhood my assurance that I and my Department are fully committed to realising the educational goals for the Indian people which are set forth in the Brotherhood's proposal.... In consultation and co-operation with the Indian organizations, my Department will begin immediately to effect the educational changes for the Indian people that they have requested.[31]

Either Chrétien lied or his bureaucrats operated without his knowledge to turn his pledges to mush. His department studied the NIB proposals for two years. Finally, a guideline stating that bands were free to create Band Education Authorities was issued, but it ensured that they would have no power. The guideline said, "When a band operates any educational program it must establish guidelines which must be acceptable to the Department."[32] The guideline described the criteria for establishing curricula, for hiring teachers and for the spending of money. It clearly stated that the funding necessary to create adult-education programs, cultural centres and to adequately subsidize university tuitions would not be forthcoming. The response to the NIB proposals meant that progress toward truly attaining what Chrétien had promised would proceed at an agonizingly slow pace.

While the struggle to improve Native education was being waged, a similar struggle to end the abduction of Native children by provincial social agencies continued. By 1980, over three thousand Native children had been taken. Native leaders had learned the futility of presenting their cases to the federal government, for it had been proven that even when ideas were publicly approved they were not quickly implemented. The new struggle to save the children was fought in the media. The most important public protest was the Indian Child Caravan, organized in 1980 in

Vancouver. Thanksgiving Day, over one thousand people staged a vigil outside the office of British Columbia's minister of human resources. Their plea was simple. They asked that their children be returned and that no more be taken. The action received national attention.

In 1981, leaders of Manitoba's Big Grassy Reserve filed an application in a Winnipeg court to stop the abduction of a child from its community. The application stated that the community would place the child in a safe home, counsel the mother, then return the child to her mother when appropriate. The court was being asked to accept the legitimacy of Native culture and traditions. The court said no. It stated that the band could not be considered a person under the law and, consequently, had no right to apply for custody. The child was taken and placed with non-Native parents.

The Big Grassy decision brought more national attention. The growing media pressure led to more court cases, and other courts began to rule against the continuing abduction of Native children and against those placing Native children with non-Native parents. The associate chief Justice for Manitoba, Edwin Kimelman, called the transfer of Native children to white homes "systemic cultural genocide."[33]

In 1982, a British Columbia Royal Commission on Family and Children's Law examined the practice. Commissioner Honourable Mr. Justice Thomas Berger noted the racism inherent in imposing the white, western style of adoption on Indian bands. His report stated,

> The North American white concept of adoption as a function of child welfare—involving the placing of children with strangers and the complete severing of natural parental ties, including the possibility of inheritance, is a relatively recent development in adoption and seems to reflect the realities of a highly mobile, nuclear-family-oriented, urban, industrial society. To impose this style of adoption on our native Indian population and to call their custom adoptions something less—i.e. guardianship—would be, in our opinion inappropriate.[34]

Later that year, laws were amended in all four western provinces to end the practice of sending Native children out-of-province. The new restrictions were an important first step. They saved many children but did nothing for the thousands who had already been taken and nothing for the families that had been shattered. One of the organizers of the Vancouver Indian Child Caravan had been the Spallumcheen band chief, Wayne Christian. In the 1960s, he and his brother had been among the stolen children. At age seventeen, his brother had found his way back to his reserve. After years in a white community, with white foster parents, he felt adrift between two worlds. One night he shot and killed himself. He was one of many.

By the mid-1980s, it had become commonly accepted that the child abduction programs had seriously, and in many cases irreparably, damaged a generation of Native children. In crippling the Native family structures the practise had done terrible harm to Native communities already damaged by generations of residential schooling. In 1985, Judge Kimelman wrote,

> The evidence would indicate they [Native parents] were correct in their claim that not only were those children lost to their own communities, the lives of the individual children were seriously and permanently impaired.... The cultural bias in the system for the past 40 years had made native people victims.[35]

Canada was waking up. Studies addressing Native education, social services, alcohol and drug abuse and other topics were beginning to create an overall picture of a people in crisis. Increasing numbers of journalists and government officials were publicly admitting the culpability of the dominant white culture and the role of systemic racism in creating and perpetuating the crisis. Meanwhile, in the eye of this and other changes, one of the most crucial segments of any democratic state was mired in eighteenth-century thinking.

•

What is left of a democracy when the rule of law is based upon race? The growth of political activism in the 1960s led to increasing numbers of questions being asked about the Canadian justice system, from the police officer on the beat to the state's highest courts. A number of provincial studies sought to discover reasons for the disproportionate number of Native people in prison. A 1969 Manitoba study, for example, noted that while Native people made up only four percent of Winnipeg's population they made up twenty-three percent of its inmate population. For too long, these and other statistics were dismissed as evidence that Native people were more criminally oriented than non-Native people. The same argument had been used to explain the number of African Americans in prisons and the number of non-whites incarcerated in South Africa. Thinking people knew there was more to the numbers.

The growing attention paid to racial matters in the late 1960s and early 1970s led the Canadian media to begin reporting improprieties in the justice system that were the obvious manifestation of systemic racism. The *Toronto Telegram* reported in October 1970, for instance, that Ontario judges were notorious for sentencing Native people far more harshly than white people. It noted many cases, including a young Native woman sentenced to six to twelve months and another to six to nine months for being drunk in a public place and breaking a window. To that point neither had a criminal record. Despite the Ontario bail reform act, a northern Ontario Native man spent nineteen days in jail awaiting trial for stealing thirty-nine cents' worth of bologna. A Kenora judge named J.V. Fregan, who also happened to be the city's former mayor, said in 1970 that he treated Native people differently from whites as a matter of course, explaining, "The Indian here is a different breed of cat.... I know jail doesn't seem to do any good, but it takes them out of circulation."[36] Two years later, Sudbury judge George Collins warned a Native youth in his court to avoid growing up to become "another stupid Indian of which we have plenty."[37] Dr. Howard Adams of the University of Saskatchewan observed that "The farther north you go, the more colonial and racist the police and judicial system becomes. In one far northern community the judge sentenced so many Natives to jail in one day that it took three days to transport them to the jail."[38] The media pressure on the government to admit that something was seriously wrong continued to build.

The Trudeau government invited two hundred Native and non-Native delegates to meet in Ottawa in 1975. The National Conference on Native Peoples and the Criminal Justice System intended to get to the bottom of the crisis. It discovered what Native people had known for generations. It found that the Canadian justice system was laced with anti-Native racism. Its fifty-eight recommendations included hiring more Native police officers, making allowances for cultural differences in prisons and affording Native nations more control over local systems of justice. The report was accepted, publicized in the media, then largely ignored. As in other matters, the wheels of change in the Department of Indian Affairs moved with glacial speed.

The need to end the systemic discrimination that riddled Canada's justice system was forced to the public's attention by several highly publicized cases. Three were of special significance. The first involved a teenaged Cree girl named Helen Betty Osborne. The high school student lived in the mill town of The Pas, Manitoba. One November evening in 1971, Osborne was walking home when she was forced into a car by four white men. She was raped by each in turn while the others watched, drank and laughed. She was stabbed more than fifty times with a screwdriver and dumped in the bush outside of town to die. Whispers around town indicated that everyone seemed to know who the four were. At a party, two of the men retold the story of the rape and murder to laughter and applause. Police conducted a cursory investigation and let the matter drop. Few were surprised that the killing of a Native girl commanded so little attention in a town where, at the time of the murder, many movie theatres, restaurants, hotels and even school cafeterias were still segregated and police brutality against Native people was still the norm.

Osborne's family, and others, maintained pressure to reopen the case. Finally, sixteen years later, a woman came forward, willing to testify that she had heard the murderers bragging about their activities. A new investigation led to an arrest and trial. Two of the four were charged. The third was granted immunity for helping with the investigation and the fourth was not charged. Only one of the four, Dwayne Archie Johnston, was convicted, but only of second-degree murder. In 1991, a massive study led by Justice Alexander Hamilton and Judge Murray Sinclair investigated the treatment of Native people by the Manitoba justice system. It examined the case and concluded that Betty Osborne was attacked because she was Native, the police failed to act because she was Native, and the long-delayed trial convicted only one of her murderers because she was Native.

The second influential case involved John Joseph Harper. In

1988, J.J. Harper was the executive director of the Island Lake Tribal Council in northern Manitoba. One March night, Winnipeg constable Robert Cross was looking for a car thief. The suspect was a slim, Native twenty-two-year-old. The first Native person Cross saw was the heavily built, thirty-six-year-old Harper, who was quietly walking home. Cross stopped Harper, demanded identification, began a barrage of questions, then grabbed Harper's arm and began to force him away. Harper refused to cooperate and a struggle ensued. Cross drew his gun and fired. Harper died at the scene.

A quick investigation concluded that Cross had done nothing wrong, but once again Native leaders were not satisfied. A new investigation was convened. This time it was revealed that Constable Cross knew before the confrontation occurred that the car thief had already been apprehended and also knew who Harper was. It was divulged that a number of police officers held dangerously racist views regarding Native people. The inquiry found that many officers had laughed about Harper's death and the first, white-washed investigation. A joke among police officers asked, "How do you wink at an Indian?" The answer was a gesture indicating the pulling of a trigger.[39]

The 1991 Hamilton-Sinclair investigation looked at the Harper case and concluded that, as in the Osborne case, Harper's murder and the shoddy investigation that followed were the result of a systemically racist justice system. The investigation found that Native people in Manitoba had for decades received longer sentences than white people when convicted of similar crimes. It found that from 1926 to 1957, when capital punishment was legal in Canada, those found guilty of killing a white person were executed twenty-six percent of the time if the murderer was also white but ninety-six percent of the time if the murderer was Native. The report stated that "In almost every aspect of our legal system, the treatment of aboriginal people is tragic.... we marvel at the degree to which aboriginal people have endured, and continue to endure what the justice system is doing to them."[40]

The third case that brought Canada's racist justice system to national attention involved a seventeen-year-old Mic Mac named Donald Marshall, Jr. Marshall was the son of the grand chief of the Mic Mac nation and next in line for that honoured, spiritual position. Around midnight on May 28, 1971, Marshall was walking through Wentworth Park in Sydney, Nova Scotia. He was with a seventeen-year-old Black youth named Sandy Seal, whom he had just met at a local bar. Marshall and Seal encountered two white men named Roy Ebsary and Jimmy MacNeill and asked them for money. Ebsary drew a knife and lunged into Seal, yelling, "This is for you, Black man!" Marshall ran to the police and reported the crime. The police took his statement and dismissed him. They did not secure the murder scene, search for witnesses or gather physical evidence. Sergeant of Detectives John McIntyre had already decided that Marshall was the murderer.

Marshall was arrested, quickly tried, and convicted. The Crown attorney was Donald MacNeil (no relation to Jimmy), who had once been reprimanded by the Nova Scotia Human Rights Commission for making racist statements about Mic Mac people. The all-white jury had been convinced by the testimony of the police and especially by two eyewitnesses who claimed to have seen Marshall kill Seal. Marshall proclaimed his innocence but was sent to prison. Two weeks after the trial, Jimmy MacNeill approached the police to turn in his friend. The RCMP conducted a new investigation but concluded that MacNeill was lying and that the initial police investigation and the testimony given at the trial, were sound. Marshall refused to rest. Psychologists promised him an early parole if he would admit his guilt, but he stubbornly refused to concede.

Finally, after eleven years, Marshall's attorney convinced the RCMP to convene another investigation. This time a proper review was conducted. RCMP officer Maynard was outraged to find that the Sydney police had ignored not only MacNeil, but also Ebsary's daughter, who had come to them two days after the murder claiming that she had seen her father discussing the incident with MacNeill while cleaning blood from his knife. Maynard was similarly shocked to find that the trial's two eyewitnesses had been selected and then coached by Sgt. McIntyre and had not even been in the park that night. Maynard then found that fibres still on Epsary's knife matched fibres from Seal's jacket. Epsary was arrested and convicted. After eleven years in prison for a murder that he did not commit, Donald Marshall was released.

In 1988, Nova Scotia created a Royal Commission to investigate the Donald Marshall case. Chair Alexander Hickman found that the Marshall case was unique only in its extremity, for it betrayed the racism that was rife in the province's justice system. He noted that

Police Sergeant of Detectives McIntyre "...shared what we believe was a general sense in Sydney's White community at the time that Indians were not 'worth' as much as Whites."[41] Racism, according to the Royal Commission, was at the root of Donald Marshall's misfortune and at the root of the mistreatment of all Native people in the province.

The Osborne, Harper and Marshall cases drew attention to the anti-Native racism that was rife in the justice system just as the shootings of young Blacks in Toronto and Montreal and racial violence in Halifax were hitting the front pages. Systemic racism became impossible to dismiss or ignore. A number of police departments were pressured into hiring more visible minorities and including anti-racism courses as part of training programs. Judges were increasingly held up for scrutiny by their peers, the media and ethnic-based interest groups regarding decisions that even hinted at racial bias. Native cultural traditions such as the sweat lodge and sweet grass were allowed to enter a number of prisons. The changes were halting half-steps but they were hopeful.

The positive trend indicated by these decisions and actions continued. Perhaps the most significant changes involved Native children. Native communities persisted in their struggle to wrest control of their children from the government and progress was made with respect to both schools and social services. The last residential school closed its doors, more on-reserve schools opened and children everywhere benefitted from more liberal curricula and non-racist learning resources.

In 1994, Donna Lewis and Dianne Marie sued the RCMP and the British Columbia Ministry of Social Services. In the 1960s, both women had been taken from their families and placed with federal government employee John Lewis. The girls were routinely physically and sexually abused. Lewis confessed to his crimes and the women won a settlement of $100,000.

This case is important beyond the settlement for the proceedings had revealed that the Ministry of Social Services had known about the abuse of Lewis and Marie but had done nothing. Officials had also known about the abuse of thousands of other children stolen and placed in foster care but had rarely acted to save them. Further, the case had brought to national attention a 1990 survey of B.C. treatment centres which showed that eighty-five percent of Native children sent to foster care were sexually abused by their foster parents.[42] The case also led to a revisiting of the 1981 Auditor General's report which had criticized the federal government for its long-standing practice of confiscating the unclaimed estates of status Indians even when it was known that the deceased's children were probably alive but simply lost in the sloppy record keeping of provincial social service departments that had stolen the children in the first place.

The momentum for change had grown with Oka, constitutional battles that first ignored then included Native concerns, well publicized court cases and Supreme Court decisions, the growing knowledge of, and disgust with, residential schools and the Sixties Scoop, and the confrontational media grabbing tactics of grand chief of the Assembly of First Nations Ovide Mercredi. The momentum was also maintained by Native people at a grassroots level. On a cool afternoon in October 1995, for example, the Vancouver sky was a deep, cloudless blue. Outside Main Street's Heritage Hall, hundreds of white balloons dotted the sky sailing toward the mountains. Upon each balloon was printed the name of a son, a daughter, a brother or a sister who had been stolen and lost. The tears of the Native people watching the balloons slowly fade from view made it clear that the struggle for justice would not and could not end.

Progress was made when, in 1996, the British Columbia government finally surrendered to pressure and passed the Child and Welfare Community Services Act. Among the Act's changes to existing legislation was a legal necessity to consult Native bands about any actions regarding the children in their communities. The Sixties Scoop was over.

More progress was made with the publication of the *Report of the Royal Commission on Aboriginal Peoples* in November 1996. The report made 440 recommendations and was the result of an exhaustive study in which the federal government, for the first time, involved not only the broader community but also Native communities in an investigation of the history of the Native experience in Canada, the current state of Native issues, and suggestions for the future. The report was shocking to those who had been blind to those matters as it tore open the curtains and let light shine on the ugliness of the systemic racism of Canada's past and the tragic legacy of that past on current Native communities. With respect to Native children the report said,

Their numbers in the population of today and their role in shaping and leading their communities and nations tomorrow make it essential for governments—aboriginal and non-aboriginal alike—to listen to their concerns and act on their priorities.... They are the current generation paying the price of cultural genocide, racism and poverty, suffering the effects of years of colonialism and public policies.[43]

For over a year, Native leaders negotiated with Department of Indian Affairs officials regarding what to do with the report. Finally, in January 1998, Minister of Indian Affairs and Northern Development Jane Stewart appeared at an Ottawa press conference to outline an action plan. Stewart prefaced her remarks with an apology to Native people for the years of systemic racism and attempted cultural genocide against which Native people had struggled. Two months later the federal government placed full page advertisements in newspapers across the country to publicize the plan which was entitled *Gathering Strength: Canada's Aboriginal Action Plan*. The advertisement quoted the document and said in part

The government of Canada today formally expresses to all Aboriginal people our profound regret for past actions of the federal government which have contributed to these difficult pages in the history of our relationship together.... Particularly to those individuals who experienced the tragedy of sexual and physical abuse at residential schools, and who have carried this burden believing that in some way they must be responsible, we wish to emphasize that what you experienced was not your fault and should never have happened. To those of you who suffered this tragedy at residential schools, we are deeply sorry.[44]

At the January press conference, recently elected grand chief of the Assembly of First Nations Phil Fontaine had cried. At age seven Fontaine had been taken to the residential school at Fort Alexander, Manitoba where he was beaten and sexually abused by the priests. He said that the apology, the program of renewal, and the $350 million healing fund was a good beginning. He praised the agreed upon process of implementation as a turning away from the paternalism of the past to a new future based upon the realization that success depended on a partnership between Native communities and the federal government and an acknowledgment that Native people must begin to make changes within themselves and their communities for substantive progress to be made.

In 1999, the largest land claim settlement in the planet's history saw the creation of Nunavut in the eastern portion of the Northwest Territories. Its creation and the progress that created it represents the boldest step yet toward Native self-government. Nunavut is yet another indication that the Canadian state is stepping off the racist ladder.

Much remains to be done. Statistics regarding Native alcohol and drug abuse, domestic violence, school drop out and incarceration rates, unemployment, and more, remain staggering. But perhaps someday hope will overtake desperation in Native communities. Perhaps that struggle is best fought one community, one family, or even one child at a time. Today over fifty-six percent of Native people are under the age of twenty-four. In this fact alone there is hope for one must always have faith in the children.

Epilogue

Building a Non-Racist Future

We must learn to live together as brothers
or perish together as fools.
—Martin Luther King

The six stories told in this book suggest that Canada has moved up and down the racist ladder. Since the Second World War, systemic racism has been increasingly under attack. Ideas essential to systemic racism, such as ethnic allegiance and social Darwinism, are still among us but have fallen into disfavour. There is a great deal about which Canadians can be proud. Native leaders have forced negotiations to recognize the legitimacy of Native culture, treaties and land claims. Cultural genocide no longer appears to be the government's goal. Immigration policies are no longer based upon race, and, while changes will always be made, it is highly unlikely that the exclusion or expulsion of entire racial groups will again be seen. Racial segregation laws have been expunged. Section 15 of the Canadian Charter of Rights and Freedoms guarantees citizens protection from discrimination based on race, national or ethnic origin, colour or religion. The clause is backed by provincial human rights codes and anti-discrimination legislation. According to sections 318 and 319 of the Criminal Code, it is illegal to incite hatred against identifiable groups.

All social institutions have played roles in the movement down the ladder. Unions have largely abandoned racist restrictions on membership. Major newspapers and magazines have adopted more tolerant editorial stances, and racial stereotypes and prejudiced beliefs are now more likely to be attacked than sanctioned. Churches have apologized for encouraging and dignifying racial intolerance through their role in Native residential schools. Provincial and territorial education ministries now have processes for reviewing textbooks and other resources and keep those betraying racist ideas or biases from the classrooms. The RCMP has apologized for infiltrating and attempting to undermine Black political action groups in the 1960s and 1970s. Many political leaders have expressed shame for the manner in which previous governments treated racial minorities. Prime Minister Mulroney, for example, extended an official apology and financial compensation to the descendants of Japanese Canadians mistreated in the Second World War. In 1994, Secretary of State for Multiculturalism Sheila Finestone admitted that many ethnic groups had suffered under Canada's systemically racist state but that to compensate them all would bankrupt the country. They would have to be satisfied with her acknowledgement and blanket apology. Native leaders accepted the 1998 apology of the Canadian government extended to all Native peoples by Minister of Indian Affairs and Northern Development Jane Stewart.

Historical plaques, museum exhibits and statues testifying to the important contributions made to Canada's development by groups and individuals of racial minorities can now be found across the country. Textbooks and new curricula, while still largely Euro-centred, are also increasingly acknowledging those contributions. Growing numbers of people from racial minorities are being elected and appointed to the country's highest political offices, earning positions of economic power, and contributing to Canada's intellectual, athletic and cultural wealth. Their ancestors, many of whom had the talent but not the opportunity to enjoy similar achievements, would be proud.

However, while Canada has stepped down the racist ladder, it has not stepped off. There remain obvious and significant economic, political and social advantages to being white, Christian and either French in Quebec or British in the rest of the country. A random poll of ten Ontario employment agencies conducted in September 1992 showed that seven categorized clients according to race and referred only white clients to prospective employers. Similar findings in previous polls indicate that the racist categorization has been happening since employment agency polls began in the 1970s.[1] Following a 1992 investigation of the beliefs and behaviour of Metropolitan Toronto police officers, Metro Toronto auditor Allan Andrews found the force rife with racism. His report stated, "These attitudes, when taken collectively, can and do produce a bias in behaviour which produces unequal treatment of individuals of different cultural or racial backgrounds."[2] A 1993 study made similar observations about the Montreal Police Department.[3] A number of investigations, including the 1991 Hamilton-Sinclair report, argued that race continues to matter in courts across the country. A federal task force on race relations reported in 1991 that an overwhelming majority of francophone and, to a lesser but still significant extent, anglophone Quebecers support laws and regulations that are racist in their nature and intent. The report stated that "Proposals for separate schools for immigrants, barring the use of all languages other than French on school property and limiting immigration to those of European and Judaeo-Christian backgrounds are just a few of the ignobilities minorities experience in Quebec."[4] Comments made by Parti Québécois officials during the 1995 referendum campaign indicated that Quebec nationalism still had room for those believing that none but "pure wool" Québécois could be real Quebecers. Quebec premier Jacques Parizeau let the Quebec nationalist's racist cat out the bag when, on the evening his side lost the referendum, he blamed that loss on "money and the ethnic vote." Meanwhile, a United Nations report issued in 1994 praised Canada for taking steps to eliminate racial discrimination but criticized the slowness of the anti-racism process. It observed that African and Asian immigrants and Native people still suffer from many manifestations of racial discrimination.[5]

We remain on the racist ladder because prejudice, stereotypes and discrimination remain firmly entrenched in Canadian society. They are the legacy of over a century of systemic racism. A nationwide poll conducted in February 1993 suggested that one out of every four Canadians holds intolerant views with respect to race. The Angus Reid–Southam poll found that fifty-seven percent of Canadians believed that minority groups should forget their native language and culture. Further, twenty-six percent believed that non-white people damage the fabric of the country.[6] Racist jokes are still told. Popular culture continues to perpetuate stereotypes. Prejudice and stereotypes still lead to acts of vandalism and physical and psychological violence. Too many blatantly racist incidents are still tolerated. For example, in the winter of 1992, twelve- and thirteen-year-old hockey players from Thompson, Manitoba, arrived in Quebec City to participate in a hockey tournament. Tournament organizers noticed that the team had six Native players and refused to billet them in the city. Organizer Alex Legare explained, "Would you have them in your home?"[7]

It is clear that while much has been done to rid Canada of racism, we have much left to do. Our first task must be to stop deluding ourselves. For too long Canadians have been like children pressing our noses against the American display window, repulsed by much of what we see but unable to tear ourselves away, yet sanctimonious in our belief that we are not like them. We are like them. With respect to race relations, we have been like them and others who harbour a racist past and a legacy of systemic racism that influences the future.

Political and social leaders must be taken to task when they attempt to perpetuate old lies. Minister of Indian Affairs and Northern Development Tom Siddon should have been challenged, for example, when in the midst of the stand-off at Oka, Quebec, in 1990 he said,

> Our country has an outstanding record of human rights. Our country has an unblemished record of standing up for the underprivileged and oppressed everywhere in the world. We're a pluralistic society...[extending] hospitality to all races and colours.[8]

Schools must play a role in helping us to face our past and build our future. Curricula that enable children to learn the real and complete history of Canada must continue to be written. The significant roles played by non-English, non-French individuals and groups must be explored and celebrated. The systemic racism that tainted Canada's development, giving rise to race riots, segregation, discriminatory laws and more, should be examined. The events and ideas should not be presented as evidence of a bad country ashamed of its past but of a great country with sufficient maturity to admit and learn from its mistakes.

While confessing our past, let us concede the present. Let us admit to the racism that still surrounds us. Amy Go became president of the Chinese Canadian National Council in 1991. She agreed that the first step in fighting racism is admitting that it exists. She argued,

We cannot ignore the fact that for visible minorities, our physical appearances, our skin colour, accent or cultural background, plays a major part in influencing every aspect of our lives—educational opportunities, employment, housing and so on…. Our goal is for society as a whole to see racism as a problem to be confronted.[9]

All of Canada's social organizations should play active roles in this effort. The media should continue to lash out against racist activities and ideas. Politicians should keep racial tolerance on the political agenda and continue to develop stronger anti-discriminatory legislation. Large and small businesses should refrain from discriminatory hiring and promotion practices and join consumers in boycotting those that perpetrate them. Organized labour should invite membership regardless of race and expose incidents of racism in the workplace. Once again, schools have a role to play. For some time now progressive schools have been teaching students to become media literate. Anti-racism should be incorporated into these programs. They should enable students to identify racism, while imbuing them with the values and intellectual tools to fight it.

With our past revealed and our present accepted, our future may be planned. We must dare to be idealistic. A non-racist society must be our goal. Young people are the key. Churches can work with schools to encourage young people to share the goal and work to attain it. Churches and schools can reach into communities by opening their buildings to young people and empowering them to develop programs to fill empty evenings and weekends. Racism can be attacked by having young people see themselves as united by similar concerns rather than divided by race.

Ethnic communities also have important roles to play. Prime Minister Trudeau declared Canada a multicultural state and created a multiculturalism ministry. Ministry funding allowed many ethnic groups to build or augment already-existing cultural centres and to organise festivals and special events to celebrate cultural uniqueness. Perhaps the ministry and some groups missed the point. Too often the cultural centres and activities emphasized differences in diet, dress and dance while ignoring the fact that people of all races share similar fears, strengths and aspirations. Everyone wants to raise his or her children in safe neighbourhoods and see that they have opportunities to follow dreams and fulfil their potentials in fair and just ways. It is essential that people learn about and feel pride in their cultural heritage. Perhaps it is time, however, that unity is promoted as a goal of diversity rather than diversity existing as an end unto itself.

The wheels of progress are greased with blood and bullshit. To create a non-racist society we must boldly tackle both. Racist violence will occur, but it must be branded for what it is and not dismissed as hooliganism, as the result of television or music, or some other easy excuse. If racist hatred is the reason for violence, then let that reason be stated clearly. Let community leaders work together with those involved to address the problem at its root and fight the emotions that feed racism by attacking the ignorance upon which they are based. It is the frightful combination of ignorance and emotion that forms the wall upon which the racist ladder rests, and without them it will fall.

Those who seek to become social or political leaders by slyly appealing to racist passions must be exposed and rejected. Appeals to curb immigration, to protect and preserve the Canadian way of life, to protect jobs from outsiders and to cut foreign aid attract those with racist beliefs. Political parties and social groups must be scrutinized carefully to discern whether thinly veiled racist ideas are being promoted by racist people to attract racist followers. In scrutinizing them, however, we must not become so entangled in our political correctness that some topics become unavailable for discussion. All racists, for instance, want to restrict immigration, but all those who discuss immigration are not racists.

In creating a non-racist future we must become sensitive to the possibility of a backlash in which attempts to end racism result in increased racial intolerance. This backlash may be part of the price paid for the shift from the promotion of racial integration to the sponsorship of that in addition to anti-racism. Patience and sensitivity must be our guides. Those fighting racism must not paranoically see enemies everywhere. For example, employment equity legislation is sometimes necessary to allow those of racial minorities to gain access to certain occupations or to smash the glass ceilings that link promotions to race. We must be diligent, however, in seeing that hiring and promotion regulations do not become racism in reverse. We must not forget merit. We must not insult ourselves by believing that every time a person from a racial minority group loses a job or promotion, is arrested or faces any of a myriad of circumstances attendant to everyday life, that a racist act has occurred.

No one knows if it is possible to create a non-racist society. We have no models. Canada has descended the racist ladder by dismantling many of the manifestations of systemic racism but remains perched upon it. The last steps to freedom will be Canada's final steps off the ladder. Only when those steps have been taken will people of ethnic minorities be free from the indignities and social and economic barriers that racism perpetuates. Only then will they will be free to fully participate in society and, in so doing, make even more significant contributions to its greatness. The last steps will enable Canada to achieve national maturity as a free and democratic society true to its constitution and its ideals.

We cannot take the last steps to freedom until we agree that the creation of a non-racist state is worth the effort. If a large proportion of Canadians continue to believe that people can be judged according to their race, then we are doomed. We will live in a society that is weakened because it allows only a few to fulfil their potential and contribute their talents to the greater good. We will live in a society fractured by suspicion and poisoned by hatred. We will live in fear of racial violence. Sadly, unless we continue to pursue the ideal of a non-racist society we will continue to believe that in creating some people, the Creator made a mistake.

Endnotes

Chapter One

1. Douglas Hill, *The Opening of the Canadian West*, p. 96.
2. James Morton, *In the Seas of Sterile Mountains*, p. 3.
3. W. Peter Ward, *White Canada Forever*, p. 27.
4. Edgar Wickberg, *From China to Canada*, p. 18.
5. *Report of the Royal Commission on Chinese Immigration*, 1885, p. xviii.
6. Ward, *White Canada Forever*, p. 11.
7. Wickberg, *From China to Canada*, p. 20.
8. Ward, *White Canada Forever*, p. 27.
9. Ibid.
10. Hill, *The Opening of the Canadian West*, p. 25.
11. Morton, *In the Seas of Sterile Mountains*, p. 6.
12. Ibid., p. 10.
13. Paul Phillips, *No Power Greater: A Century of Labour in B.C.*, p. 168.
14. W. Peter Ward, "The Oriental Immigrant and Canada's Protestant Clergy," *B.C. Studies*, no. 22 (summer 1974): 46.
15. Ibid.
16. Ibid., p. 26.
17. Morton, *In the Seas of Sterile Mountains*, p. 45.
18. Wickberg, *From China to Canada*, p. 45.
19. Ibid., p. 47.
20. Ward, *White Canada Forever*, p. 25.
21. Ibid., p. 11.
22. Wickberg, *From China to Canada*, p. 43.
23. Pierre Berton, *The National Dream*, p. 19.
24. Ward, *White Canada Forever*, p. 27.
25. Berton, *The Last Spike*, p. 197.
26. Wickberg, *From China to Canada*, p. 20.
27. Ibid., p. 49.
28. Berton, *The Last Spike*, p. 198.
29. Ibid.
30. Ibid., p. 202.
31. Ibid.
32. Ibid., p. 206.

5

33. Ibid., p. 204.
34. Ken Adachi, *The Enemy That Never Was: A History of the Japanese Canadians*, p. 39.
35. Wickberg, *From China to Canada*, p. 53.
36. *Report of the Royal Commission on Chinese Immigration*, 1885, p. 68.
37. Ibid., p. 130.
38. Ward, *White Canada Forever*, p. 41.
39. Morton, *In the Seas of Sterile Mountains*, p. 145.
40. Patricia Roy, "The Preservation of the Peace in Vancouver: The Aftermath of the Anti-Chinese Riot of 1887," *B.C. Studies*, no. 31 (autumn 1976): 47.
41. Ibid.
42. Morton, *In the Seas of Sterile Mountains*, pp. 146-47.
43. Ibid., p. 149.
44. Ibid.
45. Roy, "The Preservation of the Peace," p. 51.
46. Ibid., p. 52.
47. Ward, *White Canada Forever*, p. 62.
48. *Report of the Royal Commission on Chinese and Japanese Immigration*, 1902. p. 278.
49. Ward, *White Canada Forever*, p. 62.
50. Adachi, *The Enemy That Never Was*, p. 73.
51. Mary Hallet, "A Governor-General's Views on Oriental Immigration to British Columbia, 1904–1911," *B.C. Studies*, no. 14 (summer 1972): 54.
52. Adachi, *The Enemy That Never Was*, p. 78.
53. Ibid., p. 73.
54. Ibid., p. 74.
55. Ward, *White Canada Forever*, p. 75.
56. Hallet, "A Governor-General's Views," p. 67.
57. Hilda Gynn-Ward, *The Writing on the Wall: Chinese and Japanese Immigration to B.C.*, p. xxii.
58. Patricia Roy, "British Columbia's Fear of Asians 1900–1950," *Histoire-Sociale/Social History* XIII, no. 25 (May 1980): 168.
59. Ward, *White Canada Forever*, p. 124.
60. Patricia Roy, "The Oriental Menace in British Columbia," in *Historical Essays on British Columbia*, ed. J. Frieson and H. Ralston, p. 244.
61. Ibid., p. 246.
62. Ibid.
63. Ward, *White Canada Forever*, p. 70.
64. Gynn-Ward, *The Writing on the Wall*, p. xxii.
65. Roy, "The Oriental Menace," p. 247.
66. Ward, "The Oriental Immigrant," p. 47.
67. Roy, "British Columbia's Fear of Asians," p. 164.
68. Ibid., p. 166.
69. Roy, "The Oriental Menace," p. 250.
70. Roy, "British Columbia's Fear," p. 162.
71. Morton, *In the Seas of Sterile Mountains*, p. 115.
72. Ibid., p. 185.

73. Adachi, *The Enemy That Never Was*, p. 79.
74. Hallet, "A Governor-General's Views," p. 64.
75. Morris Davis and Joseph Krauter, *The Other Canadians: Profiles of Six Minorities*, p. 62.

Chapter Two

1. Vera Lysenko, *Men in Sheepskin Coats: A Study in Assimilation*, p. 32.
2. Howard Palmer, *Patterns of Prejudice: A History of Nativism in Alberta*, pp. 35-38.
3. Lysenko, *Men in Sheepskin Coats*, p. 16.
4. One of Selkirk's men was named Ivan Boyko. I believe I am not related, but who knows?
5. Pylypiw died in 1937 at the age of seventy-seven. He had by that time acquired a great deal of land and wealth. In 1947, he was posthumously honoured in a ceremony declaring him to be only the fourth person granted the newly created Canadian citizenship.
6. Manoly Lupul, *A Heritage in Transition: Essays in the History of Ukrainians in Canada*, p. 42.
7. Michael Marunchak, *The Ukrainian Canadians: A History*, p. 93.
8. One of those men was my great grandfather Roman Czowski. Upon his arrival in Canada, at Montreal, an immigration official gave him the Anglicized name Mallar.
9. Myrna Kostash, *All of Baba's Children*, p. 12.
10. Ibid., p. 37.
11. Jaroslav Petryshyn, *Peasants in the Promised Land: Canada and the Ukrainians*, p. 116.
12. Ibid., p. 95
13. Jaroslav Roaumny, ed., *New Soil—Old Roots: The Ukrainian Experience in Canada*, p. 21.
14. J. Lehr and W. Moodie, "The Polemics of Pioneer Settlement: Ukrainian Immigration and the Winnipeg Press," *Canadian Ethnic Studies*, XII, no. 2. (1980) 92-93.
15. Petryshyn, *Peasants in the Promised Land*, p. 100.
16. Ibid.
17. Roaumny, *New Soil—Old Roots*, p. 21.
18. James S. Woodsworth, *Strangers Within Our Gates*, p. 121.
19. Ibid., p. 136.
20. Petryshyn, *Peasants in the Promised Land: Canada and the Ukrainians*, p. 96.
21. Ibid., p. 95.
22. B. Kordan and L. Lucuik, *A Delicate and Difficult Question: Documents in the History of Ukrainians in Canada*, pp. 19-20.
23. Petryshyn, *Peasants in the Promised Land: Canada and the Ukrainians*, p. 110.
24. Roaumny, *New Soil—Old Roots*, pp. 27-28.
25. Petryshyn, *Peasants in the Promised Land*, p. 105.
26. Ibid., p. 102.
27. Lupul, *A Heritage in Transition*, p. 44.

28. Lysenko, *Men in Sheepskin Coats,* pp. 55-56.
29. Roaumny, *New Soil—Old Roots,* p. 22.
30. Ibid., p. 23.
31. Ibid., p. 25.
32. John Lehr, "Government Perceptions of Ukrainian Immigrants to Western Canada 1896–1902," *Canadian Ethnic Studies,* XIX, no. 2 (1987): 6.
33. Petryshyn, *Peasants in the Promised Land,* p. 89.
34. Kordan and Luciuk, *A Delicate and Difficult Question,* p. 29.
35. Ibid.
36. Ibid.
37. Ibid., p. 30.
38. John Herd Thompson, "The Enemy Alien and the Canadian General Election of 1917," in *Loyalties in Conflict: Ukrainian Canadians During the Great War,* ed. F. Swyripa and J. Thompson, p. 27.
39. F. Swyripa and J. Thompson, J. *Loyalties in Conflict: Ukrainian Canadians During the Great War,* p. 18.
40. Ibid., p. 16.
41. Helen Potrebenko, *No Streets of Gold: A Social History of Ukrainians in Alberta,* p. 124.
42. Swyripa and Thompson, *Loyalties in Conflict,* p. 6.
43. Ibid.
44. Lysenko, *Men in Sheepskin Coats,* pp. 116-17.
45. Swyripa and Thompson, *Loyalties in Conflict,* p. 15.
46. Donald Avery, "Ethnic and Class Tensions in Canada: 1918–1920," in *Loyalties in Conflict: Ukrainian Canadians During the Great War,* ed. F. Swyripa and J. Thompson, p. 85.
47. *Report of the Royal Commission on Bilingualism and Biculturalism,* book IV, 1970, pp. 58-59.

Chapter Three

1. I. Abella and H. Tropper, *None Is Too Many,* p. 64.
2. Irving Abella, *A Coat of Many Colours: Two Centuries of Jewish Life in Canada,* p. 20.
3. Ibid., p. 78.
4. B.G. Sack, *History of the Jews in Canada,* p. 197.
5. Gerald Tulchinsky, "Goldwin Smith: Victorian Liberal Anti-Semite," *The Whig Standard Magazine,* 22 September 1990, p. 5.
6. Yaacov Glickman, *Alberta, Aberhart and the Social Credit,* p. 47.
7. Tulchinsky, "Goldwin Smith," p. 5.
8. Abella, *A Coat of Many Colours,* p. 106.
9. Yaacov Glickman, "Anti-Semitism and Jewish Social Cohesion in Canada," in *Racism in Canada,* ed. Osmond McKague, p. 47
10. David Elliott, "Anti-Semitism and the Social Credit Movement: The Intellectual Roots of the Keegstra Affair," *Canadian Ethnic Studies,* XVII, (1985): 79-80.
11. Ibid., p. 80.

12. Ibid., p. 83.
13. Ibid., p. 81.
14. Michael Ignatieff, *Blood and Belonging: Journeys into the New Nationalism,* p. 8.
15. Abella, *A Coat of Many Colours,* p. 107.
16. Mordecai Richler, *Oh Canada! Oh Quebec! Requiem for a Divided Country,* p. 84.
17. Ibid., p. 245.
18. David Rome, *Clouds in the Thirties: On Anti-Semitism in Canada 1929–1939,* section 1. p, 14.
19. Susan Mann Trofimenkoff, *Abbé Groulx: Variations on a Nationalist Theme,* p. 237.
20. R. Levesque, *An Option for Quebec,* p. 14.
21. Rome, *Clouds in the Thirties,* section 1, p. 92.
22. Ibid., p. 25.
23. Rome, *Clouds in the Thirties,* section 2. p. 1.
24. Ibid., pp. 7-8.
25. Glickman, "Anti-Semitism and Jewish Social Cohesion in Canada," p. 48.
26. Abella, *A Coat of Many Colours,* p. 109.
27. Rome, *Clouds in the Thirties,* section 2, p. 3.
28. Abella, *A Coat of Many Colours,* p. 182.
29. Rome, *Clouds in the Thirties,* section 2, p. 17.
30. Stephen A. Speisman, *The Jews of Toronto: A History to 1937,* p. 333.
31. Rome, *Clouds in the Thirties,* section 2, p. 82.
32. Lita-Rose Betcherman, *The Swastika and the Maple Leaf: Fascist Movements in Canada in the Thirties,* p. 42.
33. Abella, *A Coat of Many Colours,* p. 182.
34. Ibid.
35. Rome, *Clouds in the Thirties,* section 1, p. 76.
36. Ibid., p. 95.
37. Ibid., pp. 101-2.
38. Ibid., p. 92.
39. Peter Desbarats, *René: A Canadian in Search of a Country,* p. 91.
40. Betcherman, *The Swastika and the Maple Leaf,* p. 5.
41. Rome, *Clouds in the Thirties,* section 1, p. 88.
42. Betcherman, *The Swastika and the Maple Leaf,* p. 10.
43. Rome, *Clouds in the Thirties,* section 1, p. 118.
44. Ibid, p. 119.
45. Abella, *A Coat of Many Colours,* p. 180.
46. Arnold Ages, "Anti-Semitism: The Uneasy Calm," *in The Canadian Jewish Mosaic,* ed. M. Weinfeld, M. Shaffir and I. Cotler, p. 388.
47. Joseph Kage, *With Faith and Thanksgiving: The Story of Two Hundred Years,* p. 88.
48. Mary Hallet, "A Governor General's Views on Oriental Immigration to British Columbia, 1904–1911," *B.C. Studies,* 14 (summer 1972): 64.
49. Rome, *Clouds in the Thirties,* section 2, p. 28.
50. Abella, *A Coat of Many Colours,* pp. 36-37.

51. Ibid., p. 9.
52. M. Weinfeld, W. Shaffir, and I. Cotler, eds., *The Canadian Jewish Mosaic*, p. 53.
53. Abella, *A Coat of Many Colours*, p. 16.
54. Ibid., p. 17.
55. Betcherman, *The Swastika and the Maple Leaf*, p. 92.
56. Rome, *Clouds in the Thirties*, section 2, p. 32.
57. Ibid., p. 68.
58. Abella, *A Coat of Many Colours: Two Centuries of Jewish Life in Canada*, p. 59.
59. Ibid., p. 50.
60. Simon Balkin, *Through Narrow Gates: A Review of Jewish Immigration, Colonization and Immigration Aid Work in Canada 1840–1940*, p. 172.
61. Betcherman, *The Swastika and the Maple Leaf*, p. 92.
62. Abella, *A Coat of Many Colours*, p. 39.
63. Ibid., p. 69.
64. Ibid., pp. 136-37.
65. Abella, *A Coat of Many Colours: Two Centuries of Jewish Life in Canada*, p. 206.
66. Robert MacIntosh, *Different Drummers: Banking and Politics in Canada*, p. 135.

Chapter Four

1. Ken Adachi, *The Enemy That Never Was: A History of the Japanese Canadians*, p. 23.
2. Ibid., p. 42.
3. Ann M. Sunahara, *Politics of Racism: The Uprooting of Japanese Canadians During the Second World War*, p. 14.
4. P. Roy, et al., *Mutual Hostages: Canadians and Japanese During the Second World War*, p. 11.
5. Adachi, *The Enemy That Never Was*, p. 142.
6. David Suzuki, *Metamorphosis: Stages in a Life*, p. 53.
7. Adachi, *The Enemy That Never Was*, pp. 144-45.
8. Roy, et al., *Mutual Hostages*, pp. 20-21.
9. Lawrence Martin, *The Presidents and the Prime Ministers: Washington and Ottawa Face to Face: The Myth of Bilateral Bliss, 1867–1982*, p. 136.
10. Roy, et al., *Mutual Hostages*, p. 37.
11. P. Roy, "A Tale of Two Cities: The Reception of Japanese Evacuees in Kelowna and Kaslo, B.C.," p. 43.
12. Adachi, *The Enemy That Never Was*, pp. 190-91.
13. Ibid., p. 191.
14. Roy, et al., *Mutual Hostages*, p. 79.
15. Suzuki, *Metamorphosis*, p. 53.
16. Adachi, *The Enemy That Never Was*, p. 201.
17. Peter W. Ward, "British Columbia and the Japanese Evacuation," *Canadian Historical Review*, 57, no. 3 (September 1976): 289-90.
18. Sunahara, *Politics of Racism*, p. 24.

19. Ibid., p. 33.
20. Roy, et al., *Mutual Hostages*, p. 83.
21. Janice Patton,*The Exodus of the Japanese*, p. 13.
22. Barry Broadfoot, *Years of Sorrow, Years of Shame: The Story of the Japanese Canadians in WWII*, p. 94.
23. Adachi, *The Enemy That Never Was*, p. 242.
24. Roy, et al., *Mutual Hostages*, p. 193.
25. Patton, *The Exodus of the Japanese*, p. 26.
26. Roy, "A Tale of Two Cities," p. 32.
27. Adachi, *The Enemy That Never Was*, p. 266.
28. Ibid., p. 286.
29. *Peterborough Examiner*, 27 February 1992.
30. Sunahara, *Politics of Racism*, p. 98.
31. Roy, et al., *Mutual Hostages*, pp. 160-61.
32. Joy Kogawa, *Obasan*, p. 185.
33. Roy, et al., *Mutual Hostages*, p. 175.
34. Adachi, *The Enemy That Never Was*, p. 311.
35. Roy, et al., *Mutual Hostages*, p. 174.

Chapter Five

1. Bruce R. Shepard, "Plain Racism: The Reaction Against Oklahoma Black Immigration to the Canadian Plains," in *Racism in Canada*, ed. Ormond McKague, p. 94.
2. Walter Stewart, *But Not in Canada!*, p. 42.
3. J. Cook and B. Britton, "The Black Canadian," *Maclean's*, XXIII, no. 1 (16 February 1911): 43.
4. Harold Martin Troper, "The Creek-Negroes of Oklahoma and Canadian Immigration, 1909–1911," *Canadian Historical Review*, LIII, no. 3 (September 1972): 281.
5. Shepard, "Plain Racism," p. 24.
6. Ibid., p. 22.
7. Ibid., p. 19.
8. Ibid., p. 16.
9. Troper, "The Creek-Negroes of Oklahoma and Canadian Immigration," p. 273.
10. Shepard, "Plain Racism," p. 17.
11. Troper, "The Creek-Negroes of Oklahoma and Canadian Immigration," p. 272.
12. Ibid., p. 277.
13. Ibid.
14. Ibid., p. 284.
15. Ibid., p. 287.
16. Shepard, "Plain Racism: The Reaction Against Oklahoma Black Immigration," p. 29.
17. Ibid.
18. James Walker, "Race and Recruitment in WWI: Enlistment of the Visible

Minorities in the Canadian Expeditionary Force," *Canadian Historical Review*, LXX, no. 70 (1989): 5.

19. Ibid., p. 11.
20. A. Calliste, "Sleeping Car Porters in Canada: An Ethnically Submerged Split Labour Market," *Canadian Ethnic Studies*, XIX, no. 1 (1987): 5
21. Headley Tulloch, *Black Canadians: A Long Line of Fighters*, p. 126.
22. Calliste, "Sleeping Car Porters in Canada," p. 5.
23. Ibid., p. 10.
24. Ibid., p. 13.
25. Tulloch, *Black Canadians*, p. 131.
26. Morris Davis and Joseph Krauter, *The Other Canadians: Profiles of Six Minorities*, p. 48.
27. Colin Thomson, *Born with a Call: A Biography of Dr. William Pearly Oliver, C.M.*, p. 84.
28. Robin Winks, "The Canadian Negro," *The Journal of Negro History*, LIII, no. 4 (October 1968): 295.
29. Adrienne Shadd, "Institutional Racism and Canadian History: Notes of a Black Canadian," in *Racism in Canada*, ed. Ormond McKague, p. 1.
30. Thomson, *Born with a Call*, p. 58.
31. Ibid., p. 64.
32. Ibid., p. 63.
33. Valerie Knowles, *Strangers at Our Gates: Canadian Immigration and Immigration Policy*, p. 85.
34. Davis and Krauter, *The Other Canadians*, p. 42.
35. Stewart, *But Not in Canada!*, p. 49.
36. Tulloch, *Black Canadians: A Long Line of Fighters*, p. 182.
37. Stewart, *But Not in Canada*, p. 52.
38. Ibid., p. 53.
39. Thomson, *Born with a Call*, p. 58.
40. Ibid., p. 98.
41. Ibid.
42. John Sawatsky, *Mulroney: The Politics of Ambition*, p. 94.
43. Donald Clairmont and Dennis Magill, *Africville: The Life and Death of a Canadian Black Community*, p. 68.
44. Ibid., p. 64.
45. Ibid.
46. Ibid., p. 151.
47. Ibid., p. 188.
48. Charles Saunders, *Africville: A Spirit That Lives On*, p. 18.

Chapter Six

1. Brian Titley, *A Narrow Vision: Duncan Campbell Scott and the Administration of Indian Affairs in Canada*, p. 34.
2. S.D. Grant, "Indian Affairs Under Duncan Campbell Scott: The Plains Cree of Saskatchewan," *Journal of Canadian Studies*, 18, no. 3 (fall 1983): 34.
3. Harold Cardinal, *The Unjust Society*, p. 28.

4. James Frideres, *Native People in Canada: Contemporary Conflicts*, p. 6.
5. James Tobias, "Canada's Subjugation of the Plains Cree, 1879–1885," *Canadian Historical Review*, LXIV (December 1983): 199.
6. J.R. Miller, *Skyscrapers Hide the Heavens: A History of Indian-White Relations in Canada*, p. 189.
7. Ibid., p. 191.
8. Ibid.
9. Ibid.
10. Ibid., p. 196.
11. Geoffrey York, *The Dispossessed: Life and Death in Native Canada*, p. 24.
12. Basil Johnston, *Indian School Days*, p. 7.
13. P.R. Bowles, et al., *The Indian: Assimilation, Integration or Separation*, p. 13
14. Cardinal, *TheUnjust Society*, p. 87
15. P. Comeau and A. Santin, *The First Canadians: A Profile of Canada's Native People Today*, p. 12.
16. *Saturday Night*, November 1959.
17. Bowles, et al., *The Indian*, p. 38.
18. Comeau and Santin, *The First Canadians*, p. 111.
19. Patrick Johnston, *Native Children and the Child Welfare System*, p. 23.
20. Comeau and Santin, *The First Canadians*, pp. 5-6.
21. *The Statement of the Government of Canada on Indian Policy*, p. 2.
22. Comeau and Santin, *The First Canadians*, p. 16.
23. Ibid., p. 13.
24. Waubageshig, ed., *The Only Good Indian*, p. 14.
25. Cardinal, *The Unjust Society*, p. 161.
26. Comeau and Santin, *The First Canadians*, p. 7.
27. Jean Chrétien, *Straight from the Heart*, p. 59.
28. Ibid., p. 58.
29. Waubageshig, *The Only Good Indian*, p. 65.
30. H.B. Hawthorne, ed., *A Survey of the Contemporary Indians of Canada: Economic, Political, Educational Needs and Policies*, p. 23.
31. Cardinal, *The Unjust Society*, p. 59.
32. Ibid., p. 84.
33. Comeau and Santin, *The First Canadians*, p. 110.
34. Johnston, *Native Children and the Child Welfare System*, p. 72.
35. Comeau and Santin, *The First Canadians*, p. 121.
36. *Toronto Telegram*, 26 October 1970.
37. *Globe and Mail*, 16 April 1972.
38. *Toronto Star*, 21October 1972.
39. *Toronto Star*, 29 August 1991.
40. *Winnipeg Free Press*, 30 August 1991.
41. Alexander Hickman, *Royal Commission on the Donald Marshall Jr. Prosecution: Digest of Findings and Recommendations*, 1989, p. 3.
42. S. Fournier and E. Crey, *Stolen From Our Embrace*, p. 121.
43. *Report of the Royal Commission on Aboriginal Peoples*, p. 156.
44. *Toronto Star*, 25 March 1998.

Epilogue

1. *Toronto Star*, 8 September 1992.
2. Ibid., 3 September 1992.
3. *Maclean's*, 1 August 1994.
4. *Peterborough Examiner*, 25 March 1991.
5. *Toronto Star*, 23 August 1994.
6. *Peterborough Examiner*, 11 April 1993.
7. Ibid., 29 October 1992.
8. J. Rick Ponting, "Internationalization: Perspectives on an Emerging Direction in Aboriginal Affairs," *Canadian Ethnic Studies* 22, no. 3 (1990): 99.
9. *Toronto Star*, 29 April 1991.

Bibliography

The following represents a sampling of the most helpful resources consulted in the preparation of this book. It is organized chapter by chapter to assist those who wish to indulge their curiosity by consulting any of the resources listed to investigate a particular area of interest.

Chapter One

Abella, Irving, and David Millar, eds. *The Canadian Worker in the Twentieth Century*. Toronto: Oxford University Press, 1978.

Adachi, Ken. *The Enemy That Never Was: A History of the Japanese Canadians*. Toronto: McClelland and Stewart Ltd., 1976.

Berton, Pierre. *The Last Spike*. Toronto: McClelland and Stewart Ltd., 1971.

———. *The National Dream*. Toronto: McClelland and Stewart Ltd., 1969.

Davis, Morris, and Joseph Krauter. *The Other Canadians: Profiles of Six Minorities*. Agincourt: Methuen Publications, 1971.

Fisher, Robin. "Gold Miners and Settlers." In *A History of British Columbia*, edited by Patricia Roy. Mississauga: Copp Clark Pitman, 1989.

Gynn-Ward, Hilda. *The Writing on the Wall: Chinese and Japanese Immigration to B.C.* Toronto: University of Toronto Press, 1974.

Hallet, Mary. "A Governor-General's Views on Oriental Immigration to British Columbia, 1904–1911." *B.C. Studies* no. 14 (summer 1972).

Hill, Douglas. *The Opening of the Canadian West*. London: William Heinemann Ltd., 1967.

Ireland, Willard. "British Columbia's American Heritage." In *Historical Essays on British Columbia*, edited by J. Frieson and H. Ralston. Toronto: McClelland and Stewart Ltd., 1976.

Lai, Chuen-Yan. "Chinese Imprints in British Columbia." *B.C. Studies* no. 39 (autumn 1978).

McDonald, Robert. "Working-Class Vancouver, 1886–1914: Urbanism and Class in British Columbia." In *A History of British Columbia*, edited by Patricia Roy. Mississauga: Copp Clark Pitman, 1989.

Mitchell, Peter. *China: Tradition and Revolution*. Toronto: Macmillan of Canada, 1977.

Morton, James. *In the Seas of Sterile Mountains*. Vancouver: J. J. Douglas, 1974.

Ormsby, Margaret. *British Columbia: A History*. Toronto: Macmillan of Canada, 1950.

———. "Canada and the New British Columbia." In *Historical Essays on British Columbia*, edited by J. Frieson and H. Ralston. Toronto: McClelland and Stewart Ltd., 1976.

Phillips, Paul. *No Power Greater: A Century of Labour in B.C.* Vancouver: B.C. Federation of Labour, 1967.

Report of the Royal Commission on Chinese Immigration. Ottawa: Printed by Order of the Commission, 1885.

Report of the Royal Commission on Chinese and Japanese Immigration. Ottawa: S.E. Dawson, 1902.

Report of the Royal Commission on Oriental Immigration. Ottawa: Printed by Order of the Commission, 1907.

Roy, Patricia. "British Columbia's Fear of Asians 1900–1950." *Histoire-Sociale/ Social History* XIII, no. 25 (May 1980).

———. "The Oriental Menace in British Columbia." In *Historical Essays on British Columbia*, edited by J. Frieson and H. Ralston. Toronto: McClelland and Stewart Ltd., 1976.

———. "The Preservation of the Peace in Vancouver: The Aftermath of the Anti-Chinese Riot of 1887." *B.C. Studies* no. 31 (autumn 1976).

———. *A White Man's Province: British Columbia Politicians and Chinese and Japanese Immigrants.* Vancouver: University of British Columbia Press, 1989.

Thomas, Roy. *China: The Awakening Giant.* Toronto: McGraw-Hill of Canada, 1971.

Waite, P.B. *Macdonald: His Life and World.* Toronto: McGraw-Hill Ryerson Ltd., 1975.

Warburton, Rennie. "Race and Class in British Columbia: A Comment." *B.C. Studies* no. 49 (spring 1981).

Ward, W. Peter. "Class and Race in the Social Structure of British Columbia: 1870–1939." *B.C. Studies* no. 45 (spring 1980).

———. "The Oriental Immigrant and Canada's Protestant Clergy." *B.C. Studies* no. 22 (summer 1974).

———. *White Canada Forever.* Montreal and Kingston: McGill and Queen's University Press, 1978.

Wickberg, Edgar, ed. *From China to Canada.* Toronto: McClelland and Stewart Ltd., 1982.

Woodcock, George. *Amor De Cosmos: Journalist and Reformer.* Toronto: Oxford University Press, 1975.

Chapter Two

Avery, Donald. "Ethnic and Class Tensions in Canada: 1918–1920." In *Loyalties in Conflict: Ukrainian Canadians During the Great War*, edited by F. Swyripa and J. Thompson, J. Edmonton: University of Alberta Press, 1983.

Barrett, Stanley. *Is God a Racist? The Right Wing in Canada.* Toronto: University of Toronto Press, 1987.

Hlynka, Isydore. *The Other Canadians.* Winnipeg: Trident Press Ltd., 1981.

Kordan, B., and L. Luciuk. *A Delicate and Difficult Question: Documents in the History of Ukrainians in Canada.* Kingston: The Limestone Press, 1986.

Kostash, Myrna. *All of Baba's Children*. Edmonton: NeWest Publishers Ltd., 1987.

Lehr, John. "Government Perceptions of Ukrainian Immigrants to Western Canada 1896–1902." *Canadian Ethnic Studies* XIX, no. 2 (1987).

Lehr, J., and W. Moodie. "The Polemics of Pioneer Settlement: Ukrainian Immigration and the Winnipeg Press." *Canadian Ethnic Studies* XII, no. 2 (1980).

Lupul, Manoly. *A Heritage in Transition: Essays in the History of Ukrainians in Canada*. Toronto: McClelland and Stewart Ltd., 1982.

Lysenko, Vera. *Men in Sheepskin Coats: A Study in Assimilation*. Toronto: Ryerson Press, 1947.

Marunchak, Michael. *The Ukrainian Canadians: A History*. Winnipeg: Ukrainian Free Academy of Sciences, 1970.

Palmer, Howard. *Patterns of Prejudice: A History of Nativism in Alberta*. Toronto: McClelland and Stewart Ltd., 1982.

Petryshyn, Jaroslav. *Peasants in the Promised Land: Canada and the Ukrainians*. Toronto: James Lorimer and Co., 1985.

Petryshyn, Roman. *Changing Realities: Social Trends Among Ukrainian Canadians*. Edmonton: The Canadian Institute of Ukrainian Studies, 1980.

Piniuta, Harry, ed. *Land of Pain, Land of Promise: First Person Accounts of Ukrainian Pioneers 1891–1914*. Saskatoon: Western Producer Prairie Books, 1978.

Potrebenko, Helen. *No Streets of Gold: A Social History of Ukrainians in Alberta*. Vancouver: New Star Books, 1977.

Report of the Royal Commission on Bilingualism and Biculturalism. Book IV. Ottawa: Information Canada, 1970.

Roaumny, Jaroslav, ed. *New Soil—Old Roots: The Ukrainian Experience in Canada*. Winnipeg: Ukrainian Academy of Arts and Sciences Canada, 1983.

Russell, Peter, ed. *Nationalism in Canada*. Toronto: McGraw-Hill of Canada Ltd., 1966.

Swyripa, Francis. *Ukrainian Canadians: A Survey of Their Portrayal in English-Canadian Works*. Edmonton: University of Alberta Press, 1978.

Thompson, John Herd. "The Enemy Alien and the Canadian General Election of 1917." In *Loyalties in Conflict: Ukrainian Canadians During the Great War*, edited by F. Swyripa and J. Thompson. Edmonton: University of Alberta Press, 1983.

Woodsworth, James S. *Strangers Within Our Gates*. Toronto: University of Toronto Press, 1972.

Chapter Three

Abella, Irving. *A Coat of Many Colours: Two Centuries of Jewish Life in Canada*. Toronto: Lester and Orpen Dennys Ltd., 1990.

Abella, I. and H. Tropper. *None Is Too Many*. Toronto: Lester and Orpen Dennys Ltd., 1982.

Ages, Arnold. "Anti-Semitism: The Uneasy Calm." In *The Canadian Jewish*

Mosaic, edited by M. Weinfeld, W. Shaffir, and I. Cotler. Toronto: John Wiley and Sons, 1981.

Balkin, Simon. *Through Narrow Gates: A Review of Jewish Immigration, Colonization and Immigration Aid Work in Canada 1840–1940*. Montreal: The Eagle Publishing Co. Ltd., 1966.

Betcherman, Lita-Rose. *The Swastika and the Maple Leaf: Fascist Movements in Canada in the Thirties*. Toronto: Fitzhenry and Whiteside, 1975.

Boudreau, Joseph. *Alberta, Aberhart and the Social Credit*. Toronto: Holt, Rinehart and Winston of Canada Ltd., 1975.

Calder, R.L. "Is the French Canadian a Jew Baiter?" *Canadian Jewish Year Book: 1939–1940*. Montreal: Woodward Press Inc., 1959.

Cook, Ramsay, ed. *French Canadian Nationalism: An Anthology*. Toronto: Macmillan of Canada, 1969.

Delisle, Jean. *The Traitor and the Jew*. Toronto: McClelland and Stewart Ltd., 1993.

Desbarats, Peter. *René: A Canadian in Search of a Country*. Toronto: Seal Books, 1976.

Elliott, David. "Anti-Semitism and the Social Credit Movement: The Intellectual Roots of the Keegstra Affair." *Canadian Ethnic Studies* XVII, no. 1985.

Glickman, Yaacov. "Anti-Semitism and Jewish Social Cohesion in Canada." In *Racism in Canada*, edited by Osmond McKague. Saskatoon: Fifth House Publishers, 1991.

Kage, Joseph. *With Faith and Thanksgiving: The Story of Two Hundred Years*. Montreal: The Eagle Publishing Co. Ltd., 1960.

MacIntosh, Robert. *Different Drummers: Banking and Politics in Canada*. Toronto: Macmillan of Canada, 1991.

Neatby, H. Blair. *The Politics of Chaos: Canada in the Thirties*. Toronto: The Bryant Press, 1972.

Nish, Cameron. *Quebec in the Duplessis Era, 1935–1959: Dictatorship or Democracy* Toronto: Copp Clark Publishing Co., 1970.

Pickersgill, J.W. *The Mackenzie King Record: 1939–1944* . Vol. I. Toronto: University of Toronto Press, 1960.

Richler, Mordecai. *Oh Canada! Oh Quebec! Requiem for a Divided Country*. Toronto: Penguin Books, 1992.

———. "Early British Columbia Jewry: A Reconstructed Census." *Canadian Ethnic Studies* 3, no. 1 (June 1971).

Sack, B.G. *History of the Jews in Canada*. Montreal: Harvest House, 1965.

Speisman, Stephen A. *The Jews of Toronto: A History to 1937*. Toronto: McClelland and Stewart Ltd., 1979.

Thomas, Lewis, ed. *William Aberhart and Social Credit in Alberta*. Toronto: Copp Clark Publishing, 1977.

Trofimenkoff, Susan Mann. *Abbé Groulx: Variations on a Nationalist Theme*. Toronto: Copp Clark Publishing, 1973.

Tulchinsky, Gerald. "Goldwin Smith: Victoria Liberal Anti-Semite." *The Whig Standard Magazine*, 22 September 1990.

Weinfeld, M., W. Shaffir, and I. Cotler, eds. *The Canadian Jewish Mosaic*. Toronto: John Wiley and Sons, 1981.

Chapter Four

Adachi, Ken. *The Enemy That Never Was: A History of the Japanese Canadians*. Toronto: McClelland and Stewart Ltd., 1976.

Angus, H.F. "Liberalism Stoops to Conquer." *Canadian Forum* 15, no. 161 (December 1935).

Bernard, Elaine. "A University at War: Japanese Canadians at UBC During WWII." *B.C. Studies* no. 35 (autumn 1973).

Broadfoot, Barry. *Years of Sorrow, Years of Shame: The Story of the Japanese Canadians in WWII*. Toronto: Paperjacks Ltd., 1976.

Cohn, Werner. "The Persecution of Japanese Canadians and the Political Left in British Columbia: December 1941–March 1942." *B.C. Studies* no. 68 (winter 1985–86).

Daniels, Roger. "The Japanese Experience in Canada: An Essay in Comparitive Racism." *Canadian Ethnic Studies* 9, no. 2 (1977).

Granatstein, J.L. *The Politics of the Mackenzie King Government 1939–1945*. Toronto: Oxford University Press, 1975.

J.L. Granatstein, and D. Morton. *A Nation Forged in Fire: Canadians and the Second World War, 1939–1945*. Toronto: Lester and Orpen Dennys Ltd., 1989.

Hallet, Mary. "A Governor-General's Views on Oriental Immigration to British Columbia, 1904–1911." *B.C. Studies* no. 14 (summer 1972).

Horibe, Kathlyn. "A Black Day in Our History." *Toronto Star*, 12 March 1992.

Ito, Roy. *We Went to War*. Stittsville: Carl Vincent Publisher, 1984.

Jamieson, Laura. "Where White and Brown Men Meet." *Canadian Forum* 21, no. 247 (August 1941).

Kogawa, Joy. *Obasan*. Markham: Penguin Books, 1983.

Marlatt, Daphne, ed. *Steveston Recollected*. Victoria: Provincial Archives of British Columbia, 1975.

Martin, Lawrence. *The Presidents and the Prime Ministers: Washington and Ottawa Face to Face: The Myth of Bilateral Bliss 1867–1982*. Toronto: Doubleday Canada Ltd., 1982.

Mertl, Steve. "Lest We Forget: Canada's Crime of 1942." *Peterborough Examiner.*, 27 February 1992.

Neatby, H. Blair. *William Lyon Mackenzie King*. Toronto: University of Toronto Press, 1976.

Patton, Janice. *The Exodus of the Japanese*. Toronto: McClelland and Stewart Ltd., 1973.

Pickersgill, J.W., and D.F. Forster. *The Mackenzie King Record 1944–1945*. Toronto: University of Toronto Press, 1968.

Roy, Patricia. "The Soldiers Canada Didn't Want: Her Chinese and Japanese Citizens." *Canadian Historical Review* LIX, no. 3 (1978).

Roy, P., et. al. *Mutual Hostages: Canadians and Japanese During the Second World War*. Toronto: University of Toronto Press, 1990.

Sunahara, Ann M. "Federal Policy and the Japanese Canadians: The Decision to Evacuate, 1942." In *Visible Minorities and Multiculturalism: Asians in Canada*, edited by K. Victor Ujimoto and Gordon Hirabayashi. Toronto: Butterworth and Co., 1980.

———. *The Politics of Racism: The Uprooting of Japanese Canadians During the Second World War*. Toronto: James Lorimer and Co., 1981.

Suzuki, David. *Metamorphosis: Stages in a Life*. Toronto: General Paperbacks, 1988.

Ward, Peter W. "British Columbia and the Japanese Evacuation." *Canadian Historical Review* 57, no. 3 (September 1976). Toronto: University of Toronto Press, 1976.

Whitaker, Reginald. "Political Thought and Political Action in Mackenzie King." *Journal of Canadian Studies* 13, no. 4 (winter 1978–1979).

Chapter Five

Bargan, Peter. *The Legal Status of the Canadian Public School Pupil*. Toronto: Macmillan Co. of Canada, 1961.

Calliste, Agnes. "Sleeping Car Porters in Canada: An Ethnically Submerged Split Labour Market." *Canadian Ethnic Studies* XIX, no. 1 (1987).

Clairmont, Donald and Dennis McGill. *Africville: The Life and Death of a Canadian Black Community*. Toronto: McClelland and Stewart Ltd., 1974.

Cook, J., and B. Britton. "The Black Canadian." *Maclean's* XXIII, no. 1 (16 February 1911).

Davis, Morris, and Joseph Krauter. *The Other Canadians: Profiles of Six Minorities*. Agincourt: Methuen Publications, 1971.

Grow, Stewart. "The Blacks of Amber Valley: Negro Pioneering in Northern Alberta." *Canadian Ethnic Studies* VI nos. 1 and 2 (1974).

Hill, Daniel. *The Freedom Seekers: Blacks in Early Canada*. Agincourt: The Book Society of Canada Ltd., 1981.

Hill, Donna, ed. *A Black Man's Toronto 1914–1980: The Reminiscences of Harry Gairey*. Toronto: Multicultural Society of Ontario, 1981.

Knowles, Valerie. *Strangers at Our Gates: Canadian Immigration and Immigration Policy*. Toronto: Dundurn Press, 1992.

Pachai, Bridglal. "The African Presence in Nova Scotia." *Dalhousie Review* 68, no. 1/2 (spring–summer 1988).

———. *People of the Maritimes: Blacks*. Tantallon: Four East Publications, 1987.

Palmer, Howard. "Reluctant Hosts: Anglo-Canadian Views of Multiculturalism in the Twentieth Century." In *Readings in Canadian History: Post Confederation*, edited by R. Douglas Fancis and Donald B. Smith. 2nd ed. Toronto: Holt, Rinehart and Winston of Canada Ltd., 1986.

Paris, Cherry. "The Universality of Human Rights: The Black Experience." In *The Universality of Human Rights: The Black Experience: A Collection of Speeches*. Dartmouth: Black Cultural Centre for Nova Scotia, 1988.

Phillips, Allan. "The Advantage of Being Black." *Maclean's* 3 (22 October 1960).

Rawlyk, G.A. "The Guysborough Negroes: A Study in Isolation." *Dalhousie Review* 48 (1968).

Ruck, Calvin. "The Development of Human Rights in Nova Scotia." In *Universality of Human Rights and the Black Experience: A Collection of Speeches*. Dartmouth: Black Cultural Centre for Nova Scotia, 1988.

Saunders, Charles. *Africville: A Spirit That Lives On*. Dartmouth: Black Cultural Centre for Nova Scotia, 1989.

Shadd, Adrienne. "Institutional Racism and Canadian History: Notes of a Black Canadian." In *Racism in Canada*, edited by Ormond McKague. Saskatoon: Fifth House Publishers, 1991.

Shepard, Bruce R. "Plain Racism: The Reaction Against Oklahoma Black Immigration to the Canadian Plains." In *Racism in Canada*, edited by Ormond McKague. Saskatoon: Fifth House Publishers, 1991.

Stewart, Walter. *But Not in Canada!* Toronto: Macmillan of Canada, 1976.

Swatsky, John. *Mulroney: The Politics of Ambition*. Toronto: McClelland and Stewart Ltd., 1991.

Thomson, Colin. *Born with a Call: A Biography of Dr. William Pearly Oliver, C.M.* Dartmouth: McCurdy Printing, 1986.

Troper, Harold Martin. "The Creek-Negroes of Oklahoma and Canadian Immigration, 1909–1911." *Canadian Historical Review* LIII, no. 3 (September 1972). Toronto: University of Toronto Press, 1972.

Tulloch, Headley. *Black Canadians: A Long Line of Fighters*. Toronto: New Canadian Publications, 1975.

Walker, James. *Identity: The Black Experience in Canada*. Toronto: Gage Educational Publishing, 1979.

———. "Race and Recruitment in WWI: Enlistment of the Visible Minorities in the Canadian Expeditionary Force." *Canadian Historical Review* LXX, no. 70 (1989). Toronto: University of Toronto Press, 1989.

Winks, Robin. "The Canadian Negro." *The Journal of Negro History* LIII, no. 4 (October 1968).

———. "Negroes in the Maritimes: An Introductory Study." *Dalhousie Review* 48 (1968).

Chapter Six

Allison, Derek. "Fourth World Education in Canada and the Faltering Promise of Native Teacher Education Programs." *Journal of Canadian Studies* 18, no. 3. (fall 1983).

Bowles, P.R., et. al. *The Indian: Assimilation, Integration or Separation*. Scarborough: Prentice-Hall of Canada, 1972.

Canadian School Superintendent. *The Education of Indian Children in Canada*. Toronto: Ryerson Press, 1965.

Cardinal, Harold. *The Rebirth of Canada's Indians*. Edmonton: Hurtig Publishers, 1977.

———. *The Unjust Society*. Edmonton: Hurtig Publishers, 1969.

Chalmers, John. "Federal, Provincial and Territorial Strategies for Canadian Native Education 1960–1970." *Journal of Canadian Studies* 11, no. 3 (August 1976).

Chrétien, Jean. *Straight from the Heart*. Toronto: Seal Books, 1986.

Comeau, P., and A. Santin. *The First Canadians: A Profile of Canada's Native People Today*. Toronto: James Lorimer and Co., 1990.

Crey, Ernie. "The Children of Tomorrow's Great Potlatch." *B.C. Studies* no. 89 (spring 1991).

Eisenberg, J. and H. Troper. *Native Survival*. Toronto: The Ontario Institute for Studies in Education, 1973.

Fisher, R., and K. Coates. *Out of the Background: Readings on Canadian History*. Toronto: Copp Clark Pitman Ltd., 1988.

Fournier, S. and E. Crey. *Stolen From Our Embrace*. Vancouver: Douglas and McIntyre, 1997.

Frideres, James. *Native People in Canada: Contemporary Conflicts*. 2nd ed. Scarborough: Prentice-Hall of Canada Inc., 1983.

———. "Native Rights and the 21st Century: The Making of Red Power." *Canadian Ethnic Studies* XXII, no. 3 (1990).

Grant, S.D. "Indian Affairs Under Duncan Campbell Scott: The Plains Cree of Saskatchewan." *Journal of Canadian Studies* 18, no. 3 (fall 1983).

Harris, Michael. *Justice Denied: The Law versus Donald Marshall*. Toronto: Macmillan of Canada, 1986.

Hawthorne, H.B., ed. *A Survey of the Contemporary Indians of Canada: Economic, Political, Educational Needs and Policies* Vol. 2. Ottawa: Indian Affairs Branch, 1967.

Hickman, Alexander. *Royal Commission on the Donald Marshall, Jr. Prosecution: Digest of Findings and Recommendations*. Halifax: McCurdy's Printing, 1989.

Johnston, Basil. *Indian School Days*. Toronto: Key Porter Books, 1988.

Johnston, Patrick. *Native Children and the Child Welfare System*. Toronto: Canadian Council on Social Development in association with James Lorimer and Co., 1983.

Joseph, Shirley. "Assimilation Tools: Then and Now." *B.C. Studies* no. 89 (spring 1991).

Mathias, J. and G. Yabasley. "Conspiracy of Legislation: The Suppression of Indian Rights in Canada." *B.C. Studies* no. 89 (spring 1991).

Miller, J.R. *Skyscrapers Hide the Heavens: A History of Indian-White Relations in Canada*. Toronto: University of Toronto Press, 1989.

Ponting, J. Rick. "Internationalisation: Perspectives on an Emerging Direction in Aboriginal Affairs." *Canadian Ethnic Studies* 22, no. 3 (1990).

Priest, Lisa. *Conspiracy of Silence*. Toronto: McClelland and Stewart Ltd., 1989. *Report of the Royal Commission on Aboriginal Peoples*. Ottawa: Canada Communications Group, 1996.

Schubert-Cardinal, Joane. "Surviving as a Native Women Artist." In *Racism in Canada*, edited by Ormond McKague. Saskatoon: Fifth House Publishers, 1991.

Seguin, Margaret. "Understanding Tsimshian 'Potlatch'." In *Native Peoples: The Canadian Experience*, edited by R. Bruce Morrison and C. Roderick Wilson. Toronto: McClelland and Stewart Ltd., 1990.

Tennant, P. *Aboriginal Peoples and Politics*. Vancouver: University of British Columbia Press, 1990.

Titley, Brian. *A Narrow Vision: Duncan Campbell Scott and the Administration of Indian Affairs in Canada*. Vancouver: University of British Columbia Press, 1986.

Tobias, John. "Canada's Subjugation of the Plains Cree, 1879–1885." *Canadian Historical Review*. LCIV (December 1983).

Waubageshig, ed. *The Only Good Indian*. Don Mills: New Press, 1970.
York, Geoffrey. *The Dispossessed: Life and Death in Native Canada*. Toronto:
  Little, Brown and Co. Ltd., 1990.

Epilogue

Ponting, J. Rick. "Internationalization: Perspectives on an Emerging Direction
  in Aboriginal Affairs." *Canadian Ethnic Studies* 22, no. 3 (1990).

Index

Bronfman, Samuel, 120
Brown, Rosemary, 16
Buck, Pearl, 147
Budka, Bishop, 75-77, 81
Bunster, Arthur, 28-29, 32
Byrne, L.D., 95

C
Cambie, Henry, 35
Canada
    anti-Semitism, 116
    as ethnic state, 10-11
    as racist state, 11, 13-14
    removing racist laws, 175
    WWII refugees, 121
    See also Black Canadians; Chinese Canadians;
    Immigration; Japanese Canadians; Jewish
    Canadians; Native Canadians; Ukrainian
    Canadians
Canada Fair Employment Practices Act, 171-72
Canadian Association of Social Workers, 203
Canadian Bill of Rights, 175
Canadian Charter of Rights and Freedoms, 223
Canadian Jewish Congress, 100, 112, 113, 118,
    120
Canadian Labour Congress, 172, 183
Canadian Métis Society, 206
Canadian Pacific Railroad (CPR)
    Black Canadians, 170-72
    Chinese Canadians and, 32-37
Cantonese, in Canada, 19
Cardinal, Harold, 200
    Citizens Plus, 208-9
Carmen, Reverend A., 45
Cartier, Jacques, 158
Carvery, Aaron "Pa", 184
Catholic Church, in Quebec, 96
    anti-Semitism, 98, 108, 110, 115-16
    Japanese Canadians and, 150
Chain migrants from China, 19, 20
Chambers, Alan, 139
Chapleau, Dr. Joseph Adolphe, 37
Chi, Ah, 22
Chinese Canadians, 9, 17-54
    1923-47 exclusion, 54
    and railway, 32-37
    during Japanese internment, 15-16
    economic segregation, 39
    immigration, 38, 45
    Laurier and, 44-45
    legal disabilities, 44
    unions and, 39
Chinese Canadians, in B.C., 19-20, 34
    1905 violence, 46-47
    1922 Act, 53-54
    after 1871, 27
    anti-Chinese agitation, 23-24
    before 1871, 19-27
    Brighouse Estate, 40-44
    Chinese-owned businesses, 22-23
    Gold Rush, 19-20
    head tax, 28, 38, 44-45
    land ownership, 50-51
    local media, 24-25, 29, 36-37, 39-40, 43, 50
    Macdonald and, 27, 31-33, 36, 37, 38-39

mining, 22
Natal Act riot, 48-49
pejorative terms, 24
railway and, 31-37
road work, 21
segregated schools, 46
vote, 38-39
Chinese Consolidated Benevolent Association, 46
Chinese Immigration (Exclusion) Act, 54
Chong, Lee, 22
Chrétien, Jean, 15
    Native concerns and, 206-7
    Native education, 212
    White Paper, 205-6, 210
Christian, Wayne, 214
Christianity. See Churches
Christie Pitts riot (Toronto), 102-3
Churches, 14
    B.C. Chinese and, 26
    Black Canadians, 160-61, 176
    Japanese Canadians and, 152, 153, 154
    Native Canadians and, 211
    racism in, 52-53
    residential schools, 196-203.
    See also Catholic Church, in Quebec
Climate, as excuse for racism, 177
Clute, R.C., 45
Coleman, D.C., 84-85
Collier, Robert, 22
Collins, George, 149
Commonwealth Immigration Act, 178
Communism. See Ukrainian Canadians, Bolshevik
victory and
Connor, Ralph. See Charles Gorden
Conservative Party, 121
    anti-Semitism and, 110
Cooperative Committee of Japanese Canadians,
    154
Cooperative Commonwealth Federation, 121, 153
Courchene, David, 206, 207
Cowichan, 17
Craig, Malin, 135
Cree. See Plains Cree
Crerar, 120
Crowfoot, 186
Culbertson, Ely, 70-71
Cultural genocide, 13. See also Native Canadians,
    cultural genocide

D
da Costa, Matthieu, 158
Dafoe, J.W., 77
Darwin, Charles, 10. See also Social Darwinism
David, Athanase, 106
Daye, Buddy, 179
De Cosmos, Amor, 24-25, 32
Department of Indian Affairs, 196. See also Native
    Canadians
Desmond, Viola, 173-74
    legal victory, 175
Dewdney, Edgar, 189-90, 191
Diefenbaker, John, 175
Discrimination, 175-76
    explained, 12. See also Black Canadians;
    Chinese Canadians; Japanese Canadians;

This is John Boyko's second book. His first, *Politics: Conflict and Compromise* (Oxford University Press), quickly became the senior level politics text in secondary schools across Canada. John is the History and Social Science Curriculum Leader and a teacher at Lakefield College School in Lakefield, Ontario.